Policies for America's Public Schools: Teachers, Equity, and Indicators

CHILD AND FAMILY POLICY

SERIES EDITORS
JAMES J. GALLAGHER AND RON HASKINS

Policies for America's Public Schools: Teachers, Equity, and Indicators

RON HASKINS and DUNCAN MACRAE
EDITORS

Ablex Publishing Corporation
Norwood, New Jersey   07648

Library of Congress Cataloging-in-Publication Data

Policies for America's public schools.

  (Child and family policy;   v. 6)
  Bibliography: p.
  Includes index.
  1. Public school—United States.   2. Education and state—United States.   3. Education—United States—Evaluation.   I. Haskins, Ron.   II. MacRae, Duncan.   III. Series.
LC89.P63   1988   371'.01'0973   87-27057
ISBN 0-89391-444-4

Ablex Publishing Corporation
355 Chestnut Street
Norwood, New Jersey 07648

CONTENTS

ABOUT THE AUTHORS

William W. Cooley. Ed. D. from Harvard; Director of Evaluation Research, Learning Research and Development Center, University of Pittsburgh, Pittsburgh, PA, 15260.

David D. Dill. Ph.D. in education from the University of Michigan; Associate Professor of Education and Assistant to the Chancellor for Planning at the University of North Carolina at Chapel Hill, South Building 005A, Chapel Hill, NC, 27514.

Ron Haskins. Ph.D. in developmental psychology from the University of North Carolina at Chapel Hill; Professional Staff Member, Committee on Ways and Means, U.S. House of Representatives, Room 1106 Longworth HOB, Washington, D.C., 20515.

Joyce L. Eptsein. Ph.D. in sociology from Johns Hopkins University; Principal Research Scientist, Center for Research on Elementary and Middle Schools, Johns Hopkins University, 3505 N. Charles Street, Baltimore, Md, 21218.

Ernest R. House. Ed.D. from the University of Illinois at Urbana-Champaign; Director of the Laboratory for Policy Studies, School of Education, University of Colorado at Boulder, Boulder, CO, 80309.

James J. Gallagher. Ph.D. in clinical psychology from the Pennsylvania State University; William Rand Kenan, Jr. Professor of Education, Frank Porter Graham Child Development Center, 500 NCNB Plaza 322A, University of North Carolina at Chapel Hill, Chapel Hill, NC, 27514.

Stephen D. Lapan. Ph.D. in education from the University of Connecticut; Associate Professor of Gifted Education, Center for Excellence in Education, Northern Arizona University, Room 222B-Box 5774, Flagstaff, AZ, 86011.

Mark W. Lanier. Ph.D. candidate in the Department of Political Science, Hamilton Hall 070A, University of North Carolina at Chapel Hill, Chapel Hill, NC, 27514.

Duncan MacRae, Jr. Ph.D. in social psychology from Harvard; William Rand Kenan, Jr. Professor of Political Science and Sociology,

Hamilton Hall 070A, University of North Carolina at Chapel Hill, Chapel Hill, NC, 27514.

John U. Ogbu. Ph.D. in anthropology from the University of California at Berkeley; Professor of Anthropology, Department of Anthropology, University of California at Berkeley, Berkeley, CA, 94720.

Paul E. Peterson. Ph.D. in political science from the University of Chicago; Benjamin H. Griswold III Professor of Public Policy and Director of the Center for the Study of American Government, Johns Hopkins University, 3411 Ashley Terrace, NW, Washington, DC, 20008.

Donald J. Stedman. Ph.D. in education from George Peabody College for Teachers (now part of Vanderbilt University); Associate Vice President for Academic Affairs, University of North Carolina, UNC General Administration, P.O. Box 2688, Chapel Hill, NC, 27514.

Preface to the Series

JAMES J. GALLAGHER

Emergence of the new field of social policy analysis, starting in the 1960s, but accelerating in the 1970s, is an intriguing phenomenon in the academic world that is worthy of study in its own right. This evolving discipline is clearly multidisciplinary in nature, drawing interest and contributions from such diverse bedfellows as the health sciences, economics, sociology, psychology, and education, among others.

Even more interesting than this multidisciplinary thrust from the academic community is that those in positions of power seem to be aware of this new movement and are generally attentive. The relationship between the keepers of knowledge and holders of power has always been a strained one. Truth, particularly when unpleasant, has rarely been welcomed by those at the seat of power. Those messengers who deliver such unpleasant truths run some very real risks, more psychological than physical these days. On the other hand, the academician rarely has a sense of the multitude of conflicting pressures and compromises that are the daily menu of the practicing politician, and often doesn't appreciate the many changes in directions that often must be taken to reach a political (policy) goal.

To appreciate this continued strain between knowledge and power, one need not invoke the memories of Galileo or Sir Thomas More. The current difficulties are well expressed in the agonies of the atomic scientists, aptly delineated in an extraordinary series of novels by C. P. Snow. Given this obvious and continued strain, why is there a current interest in pursuing what academia can bring to social policy formulation and implementation?

My own view is that the public policies of the 1960s are the stimuli for this review of relationships. Those policies were, by and large, designed to lead to a better life for all our citizens through improving the delivery of health, social, and educational services. The consensus held by both the political community and the lay public appears to be that after 15 years, the programs have largely come to grief, or have attained much less than was originally intended. Whether this outcome is the result of unrealistic expectations, poor policy formulation, or inadequate policy implementation is still a matter of personal interpretation.

Currently, there is a growing realization that attempts to improve American society can no longer be based on a "seat-of-the-pants," largely uncorrelated, and uncontrolled set of innovations. Such a strategy yields uncontrolled budgets and a corrosive cycle of over-expectation, disappointment, and despair. There appears to be a new willingness, tinged with some skepticism, to pursue what academia has to offer in improving policy design and implementation. What does academia have to offer? What it always has—the ability to organize systems of ideas into a pattern that allows us to bring order and new insights to the phenomenon under study.

This series on social policy analysis summarizes some of the latest ideas and methods that are being utilized by those social and health scientists most directly concerned with policy relating to children and families. Each volume in the series will be built around a particular theme so that contributors to a given volume will be focusing on a common topic. In this first volume, the theme is the development of models for analyzing social policy. Such model development is presented from a multidisciplinary perspective as we seek some usable procedures to bring clarity and comprehension to complex policy topics. In subsequent volumes, we will focus upon policy issues such as parent education, the needs of handicapped children and their families, maternal and child health, and children and families in poverty. In each of these volumes, there will be a mixture of general descriptions on the topic area plus the inclusion of specific policy analyses that attempt to bring insight into particular topics within the theme.

It would be inappropriate to conclude these introductory remarks without giving credit to the Bush Foundation of St. Paul, Minnesota, whose forward thinking has provided financial support for much of the analytic work that will be included in these volumes. The Bush Foundation has established training programs at four major universities—Michigan, Yale, UCLA, and North Carolina—and while the papers in this series will be based, to a large degree, on the work at North Carolina, the ideas and concepts in this series will undoubtedly reflect the interests of all four Bush centers.

PREFACE TO THE VOLUME

The nine papers in this volume, excepting the introductory and summary chapters, were originally prepared for a colloquium series on "Public Education Policy for the 1990s" at the University of North Carolina in the spring of 1985. Six of them were presented as public lectures and three additional papers were invited.

We chose to deal with public but not private schools because we believe the most important problems of publicly supported, pre-collegiate education cannot be dealt with adequately by competition between public and private schools. We nevertheless favor the study of competitive processes for rewarding educational effectiveness, and recognize that in a broader perspective public policies affecting private schools can be helpful.

Within the general domain of policies for the public schools, we chose contributors whose topics related to three particular policy areas: teachers and teaching, equity, and information and indicators. These topics do not include all the policy issues faced by the schools and addressed by the numerous educational commissions that have reported to the American public in recent years, but we elected to treat what seemed to us the most critical issues and then deal with them in depth.

Our contributors are associated with universities, but they are here addressing citizens, teachers, school administrators, and public officials as well as fellow academics. The arguments presented in this volume are thus intended to link academic research with public policy. They are more academic and refer more to the scholarly literature than the major critical reports and commission proposals that have been published recently. They are also more valuative and speculative than most articles in the journals of basic social science. We hope there will continue to be a vigorous literature connecting educational research and policy in this way—seeking both relevance and rigor, however difficult that may be.

In preparing this volume, we have accumulated numerous debts.

The Bush Foundation of St. Paul, Minnesota provided funds to the Bush Institute for Child and Family Policy at the University of North Carolina to sponsor the colloquium series. Stan Shepard of the Bush Foundation has assisted us in every possible way over the years; we owe special gratitude to the Foundation and Stan Shepard for their generous help.

After the initial papers had been presented to an audience of scholars and students in Chapel Hill, the authors met with faculty and fellows of our Bush Institute to discuss their papers in detail. We hope the authors were helped by these sessions; we know our faculty and fellows were.

Following each of the colloquium presentations, we asked a scholar or practitioner of public education to present a formal reaction to the presentation. These reactions often provided both the authors and the audience with alternative perspectives, new information, or compelling arguments either supporting or opposing the author's policy conclusions. The reactions also stimulated comments and discussions from the audience. Thus, we remain grateful for the assistance of the scholars and practitioners of education who served as reactants: Mark Appelbaum, Frank Brown, David Dill, Howard Maniloff, Pamela Mayer, and Marvin Wyne.

We also thank James J. Gallagher, who, as Director of the Bush Institute as well as the Frank Porter Graham Child Development Center, helped bring both the colloquium series and this volume to fruition. He provided excellent advice during the process of selecting topics and speakers. Further, he agreed, despite a demanding schedule, to participate in the colloquium series by delivering a paper and writing a chapter on education of the gifted. Although neither of us would claim any expertise in education of the gifted, it quickly becomes apparent to anyone who even dabbles in this field that James Gallagher is one of its two or three leading scholars. We also acknowledge the rather spirited, one might even say pungent, criticisms Jim offered on several of the papers in this volume—including, we regret to say, the introductory and summary chapters.

As is always the case in scholarly books and papers, the authors who receive such public credit as affixes to the final product are actually supported by a cast of people whose contributions go largely unrecognized—but, at least in this case, not unappreciated. Stacy Reynolds typed several versions of four chapters in this volume. In the process, she kept Federal Express in business for at least three months firing manuscripts back and forth between Washington, D.C. and Chapel Hill. We also received excellent and timely help administering the colloquium series from Flo Purdie and Tom Richey. Finally, we thank the Bush doctoral students and professional fellows who helped administer the colloquium series and who provided the authors with perceptive reactions and questions.

May, 1987   Ron Haskins
                                                             Duncan MacRae, Jr.

ONE

REFORMING THE PUBLIC SCHOOLS: THE COMMISSION REPORTS AND STRATEGIES OF REFORM

RON HASKINS, MARK W. LANIER, and
DUNCAN MacRAE, JR.

Since 1983 the United States has been besieged by a series of reports that severely criticize the nation's public school system. In prose befitting a public relations firm preparing the nation for war, the reports discover massive problems in the schools and recommend hundreds of solutions that, taken together, would cost about as much money as a major war.

In this volume, we have assembled a set of papers by leading scholars of education that address some important problems faced by American public schools and propose a variety of policies to deal with these problems. By way of introduction, in this chapter we summarize the findings of the education commissions that provided the impetus to the current reform movement, propose and briefly discuss a typology of the possible reforms that policymakers could use to improve the public schools, and provide an overview of the chapters that follow.

OVERVIEW OF COMMISSION REPORTS

What is wrong with American education? When one sifts through the various reports, the major problem appears to be that students are not learning enough. The evidence cited includes dropout rates, international comparisons of school performance, standardized achievement test scores, and illiteracy rates. From this evidence, it follows that today's students are prepared neither to achieve "excellence"—a word much in vogue—nor to augment the nation's international economic position. Japan and other foreign competitors constantly lurk in the background, ready to steal our markets if our high school students don't begin studying 2 hours each night (Task Force of the Business–Higher Education Forum, 1983).

Although the reports propose a host of solutions to the problem of poor achievement, four categories of recommendations stand out: goal setting, improved teaching, revised school curriculum, and better school organization and leadership. The reports offer a few recommendations that do not fit into these categories, but nearly all the major recommendations are captured by these four issues—perennial issues of American education. One can go back to the commission reports of earlier times (e.g., National Commission, 1973; National Panel, 1976), to yearbooks of the National Society for the Study of Education, or to classic works by Dewey (1916, 1938), Rickover (1963), William James (1958) and similar writers and find discussions and recommendations about many of these same issues.

Setting Goals

Perennial or not, the issues raised and solutions proposed by the reports can be summarized by a brief overview of the four major aspects of school reform addressed by their recommendations—beginning with goal setting. Recommendations concerning goal setting are as universal as they are unremarkable. Especially in an era of program evaluation, most professionals and politicians are well aware that effective organizations must have clearly defined goals. Indeed, many state and local school systems, as well as individual schools, have defined elaborate sets of goals over the past two decades; some of these are so specific that they identify the year and semester in which children will learn the alphabet, addition of one-digit numbers, and so forth.

Even so, most of the reports recommend a clear statement of goals by both school systems and individual schools. Ernest Boyer's (1983) report on high school for the Carnegie Foundation for the Advancement of Teaching is typical. He believes that, to be effective, high schools must have a shared vision of what administrators, teachers, parents, and students are trying to accomplish. Every school should establish written goals; the goals should focus on language learning, a core of other common learning, preparation for work or further education, and civic service. Similarly, John Goodlad's *A Place Called School* (1983) emphasizes goals, but Goodlad would make the goals broad at the state and school system level, leaving ample room for flexibility and initiative at the building level. On the other hand, Theodore Sizer, in his report *Horace's Compromise: The Dilemma of the American High School* (1984), argues that the schools already have too many goals. He recommends streamlining the goals to be certain the basics take precedence over driver education, extracurricular activities, school trips, and the like. Nonetheless, Sizer's report, like most of the others, emphasizes the importance of goal setting.

Teachers and Teaching

Rising above all other concerns expressed by the reports is the unanimous view that teachers and teaching are the most important focus for education reform. The facts here are widely known and accepted: Comparatively low achievers enter the teaching profession; teachers who score highest on standardized tests tend to leave the profession; teacher certification procedures are not very stringent and do not necessarily bear any relation to performance; teachers are the lowest paid of all professionals, averaging about 20% less than accountants (Carnegie Forum, 1986). Thus, it is no surprise that all the commissions have something to say about teachers and teaching; the major recommendations can be summarized in four points.

First, the teaching profession must be made more attractive. Higher pay, to be discussed in greater detail below, is one mechanism to achieve this end, but several others are also recommended. Boyer recommends a cadet teaching corps in U.S. high schools; *A Nation at Risk* (National Commission, 1983) calls for grants for outstanding students to enter teaching; several of the reports call for a federal role in providing scholarships or grants for students who plan to become teachers.

Second, and closely related to making the teaching profession more attractive for new entrants, most reports call for improved working conditions to raise the morale of current teachers and to attract and retain the best. If teachers are professionals, why must they perform bus duty, lunchroom duty, hall duty, and similar menial tasks? An especially undesirable feature of these responsibilities is that they involve little or no professional competence but frequently bring teachers into conflict with students. Thus, Boyer's report and several of the others recommend an outright prohibition on assigning such responsibilities to teachers.

Another means of making teaching more attractive is to give teachers fewer classes and ensure that they have at least one period each day for preparation. This recommendation is especially important for teachers who must grade compositions. The reports call for extensive homework and written assignments in class; if these are to do any good they must be carefully graded.

A point made by a number of the reports is that teaching could be made more attractive if teachers were given more recognition and respect. Boyer, for example, recommends that local districts create a teacher excellence fund to distribute money to quality teachers. The Twentieth Century Fund (1983), the Task Force on Education for Business Growth, and Sizer also propose means by which teachers could be given greater recognition by their schools or districts. Sizer even favors giving teachers greater control over students and their schedules. Most of the reports, although calling for an increased role for principals, seem to envision a collective decision-making process at the schoolbuilding level, with teachers and principals making most decisions that affect the academic process. In short, the schools should increase the professionalization of teaching by replacing duties that amount to babysitting with responsibility for making decisions about the instructional process.

In a third broad area of agreement about teachers, the reports are very critical of current approaches to teacher education. Points of agreement across the reports include the recommendation that high school teachers, and perhaps elementary-school teachers (Bennett, 1986), take a liberal arts or sciences undergraduate major and then take education courses after completing their degree in a substantive area. Commission members seem to believe that education courses are less important than thorough knowledge of a discipline or disciplines. Moreover, the reports agree on the principle that teacher preparation should include extensive experience in the classroom under the supervision of competent senior teachers.

Part of teacher preparation is certification. All professions, in the attempt to regulate membership and ensure a minimum level of competence, give tests as part of their certification procedures. There appears to be a general recognition across the reports that the process of teacher certification, including standardized, national testing, is weak—it neither identifies teachers who will be excellent nor eliminates teachers who will be ineffective.

By far the most specific and thorough set of recommendations concerning teacher certification comes from the Carnegie Forum on Education and the Economy. The members of this commission propose that teacher certification be performed by an organization composed primarily of teachers themselves. After all, they argue, a sine qua non of a profession is a mechanism of self-certification and policing. To this end, the Carnegie Report proposes the creation of a National Board for Professional Teaching Standards. A majority of board members would be certified teachers, but public representatives, parents, chief state school officers, and governors would also be represented. Teacher members would be elected on a state or regional basis; teachers who are members would in turn elect the other members.

The board would have four primary responsibilities: setting standards for certification and certifying, establishing a code of ethics, disciplining violators of the code, and maintaining a register of certified teachers. Certification, the central function of the board, would require assessment of knowledge of subject matter, knowledge of general principles of instruction, and mastery of the techniques required to teach specific subjects (Carnegie Forum, p. 66). Assessment procedures would include both written tests and observation of candidates by experienced teachers.

The fourth recommendation concerning teachers, and perhaps the most important and controversial, is to increase teacher pay. All the reports agree that Americans pay their teachers far less than they should. Indeed, teachers make about half as much as attorneys, about $7,000 less than accountants, and nearly $1,000 less than mail carriers (Carnegie Forum, p. 37). The most straightforward solution, of course, is simply to give teachers an across-the-board salary hike. Boyer recommends that teachers receive a 25% (above inflation) salary increase over 3 years. A Nation at Risk recognizes the importance of more money, but wants pay increases tied to a system of promotion, tenure, and retention that is based on a carefully planned evaluation system. Similarly, Sizer and the Twentieth Century Fund Report are less specific, but call for some type of career ladder that leads to increased responsibility and compensation.

Again, the most specific and detailed recommendations regarding teacher pay are made by the Carnegie Forum on Education and the Economy. The forum outlines a comprehensive plan for education reform, the central element of which is a set of recommendations regarding teachers. The recommendations encompass all the areas summarized above: an improved environment for teachers, new standards for teachers, a radically revised program of teacher education, an incentive and performance-based system of advancement, and across-the-board pay increases. Regarding the last proposal, the forum recommends a much wider range of salaries than presently exists. Licensed (beginning) teachers would start at about $20,000 to $24,000 and advance through a total of four pay and status levels until they were lead teachers with salaries in the range of $55,000. Advancement and pay would be based on four factors: level of responsibility (especially in supervising younger teachers), level of certification, seniority, and productivity as measured by student performance.

The various recommendations on teachers by the commissions display a certain commonality at a general level of abstraction: Teaching should be a more attractive job, teacher certification is inadequate, teacher education should be improved, teachers should make more money. As one reviews the specific recommendations that underlie this general agreement, however, great diversity quickly becomes apparent. Moreover, few of the commissions attempt to estimate the costs of their recommendations, some of which would be enormous, and fewer still explain how the recommendations are to be implemented. Not unexpectedly, then, the commission reports point to serious problems and broad solutions, but specific blueprints for reform are left to others.

Curriculum and Teaching the Basics

A third consistent theme in all the reports is that schools must make a renewed commitment to teaching the basics. English and mathematics are mentioned in every report, and some of the recommendations are very specific. Boyer puts language at the center of the curriculum and even recommends that English be assessed before entrance to high school and that all students exhibit a basic proficiency before they be allowed to proceed. Similarly, *Making the Grade* by the Twentieth Century Fund makes proficiency in language the center of the school curriculum; the fund even recommends that bilingual education be eliminated and that the money saved be used to promote remedial instruction in English.

Agreement among the reports on curriculum matters extends beyond the central importance of language. Nearly all the commissions agree that there should be more instruction in math, science, and social studies and that students should have fewer elective and more required courses. The National Commission on Excellence in Education recommends 4 years of English, 3 years of math, 3 years of science, 3 years of social studies, and a half-year of computer instruction for all students. Mortimer Adler's *Paideia Proposal* (1982) would eliminate all specialized courses, such as vocational education, and make the entire curriculum, which would consist primarily of the basics and the humanities, required for all students.

Adler's recommendations also show another common thread in the curriculum recommendations of the various reports; namely, the development of thinking skills. Inducing disciplined thought and original thinking in students are the primary objectives of the curriculum proposed in the *Paideia Proposal*. The development of thinking skills also occupies a central position in the curriculum recommendations of Boyer, Sizer, and Goodlad.

Despite this similarity across the reports in emphasizing the basics and thinking skills in school curriculum, a few of the reports contain interesting, even radical, proposals for changing the curriculum or the organization of instruction. Goodlad, for example, would have children begin school at age 4 and leave at about 16. Further, he would reorganize the high school into smaller "schools within a school" (p. 309), each with its own complement of students (500 or fewer is recommended) and teachers. Although the individual schools would share some common facilities, such as the library, gym, and playing fields, they would do so at different times of the day to promote the self-contained nature of each school. The main advantage Goodlad sees in this organization would be increased interaction between students and teachers, who would come to know each other personally. If this approach were successful, the isolation and anomie of large high schools could be reduced. Under such circumstances, academic performance as well as classroom behavior might improve.

Nor are Sizer and Boyer any less innovative in their recommendations regarding curriculum and organization for instruction. Sizer wants to eliminate age grading in order to allow students to progress at their own rate. The public schools are so wedded to organization by age groups that one could hardly think of a more radical—or less likely— reform than its elimination. Sizer, like Goodlad, would end tracking and, what is really but an extension of the tracking principle, magnet schools, and require that all students take their instruction in basic courses in heterogeneous groups.

Similarly, Boyer recommends sweeping changes in the curriculum and school organization. Like several other reports, Boyer's *High School* supports a core curriculum of English and literature, math, history, and science. Boyer's report also is similar to a few of the others in recommending a new emphasis on foreign language, the arts, health, and technology. A major innovation of Boyer's curriculum, however, is an emphasis on the transition from high school to work or advanced learning. He wants students in the last 2 years of high school to have more elective courses and substantial experience outside the school building. Especially notable here is his recommendation of required volunteer work in the community and a senior project for all students.

Along with these reforms of the curriculum and the organization of instruction, the reports are nearly universal in their emphasis on three factors that condition learning. First, there is nearly unanimous agreement that schools should assign more homework and that parents should create the home conditions conducive to daily homework. Second, there is a call for more discipline. *A Nation at Risk* is especially insistent in calling for increased emphasis on correct behavior in the schools, particularly through the use of discipline codes. Third, several reports recommend that more time be devoted to education. They point out that Japanese and European children have longer school days and longer school years than American children; how then can we expect to keep up? The obvious solution is to lengthen the school day and the school year. *A Nation at Risk* recommends a 7-hour academic day and a 200–220-day year.

School Leadership: The Central Role of Principals

The fourth area of reform emphasized by many of the reports is the role of principals. Goodlad is especially provocative in recommending a revised and clarified division of authority and responsibility for local schools. He would have the states set broad goals for education but allow local flexibility. School districts, in turn, would set broad, system-wide goals, but leave considerable flexibility at the building level. Within this framework, the role of the principal would be considerably enhanced. Our educational system has fallen into the habit of promoting good teachers to principals and good principals to assistant superintendents. If principals are crucial in the educational process, such "promotions" may not be in the best interests of students. Indeed, there is a general understanding across the reports, based in large part on the effective schools literature (Cohen, 1983), that principals are a key to both education reform and quality schooling for our children. Thus, recommendations involve better selection of principals, more adequate compensation, and above all greater authority for principals in allocating resources, organizing instruction, and choosing teachers (Task Force on Education for Economic Growth, 1983).

Given the controversy surrounding each of the four common issues addressed by the reports, it is no surprise that the commissions themselves received thorough criticism (*New Republic,* 1983; Passow, 1984; Peterson, 1983; Stedman, 1985; Symposium, 1984). Commissions and their overwritten, often simplistic reports make an easy target (Haskins, 1983; Peterson, 1983). But whatever their faults, the education commissions did focus national debate on an important issue of social policy. In this volume, we intend to advance this debate in a modest way by using the commission reports as a point of departure. Throughout, we seek feasible policies designed to deal with the problems identified by the reports. We begin, however, by defining and discussing a typology of possible education reforms. Our purpose in offering this typology is both to organize debate about reform and to highlight the particular types of reforms taken up in this volume.

A TYPOLOGY OF EDUCATIONAL REFORM

Table 1 presents one possible typology of educational reforms. The typology is divided into four panels: teachers and teaching; curriculum

TABLE 1: TYPOLOGY OF EDUCATIONAL REFORMS

Teachers and Teaching

A. Financial incentives for attraction, retention, development, and performance
   1. Uniform salary increases
   2. Entry pay increases
   3. Differentiated pay plans (career ladders, career development, merit pay, master or mentor teachers, etc.)
   4. Selective incentives (in specific content or geographical areas)
   5. Scholarships and grants for prospective teachers
B. Nonmonetary reward and recognition programs
C. Preparation and training
   1. Standards for prospective teachers
   2. Curricular and program reforms in schools of education
   3. In-service training and professional development
   4. Lateral entry plans
D. Criteria for certification
   1. Standards for preparation
   2. Competency testing
E. Evaluation procedures
F. Working conditions
   1. Class size
   2. Reduction or elimination of nonteaching tasks
   3. Increased authority

Curriculum and Instruction

A. Emphasis on basics (English, math, science, social studies)
B. Emphasis on information age subjects (science, math, computers, foreign languages, etc.)
   1. Teachers (supply, preparation, retention)
   2. Centers for coordination/development
   3. Boarding schools
C. Emphasis on standards for students
   1. Promotion and retention policies
   2. Testing programs (minimum competency, assessment, etc.)
   3. Requirements for extracurricular participation
   4. High school course requirements and graduation standards
   5. Entrance standards in higher education
D. Emphasis on school-to-work transition
   1. Improved guidance and counseling
   2. Vocational education and school-to-work transition programs
   3. Linkage with higher education
E. Instructional methods
   1. Advocacy of specific methods
   2. Ability grouping policies
F. Policies for unserved or underserved student populations
   1. Gifted and talented
   2. Remediation
   3. Handicapped
   4. Students at risk of dropping out
   5. Minorities and females

(continued)

TABLE 1:   (*Continued*)

Curriculum and Instruction (*cont.*)

G. Addition of instructional materials, supplies, equipment, etc.
H. Quantity of schooling
    1. Longer school days and/or years
    2. Preschool programs
    3. Saturday and summer programs
    4. Attendance
    5. Discipline
    6. Homework

Systemic Reforms

A. Reforms based on existing research concerning effective schools and learning climates
B. Administrative and management systems, including student discipline
C. Policy-making systems
D. Financing systems
E. Use of information and educational indicators

Research, Experimentation, Evaluation, and Diffusion

A. Identification of effective/ineffective schools, programs, practices, and policies
B. Diffusion/institutionalization of effective programs, practices, and policies
C. Development of acceptable, valid teacher evaluation procedures
D. Other research, development, and diffusion activities

---

and instruction; systemic reforms; and research, experimentation, evaluation, and diffusion. The first two panels correspond to the second and third categories we used to classify proposals from the commission reports. Our third panel, systemic reforms, includes the reports' emphasis on leadership but also deals more broadly with structural change in schools and school systems. The fourth panel includes not so much specific reforms but processes, such as research and evaluation, that lead to and, we hope, shape reform. The reports did not emphasize these processes, as their general approach was to identify policies thought to be effective in addressing the schools' problems. Nonetheless, in both this typology and this volume we highlight linkages between research, evaluation, and policy.

Teachers and Teaching

Many of the most important reforms concern teachers and the teaching profession (Table 1, first panel); we address these reforms in Part I of this volume. The importance of policies that lead to recruitment, preparation, retention, and continued development of quality teachers can hardly be overstated. Most critics hoping to attract the best and brightest into the profession have noted the financial opportunities available outside the profession and then demanded increased teacher salaries. These increases are variously concentrated at the entry level or more senior levels, or not concentrated at all. Selective incentives are also commonly proposed as means of attracting and retaining certain groups of teachers, notably those teaching math and the sciences.

Teacher education has also received a great deal of attention. Higher standards for entrance into teacher education programs, changes in the balance of core and specialty courses, and the addition or expansion of internships are some of the reforms advocated most frequently. In addition, educators are now giving critical attention to the certification of teachers. A basic thrust of this attention to certification is to restrict the admission of new people into the teaching profession—precisely the opposite course from that recommended below by Peterson (Chapter 2 in this volume). Once in the profession, teachers might be influenced by a host of recently enacted or proposed reforms dealing with in-service training, continuing education, and performance evaluation.

The final reform directly involving teachers as professionals is modification of teachers' working conditions, including reduction of class size. Many observers have suggested that improvement will result from strictly enforcing current class size limits or from adding teachers to reduce these limits. Alternatively, some have argued for selective reductions in certain subject areas or at certain grade levels. Such reductions in class size are examples of additive (i.e., "more is better") reforms, as are reforms discussed below in relation to quantity of schooling or additional materials and facilities. In contrast, increases in class size, as might be possible through the use of computer-assisted instruction, have been offered as a means of freeing resources for other educational purposes (see Peterson's chapter). Other reforms in working conditions include reducing the time devoted to nonteaching tasks, and increased authority for teachers both within the classroom and in school governance.

Curriculum and Instruction

A second general area in which numerous reforms have been enacted or proposed is curriculum and instruction (Table 1, second panel). We have previously noted the emphasis placed by the commission reports on instruction in the basics. Curriculum reform proposals also stress effectiveness and excellence—especially as related to economic productivity—but some also focus on equity. As in the reforms that followed the launching of Sputnik, much recent concern has focused on subjects such as math and science, foreign languages, and information processing. This focus has led to proposals for attracting, preparing, and retaining teachers in these subject areas and for creating a variety of new institutions to promote and improve instruction in these subjects.

"Standards" is one of the catchwords in the current reform era. When critics say that standards should be raised, they often mean that students should have more coursework, especially in the basics. A second type of standards reform goes beyond course content and specifies outcome measures. Outcome measures take many forms and can serve many purposes, as suggested by the chapters on educational indicators below (Chapters 8, 9, and 10). A tightening of entrance standards by institutions of higher education has also been advanced as a means of encouraging greater effectiveness at earlier levels. The emphases on "information age" subjects and on standards are entirely consistent with the current linkage between education and economic growth. Yet, nowhere is this linkage clearer than in the renewed attention given to career guidance, vocational education, and cooperation between the public schools and community colleges and universities.

The press for effectiveness, although not necessarily for economic growth, is also partly responsible for recent advocacy of specific methods of academic instruction, such as direct instruction or computer-assisted instruction. Reforms in ability-grouping practices (see Epstein, Chapter 5) have been recommended, reflecting a widespread concern for both effectiveness and equity. Epstein also presents a more detailed typology of particular features of school and classroom organization that can be manipulated to increase educational effectiveness.

A variety of perspectives are apparent in proposals to reform programs dealing with students deemed to be unserved or underserved. The interests of these populations—the gifted and talented, those in need of remediation or at risk of dropping out, the handicapped, minorities, and females—are often promoted under the rubric of educational equity. Their problems and needs can be addressed through many policies broader than those involving curriculum and instruction; e.g., selection of teachers, research and experimentation, and systemic reforms (see below). Teaching these populations may impose costs; for example, "placing a handicapped child in a regular classroom might alter the quality and generosity of time a teacher can give nonhandicapped students, and, depending on the handicapped child, might cause disruptions in the classroom" (Turnbull et al, 1983, p. 510). Nonetheless, several recent policy recommendations focus on the needs of these special populations from the perspectives of both equity and effectiveness.

Three of these populations—those needing remediation, minorities, and the gifted—are the special concern of the contributors to Part II of this volume.

The last two subheadings under curriculum and instruction are, like class-size reforms, additive rather than qualitative reforms. Practitioners, especially in resource-poor districts, often describe the problems resulting from students having to share textbooks or reuse textbooks. Their suggestion that more resources be devoted to instructional materials and supplies must be taken seriously. The quantity of schooling issue has led to recommendations to extend the school year or school day, to offer preschool programs, and to offer optional or mandatory Saturday or summer programs. Moreover, proposals to revise attendance, discipline, and homework policies have the goal of increasing the time students devote to learning.

Systemic Reforms

The third set of reforms (Table 1, third panel), sometimes called "systemic" reforms, is relevant at the federal, state, local, or building level. Some of these reforms have been addressed by the effective schools movement and by the commission reports' emphasis on school leadership. Others, however, have received relatively little attention by reformers over the past 4 years. Particularly neglected has been the federal level, perhaps because the major responsibility for education in our system of government has always been held by states and localities.

The policies classified as systemic in this typology include the use of effective schools research, managerial and administrative reform, governance or policy system reform, and financial reform. At the local level, reform of the role of school boards has been proposed by the Institute for Educational Leadership (1986). Various factors that contribute to effective learning climates, such as clear academic mission, safe and orderly environments, and time on task, are related to entries elsewhere in the typology and to recommendations made by the commission reports. As examples, the monitoring of student progress is directly related to the use of testing programs as part of the current emphasis on standards; teacher preparation must include the instilling of classroom management skills necessary for adequate student time on task; principals must be trained to be instructional leaders, and so forth. These examples again remind us of the interrelatedness of educational reforms. They also suggest that levels of policy making above the school or district level can use effective schools research by investing in testing programs, teacher preparation, training principals, and new facilities.

State and local managerial reforms have focused on programs such as the introduction of computers into management, the training of administrators at various levels, the provision of business and finance managers for districts and schools, the creation of private sector–public education partnerships, and increased cooperation between higher education and the public schools. Some reforms call for a greater role for teachers in school governance. Discipline, as a supplement to positive leadership in maintaining learning climates, is also a relevant part of school and classroom management. Reforms of policy-making systems, such as the methods for selecting school boards and officers, have been concentrated at the state level. Although such changes have been frequent in the last several decades and proposals have regularly surfaced more recently, the effect of such changes on student learning has been continually questioned. Several states have also proposed or enacted substantial financial reforms, often intended to provide educational equalization among areas and groups. Recent financial reforms have included state assumption of responsibility for new facilities, and proposals at the federal level to increase competition between public and private schools through the use of vouchers, and parental choice.

A final type of systemic reform, which will be treated in Part III of this volume, concerns the use of information and educational indicators as means to guiding and improving schools. This reform is germane to all the reforms outlined up to this point because the information used expresses goals and values, and facilitates evaluation and improvement of substantive policies.

Research, Experimentation, Evaluation, and Diffusion

Although some programs in the areas of research, development, experimentation, innovation, and evaluation (Table 1, last panel) have been proposed and adopted recently, these policies have received less attention than other policies summarized in Table 1. Some of the relatively recent activities in these areas, such as the search for effectiveness and the diffusion of policies furthering it, continue to receive support. Moreover, the development of procedures for school and teacher evaluation has received much attention from researchers, and was mentioned frequently by the commission reports. However, many other policies designed to increase and use educational knowledge can also be advanced through research, trial, evaluation, and diffusion. If this process is carried out according to conventional models of technical rationality, its immediate usefulness may be limited (see House & Lapan, Chapter 4); but a longer-term approach, including teacher participation, may yield greater benefits. Several contributors to this volume, including Peterson (Chapter 2), House and Lapan (Chapter 4), Epstein (Chapter 5), Gallagher (Chapter 7), and MacRae and Lanier (Chapter 9), emphasize the need for research, development, evaluation, and use of repeated trials in initiating educational reforms.

Our purpose in presenting this typology of educational reform has been simply to bring some coherence to the wide variety of proposals currently under discussion. In addition, the typology can be used to show what we included and omitted in our choice of topics treated in this volume. No single volume could hope to consider all the possible reforms listed in Table 1. The major issue faced by those who would join the reform debate, then, is which specific types of school reform are most likely to make a lasting contribution to improving the public schools. We voted with our invitations to authors, selecting scholars to address the problems of teachers and teaching, equity and diversity, and the uses of educational information and indicators. We defend these selections with the chapters that follow.

OVERVIEW OF VOLUME

Having set forth the perspective from which recent educational reform efforts arose, and outlined the wide range of possible policies that might be undertaken, we turn now to a brief overview of the chapters that follow. These chapters address educational reform selectively, departing considerably from the commission reports that defined the problem for the public. In particular, the chapters differ from the commission reports in being more oriented to research, and in placing greater emphasis on equity and diversity and less on excellence. They also address important underlying problems that are not simply matters of educational policy but more nearly "meta-policy," particularly ways of generating and rewarding educational innovations and the nature of the knowledge that is relevant to those innovations.

Policies Concerned with Teachers and Teaching

A major concern in the movement for more effective and efficient public education has centered about teacher quality. Paul Peterson (Chapter 2) sets the stage for considering the wide variety of policies that affect teachers. He points out the need for adequate finances in support of teacher salaries, tracing the relations between the real (inflation-adjusted) salaries of teachers in comparison with nonteachers. In spite of a widespread concern with the need for high quality in teaching, many of the initially proposed remedies have ignored the economic incentives that affect the pool of potential teachers, and their budgetary cost in a period of fiscal stringency. Unnecessary state regulations may constrict the supply of teachers by limiting lateral entry or part-time work. Teachers' productivity may be increased through greater use of computers in instruction, though this improvement is likely to be slow and may await a new generation of teachers who will learn the new skills.

The present resistance to federal taxation and spending, Peterson points out, leads us as citizens to seek the resources needed for educational reform from the states; or leads some, usually wealthy, parents to the private schools. These trends often bypass the value of equity that played so large a part in educational policy making in the 1970s. Still, increased state support for education has been provided in the South, which has progressed economically, relative to other regions, but now requires educational improvement to match this economic progress.

The quality of teaching can be improved, not only through the attraction of able persons into the profession, but also through well-designed programs to prepare and retain teachers and improve their skills. Having been closely involved in educational reform in North Carolina, Donald Stedman (Chapter 3) traces some of the initiatives taken in that state, reviews them critically, and proposes further innovations in teacher education. He proposes greater emphasis on graduate training for teachers, especially for those who will teach in junior and senior high schools, and on programs provided by major research universities. His proposals are generally compatible with those of the recent Carnegie Forum Report (1986), particularly in the emphasis on prospective teachers' specializing in subjects other than education as undergraduates. His proposals also lead to great flexibility in designing teacher career plans, much like those proposed by the Carnegie Forum.

The teacher is a central figure in educational improvement, not only as someone who responds to the market, or who can become a more efficient producer, but also as a person whose perspectives are at the center of a wide variety of changes in the educational system. Ernest House and Stephen Lapan (Chapter 4) argue that the teacher is the "driver of the classroom" and that reformers who ignore the teachers' perspective are doomed to failure. They take issue with a widespread view, that of "technical rationality," according to which research conducted without input from teachers must be the central guide to educational innovation and reform. Teachers, they contend, tend to operate in isolation and learn from their own experiences rather than from communication with researchers.

If teachers learn only from their own experiences, then researchers or analysts who wish to improve teaching must enter into that experience. The researchers might begin by studying what teachers actually do, so as to be able to suggest modifications consistent with the teachers' perspective. Researchers might help in the selection of teachers who perform best in the classroom, and thus help other teachers find models for improvement. Researchers might also conduct case studies of entire teaching programs and try to introduce other teachers to these programs. They might engage in action research, forming teams to study problems. Or, as a more fundamental approach to the teachers' situation, they might seek institutional changes that would break down the isolation of teachers and help them help one another. This last sort of change requires trust among teachers, and might be undermined by incentive systems that pit one teacher against another or expose teachers to criticism and publicity in the media.

Policies Concerned with Diversity and Equity

The recent wave of educational reform has stressed "effectiveness" and "excellence", but has sometimes been criticized as neglecting the diversity among pupils and schools, and the needs both for differential treatment of some students and for grouping students together because of their mutual educational influences. One type of diversity is addressed by Joyce Epstein (Chapter 5) in her chapter on effective schools and effective students. In dealing with the social organization of remediation, she argues that some pupils who fall behind are placed inappropriately in social roles by the school system (e.g., by tracking or by having to repeat a grade), when in a better system they need not be so placed. Such a definition of pupils' roles may be, at least in part, an artificially constructed type of diversity.

Epstein deals not only with the value of rapid remediation, but also with the means of accomplishing it and the sorts of research needed to find these means. She reports research in which her colleagues at Johns Hopkins have developed a possible method for remediation that involves teamwork by students. This peer teaching and learning process represents an innovation that would not necessarily have emerged from the day-to-day experiences of teachers, nor perhaps from incentives for remediation. Epstein claims, in other words, that research and experimentation are vital tools for educational innovation—not only to further equity but in any realm of educational reform. In this respect her work represents a different approach from that of House and Lapan. It is important, then, to see how innovations like those discussed by Epstein are diffused and reconciled with the perspectives of the teachers who are to use them.

A second type of diversity is treated by John Ogbu (Chapter 6). He is concerned with differences between pupils belonging to two culturally diverse groups in a caste-like relation—a difference of power as well as of culture. He deals, in an anthropological approach, with an ideal-typical situation in which the groups are clearly delimited and culturally separate. His ingenious distinction between immigrant and nonimmigrant minorities is used to explain the considerable difference between minorities who were brought against their will into American culture and those who entered it by free choice. In addition to differences in historical background and motivation, the different experiences and outlooks of the two types of minorities help explain a "low academic effort syndrome" among nonimmigrant minorities (such as Blacks); this syndrome leads in turn to low achievement, which is sustained by a continuing alienation from the goals of the school. This alienation can be reduced, he contends, in several ways: by making the transition from school to the occupational world more rewarding for nonimmigrant minorities; by making the school not a "scene of battle" but a scene of cultural reconciliation through "learning how to go to school"; by continuing efforts to eliminate the vestiges of racism in American society; and by involving parents in school decisions. Though Ogbu expresses some hope that the schools can contribute to bringing nonimmigrant minorities into the social and economic mainstream of American culture, his analysis shows quite clearly that low achievement and alienation among some groups find their causes—and perhaps their most efficacious solutions—outside the schoolbuilding.

James Gallagher (Chapter 7) examines a third type of diversity in his chapter on education of gifted students. In this case, diversity is based on student characteristics that are assumed to be relatively permanent. Gifted children, he argues, should be given special programs of study in a resource room at the elementary level and in special classes at the secondary level. We should continue to support quality programs for the handicapped and other groups at the opposite end of the achievement spectrum from the gifted, but Gallagher contends that our economic, military, and cultural survival rests disproportionately on the achievements of the gifted. In the past, we have foolishly ignored the special educational needs of this group. Thus, Gallagher argues that now is the time to direct greater resources, including federal dollars, to their education.

Uses of Information and Educational Indicators

Our national concern with the state of the public schools was heightened by trends in scores on the Scholastic Aptitude Test (SAT) and by comparisons between the test scores of American children and children in other countries (e.g., Stevenson, Shin–Ying, & Stigler, 1986). Defining public problems by use of standardized tests takes us back to an underlying question—that of how best to measure educational achievement and the effects of the schools in producing it. The recent enthusiasm for reform has produced many proposals for testing of both teachers and pupils. Not all have worked in practice. Some have been held back by the resistance of teachers, who have not only special expert knowledge but also vested interests. Others, depending on stable measurement of the schools' contributions, have been hampered by statistical problems, since the measurement of school effects turns out to be quite difficult. In this section of the volume, three chapters deal with the uses of statistics or indicators to define educational problems, to assess outcomes, and to stimulate subsequent innovation.

William Cooley (Chapter 8) emphasizes the special importance of using statistics at the district or school level. Statewide incentive systems tied to indicators have encountered special difficulties. Some incentives created by the use of indicators have led merely to public embarrassment of schools rather than improvement. Others have led to efforts to manipulate the test results themselves. Cooley argues, therefore, that educational statistics must be used primarily at the local level, in a manner designed to address the needs of local participants, such as school boards, over a continuing period in which the users can participate in the choice and use of the data. Similarly, indicators used in a single schoolbuilding should be integrated into the daily procedures of the teachers rather than being a foreign object over which teachers have little control.

MacRae and Lanier (Chapter 9) move to the state or district level in discussing the use of student improvement scores in incentive systems. They take up the notion, often proposed since at least the early 1970s, of a market-like arrangement whereby schools or teachers are rewarded for gains in learning by their pupils. Proposals of this sort have become much more numerous during the recent wave of reform. The underlying principle of rewarding success seems well recognized in many sorts of competitions, but has not yet been applied with great success to competition among teachers or schools. The authors discuss the results of recent reform efforts of this type; the efforts have varied in their degree of success although many are still continuing and remain to be judged.

MacRae and Lanier also discuss the statistical problems that arise in measurement of school or teacher effects on pupil improvement. Instability from one year to another has been a problem not fully recognized in recent proposals for incentive systems. Further research comparing various statistical measures, and policies using them, is required.

More important, however, is the motivation of participants to resist or manipulate the measures involved. Teachers or administrators whose careers are put at risk by incentive systems cannot easily tolerate a new type of uncertainty introduced by outsiders. It thus becomes especially important to seek out incentive systems that have been used successfully in other schools over a period of time, and to involve teachers in the design and implementation of the incentive procedures. Through such involvement teachers may be able to develop new job expectations that will help incentive systems succeed.

A central condition for the workability of these incentive systems is the supplementation of statistical information with qualitative and personal information (Cooley, 1983; Cooley & Bickel, 1986, pp. 270–271). A system based solely on test results, gathered and used by persons outside the school system being judged, is an invitation to both accusations of invalidity and efforts at manipulation. Test results can be rendered invalid by use of inappropriate tests, by accidental poor performance of pupils, or by manipulation by teachers. If, however, evaluating groups use measures of pupils' improvement together with personal knowledge and other information about the teachers or schools involved, this combination can give greater assurance that invalid results will be detected. Such "other" information might include indirect measures of performance, including reactions of students, former students, and parents; ratings of skill in classroom management; and assessments of process variables such as curriculum organization, use of discipline, and relations with parents. Incentive systems that incorporate such multiple measures have promise of lasting longer and perhaps succeeding. So, too, do reward systems that associate lesser rewards and threats with measures of performance (Wynne, 1984). Successive trials of modest incentive systems may contribute more in the long run than ambitious, salary-linked proposals initiated at the state level.

Since national concern was generated in part by test statistics, it is important to ask what use should be made of national statistics in the future. David Dill (Chapter 10) addresses this issue in his chapter on national educational indicators. He observes that the decentralization of American school systems makes it difficult to set national goals, but argues that a system of national indicator statistics, including measures of pupils' gain, could be of great value in guiding educational policy. While acknowledging the controversial nature of this proposal, he outlines the considerable advantages of such a system and rebuts arguments that might be raised against it.

The general issues of teacher quality, student diversity, and the use of indicators are a selection among the many questions that have been raised in recent years about education policy. Yet these issues, and others that the authors raise in discussing them, have a broad relevance to current and future policies for our public schools. By design, the contributors have made a special effort to state the policy implications of their work. Summarizing these policy implications in the final chapter will give us an opportunity to propose a moderately coherent set of policies that would promote achievement while serving equity in the public schools.

REFERENCES

Adler, M. J. (1982). *The Paideia proposal*. New York: Macmillan.

Bennett, W. J. (1986). *First lessons: A report on elementary education in America.* Washington, DC: U.S. Government Printing Office.

Boyer, E. (1983). *High school: A report on secondary education in America.* Princeton, NJ: Carnegie Foundation for the Advancement of Teaching.

Carnegie Forum on Education and the Economy, Task Force on Teaching as a Profession. (1986). *A nation prepared: Teachers for the 21st century.* Hyattsville, MD: Author.

Cohen, M. (1983). Instructional, management, and social conditions in effective schools. In A. Odden & L. D. Webb (Eds.), *School finance and school improvement: Linkages for the 80s.* Cambridge, MA: Ballinger.

Cooley, W. W. (1983). Improving the performance of an educational system. *Educational Researcher, 12*(6), 4–12.

Cooley, W. W., & Bickel, W. E. (1986). *Decision-oriented education research.* Boston: Kluwer–Nijhoff.

Dewey, J. (1916). *Democracy and education.* New York: Macmillan.

———. (1938). *Experience and education.* New York: Collier Books.

Goodlad, J. I. (1983). *A place called school: Prospects for the future.* New York: McGraw–Hill.

Haskins, R. (1983). Presidential and congressional commissions: The Select Panel in context. In R. Haskins (Ed.), *Child health policy in an age of fiscal austerity: Critiques of the Select Panel Report* (pp. 162–197). Norwood, NJ: Ablex.

Institute for Educational Leadership. (1986, November). *School boards: Strengthening grass-roots leadership.* Washington, DC: Author.

James, W. (1958; 1899). *Talks to teachers.* New York: Norton.

National Commission on Excellence in Education. (1983). *A nation at risk: The imperatives for educational reform.* Washington, DC: U.S. Department of Education.

National Commission on the Reform of Secondary Education. (1973). *The reform of secondary education.* New York: McGraw–Hill.

National Panel on High School and Adolescent Education. (1976). *The education of adolescents.* Washington, DC: U.S. Government Printing Office.

New Republic. (1983, November 7). *189* (Issue No. 3590).

Passow, A. H. (1984). Tackling the reform reports of the 1980s. *Phi Delta Kappan, 65*(10), 674–683.

Peterson, P. E. (1983). Did the educational commissions say anything? *Brookings Review, 2*(2), 3–11.

Rickover, H. G. (1963). *American education: A national failure.* New York: Dutton.

Sizer, T. R. (1984). *Horace's compromise: The dilemma of the American high school.* Boston: Houghton Mifflin.

Stedman, J. B. (1985). *Education in America: Reports on its condition, recommendations for change* (IB83106). Washington, DC: Congressional Research Service.

Stevenson, H. W., Shin–Ying, L., & Stigler, J. W. (1986). Mathematics achievement of Chinese, Japanese and American children. *Science, 231*, 693–699.

Symposium on the year of the reports: Responses from the educational community. (1984). *Harvard Educational Review, 54*(1), 1–31.

Task Force of the Business–Higher Education Forum. (1983). *America's competitive challenge: The need for a national response.* Washington, DC: Business–Higher Education Forum.

Task Force on Education for Economic Growth. (1983). *Action for excellence: A comprehensive plan to improve our nation's schools.* Denver: Education Commission of the States.

Turnbull, H. R., III, et al. (1983). A policy analysis of "least restrictive" education of handicapped children. *Rutgers Law Journal, 14*, 489–540.

Twentieth Century Fund Task Force on Federal Elementary and Secondary Education Policy. (1983). *Making the grade.* New York: Twentieth Century Fund.

Wynne, E. A. (1984). School award programs: Evaluations as a component in incentive systems. *Educational Evaluation & Policy Analysis, 6*(1), 85–93.

PART ONE

TEACHERS AND TEACHING

Two

Economic and Political Trends Affecting Education[1]

PAUL E. PETERSON

In the next quarter of a century American education could divide into two distinctive parts: (1) an improving, expanding private sector, utilizing new technologies to provide more sophisticated education to children of two-income families who, with the aid of tax credits, are able to purchase a quality, private education; and (2) a declining, increasingly minority-dominated public sector for children from families of lesser income; it could more closely resemble the charity schools of the past than contemporary public schools. I do not think these developments are the most likely outcome of current trends in public education. The public schools have proven in the past to have a resilience that has withstood both economic recessions and racial turmoil. But certain developments, if extrapolated, have made a dual system of education a possibility in a society where such an outcome might have once seemed remote.

The trends of which I speak are demographic, economic, and political. They include the ever-increasing cost of teacher quality, the conservative, tax-minded mood in Washington, the increasing percentage of minorities among the youth population, especially in snowbelt cities, and the revivification of the nonpublic school. They are not offset by the optimistic mood set in train by the National Commission on Educational Excellence and other studies calling for educational reform. These studies, as a whole, propose solutions that are little more than political palliatives instead of serious responses to underlying economic and social developments (Peterson, 1983a). In this chapter I shall show how a diverse set of forces poses significant new problems for American educa-

---

[1]Research assistance for this chapter was provided by Carol Peterson, Joel Ostrow, and Nathan Teske.

tion. In all probability the system will respond successfully; but the outcome is sufficiently problematic to deserve serious discussion by the educational community.

THE QUESTION OF TEACHER QUALITY

Since the National Commission on Educational Excellence announced its discovery of a "tide of mediocrity" sweeping American education, a flurry of studies, reports, proposals, enactments, and policy initiatives have taken place. According to the Department of Education's own official report, 28 states have enacted teacher preparation or certification alterations, 14 have raised teacher salaries, 6 have instituted career ladders for teachers, others have required competence tests for high school graduates, and in some, teachers are themselves required to take a minimum competency test.[2]

Much is to be said for this as for other periods of reform and renewal in education. As practices become standardized, programs routinized, and organizational relationships institutionalized, much of the original energy and purpose that motivated schools and educators becomes enmired in trivial pursuits. But too often the call for reform, especially when pronounced from on high by national commissions and major political figures, is followed by nostrums and panaceas that can hardly address the problems at hand. Significant reform is likely to be financially costly, organizationally disturbing, and politically unsettling. Those who gain will do so only some time in the future, while the burdens will immediately be felt. The beneficiaries are likely to be only vaguely identified and poorly organized, while the losers will be self-consciously attentive and involved from the beginning.

It is tempting under such circumstances to claim to have found serious problems, but actually to propose changes that are likely to modify the status quo only slightly. Indeed, sometimes steps taken in the name of reform are advances to the rear.

In the present call for educational reform the teacher has received special attention. Given the labor-intensive character of the educational industry, such concentration on the quality of teaching is well advised. Yet many of the reforms designed to enhance teacher quality seem to be designed for media and popular consumption rather than solutions to the problems that have been identified. For example, the Department of Education has denoted some schools as excellent and a few teachers as

---

[2]For these and other examples of state and local reform efforts see United States Department of Education (1984b).

masterful, but the applause these individuals have received is hardly likely to change the modus operandi of thousands of others. Some states have provided salary bonuses for teachers who agree to participate in a master teacher program. As useful as this innovation may be, it's hardly a significant structural change in teacher policy. Some states have increased teacher salaries, but on the whole these increases are only barely keeping pace with increases in the cost of living.

The Cost of Quality Teachers

Many reformers imply that school improvement can be achieved at little or no additional financial cost. While the National Commission on Educational Excellence avoided explicit discussion of the financial costs of its recommendations, its warm reception by an administration otherwise committed to cutting federal expenditures for schools carries with it the implication that schools can be improved by more efficient use of existing resources. In fact it is noteworthy that the commission, though emphasizing many signs of educational decline, failed to mention one of the areas in which decline was both unmistakable and easily documented—the drop in teacher salaries. As can be seen in Table 1, teacher salaries, in real dollars, fell in the decade between 1970 and 1983 from $23,334 to $20,432, a decrease of some 12%. (This is a conservative measure; the drop from 1972 to 1982 was 22%.) To some extent, the decline in teacher salaries is understandable. The teacher market

TABLE 1:   AVERAGE SALARIES FOR ELEMENTARY AND SECONDARY SCHOOL TEACHERS, COMPARED WITH FULL-TIME EMPLOYEES IN ALL INDUSTRIES, 1929–30 THROUGH 1982–83

	Average annual teacher salary		Average earnings of full-time employees in industry		Percentage higher teacher salaries
	Current $	Constant $[a]	Current $	Constant $[a]	
1929–30	$ 1,420	$ 8,366	$ 1,386	$ 8,165	2.4%
1939–40	1,441	10,287	1,272	9,152	12.4
1949–50	3,010	12,518	2,930	12,186	2.7
1959–60	5,174	17,545	4,632	15,707	11.7
1969–70	8,840	23,334	7,334	19,358	20.5
1979–80	16,715	21,495	15,094	19,406	10.7
1982–83	21,229	21,568	18,979[b]	19,283[b]	11.8

[a]1983 = 100.   [b]Preliminary data.
Source. National Center for Education Statistics, 1984, p. 55; and National Education Association, 1984, p. 457.

changed from one in which teachers were in short supply to one in which the number of new graduates exceeded the demand for them. At the very time the baby boomers were graduating from college the baby bust generation was in grade school. Trying to keep teacher salaries high when supply increased and demand decreased would have defied the laws of the marketplace.

But in the process of adjusting to new market conditions, teacher salaries fell, relative to the salaries of employees in the other industries. Whereas teachers in 1970 received about 20% more than did the average employee in all industries, that percentage fell to 14% in 1983 (see Table 1). In other words, for the college graduate entering the labor market, teaching had become a comparatively less attractive profession to pursue.

As teacher salaries have fallen, demographic trends began to move in a direction opposite from those of the 1970s. On the one side, the baby bust generation is now entering college, and if the percentage of college graduates entering the field of teaching remains at current levels, the numbers will fall (see Figure 1).

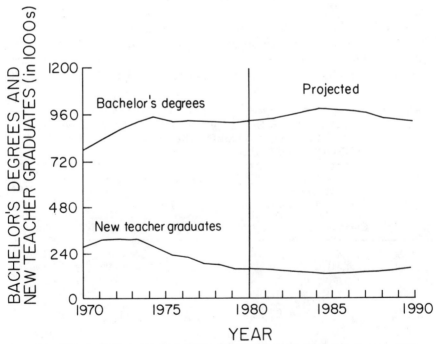

FIGURE 1:   Bachelor's degrees and supply of new teacher graduates, 1969–70 to 1990–91 (National Center for Education Statistics, 1982b, p. 76.)

At the same time that the supply of teachers is becoming more limited, the demand is growing. A new baby boomlet, the children of those baby boomers who are now in their child-rearing years, are entering elementary school. The elementary school-age population, which has been quite stable for the past few years, is expected to increase by more than 10% by 1990 (Table 2). While these increases will be offset somewhat by declines at the secondary level, the overall demand for teachers now appears to be intensifying for the first time in more than a decade.

Given these changes in demography, one can confidently predict that school boards must increase teacher salaries, if teacher quality is not to fall precipitously. However, few recognize the size of the increments that are needed. First, salaries must increase by 4% or 5% a year merely to keep pace with inflation. Second, increases of 2.5% a year beyond that amount are probably necessary if teacher salaries are to remain competitive with those in other industries. Such an increase will be necessary if productivity in the United States economy as a whole improves by 2% to 3% per annum and if workers realize these productivity gains result in increases in real wages. The Reagan administration optimistically predicts a 4% growth in productivity over the next 5 years. If this projection is accurate, teacher salaries will have to increase by an even faster rate, merely to keep competitive.

Third, salary increases higher than these levels will be necessary if schools are to attract more than the current 17% of college graduates necessary to teach the larger number of elementary school pupils anticipated by 1990 and to offset the increased rate of retirement that analysts expect in the next few years. In addition, still larger salary increments will be necessary to attract better quality personnel into the field of teaching that the National Commission on Excellence in Education

TABLE 2:　　SCHOOL AGE
　　　　　　　POPULATION, 1960–90

	5–13 years old (thousands)	14–17 years old (thousands)
1960	32,965	11,219
1970	36,672	15,924
1980	31,080	16,139
1985	29,654	14,731
1990	32,189	12,950

Source. U.S. Bureau of the Census, Current Population Reports, "Population Estimates and Projections," Series P-25.

TABLE 3: AVERAGE SALARIES
OF ELEMENTARY AND
SECONDARY PUBLIC SCHOOL
TEACHERS, 1929–30 THROUGH
1990–91

	Current Dollars	Constant Dollars[a]
1929–30	$ 1,420	$ 8,366
1939–40	1,441	10,287
1949–50	3,010	12,518
1959–60	5,174	17,545
1969–70	8,840	23,334
1979–80	16,715	21,564
1985–86	21,229[b]	21,568[b]
1990–91	46,238[b]	34,215[b]

Note. An inflation rate of 5% per annum is assumed.

[a]1983 = 100. [b]Projected, assuming an inflation rate of 5%, a salary comparable to 1970 wage levels, a 20 percent salary increase, and an increase in real wages of 2.5% a year.

Source. National Center for Education Statistics, 1984; National Center for Education Statistics, 1982b; National Education Association, 1983.

(1983) calls for. It is difficult to specify the exact percentage by which salaries will have to increase, but if they are to regain by 1990 the same competitive edge vis-à-vis other occupations they had achieved in 1970, they will have to reach a level of $44,772 in current dollars and receive the 20 percent bonus that educational reformers think necessary to improve teacher quality, (See Table 3).

In short, to keep up with inflation and expected salary increases in other occupations and to regain the competitive advantage that teachers had in 1970, and to implement educational reforms teacher salaries will need to double in nominal terms by the end of the decade from where they were in 1982–83.

Unfortunately, even with the current wave of reform, it is unlikely that such a dramatic turn around in teacher salaries will occur. For that to happen Americans would have to agree to more than double their nominal spending on public elementary and secondary schools from $97 billion in 1981 to $242 billion by 1990.

It is true that Americans have done this in the past. Between 1949 and 1975 we more than doubled the percentage of the gross national product allocated to the public schools (Table 4), from 1.8% in 1949 to 4.1% in 1975. But between 1975 and 1982 the percentage fell to 3.3%, both as a function of declining numbers of pupils and of decreasing teacher salaries. As a nation, we might return to our previous perfor-

TABLE 4: PERCENTAGE OF THE GROSS NATIONAL
PRODUCT SPENT ON PUBLIC
ELEMENTARY AND SECONDARY
EDUCATION, 1949–85

	GNP	Public Elementary and Secondary Current Expenditures	% of GNP
	(billions—unadjusted dollars)		
1949	$ 258.0	$ 4.7	1.8%
1959	486.5	12.3	2.5
1969	935.5	34.2	3.7
1975	1,528.8	62.1	4.1
1979	2,395.4[a]	87.0[a]	3.6
1981	2,954.1[b]	101.1	3.4
1982	3,073.0	108.1	3.5
1990	5,726.9	265.0	4.2

Note. The school year beginning in September of the listed year.
[a]Based on 1978 GNP of $2,106.6. [b]Based on 1980 GNP of
$2,626.1. [c]Projected, Brookings Institution. [d]Projected, Department of
Education, using projected CPI.
Source. National Center for Education Statistics, 1984, pp. 80–81; National Center for Education Statistics, 1982b, p. 104; Perry, 1985.

mance but the gains in the 1950s and 1960s occurred at a time when the public seemed prepared to accept a shift in expenditures from the private to the public sector. Now that tax cutting has proven politically popular at all levels of government, and proposals to raise taxes have been "the kiss of death," it is difficult to see how current trends can be reversed so that in just a few short years real expenditures for public education can grow by a rate equivalent to that of the 1950s and 1960s. This point is elaborated in detail in a later section.

These trends in education are what are necessary if the United States is to improve the quality of its existing teaching force, given an educational system organized as we know it today. Over the long run, education competes with other industries for its personnel. If its level of compensation steadily falls, relative to that of other industries, it must be expected that the quality of those attracted to the industry will also gradually decline.

These changes in teacher quality will not happen precipitously. In the short run, compensation levels can rise or fall decidedly without any apparent effects on performance. Many people working in a declining industry have already so committed themselves to this particular occupation that they cannot readjust without great personal and financial cost. One of the fallacies made by reformers in the 1960s was to expect immediate results in educational performance as a function of increased resource commitments to education. The reverse fallacy is now being made; whenever people do not see immediate institutional decline as revenues become more scarce, they conclude we can get by with less. But over the long run changing compensation levels will have their effects. Young people making their first occupational choice can be expected to choose the more rewarding career. Many people in education have discovered early in their careers the advantages of switching to more lucrative lines of activity. This will happen with even greater frequency in a future of declining relative salaries. In these and in countless other ways, marginal shifts in occupational choice can be expected to have a slow but steady impact on the quality of the teaching profession.

Already, we have evidence that the quality of those choosing education as a career has declined in response to falling compensation for educators. As can be seen in Figure 2, SAT scores for those choosing education as their major not only declined throughout the 1970s but, more significantly, the decline was steeper for this group than for college-bound seniors more generally. These data are perfectly consistent with the decrease in teacher salaries relative to earnings in other professions. One can hardly expect a reversal of this downward trend in teacher quality, unless salary declines are reversed.

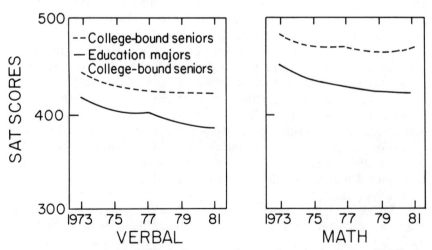

FIGURE 2:   Academic ability of prospective teachers is declining (Darling–Hammond, 1984, p. 2).

Reducing Restrictions on Labor Supply

Short of major salary increases, there are only two alternative ways of addressing the question of teacher quality. Neither can act as a complete substitute for improved compensation and both are likely to encounter strong political resistance, but both are likely to be pursued at least to some extent. First, one could try to check the decline in teacher quality by reducing current limitations on the supply of teachers available to the public schools. In most states teacher recruitment is restricted by many state laws and local regulations. Teachers are required to take a very specific set of courses in college; they must undergo a well-defined set of practice teaching experiences; they must pass certain tests; they must be paid according to a previously set schedule that usually takes into account only years of education and years of work experience; they typically must be hired on a full-time basis; and if they move to another state, they often must meet a new set of certification requirements.

As a result, many people whom local school administrators regard as potentially excellent teachers simply cannot be hired because they do not have the formal qualifications. Other people avoid the field of education altogether because they object to the training they are required to take. The net result is an artificial limit on the supply of available people for teaching. Schools are forced to accept less able, lower quality teachers than their salaries otherwise might be able to entice. The problem is especially severe in subject areas such as mathematics, science, and computer education, where salaries in industry are particularly high.

If states and school systems could introduce greater flexibility into their requirements for entering into the teaching profession, local school districts could select teachers from a wider pool. If they could pay more for those teachers whose skills are in short supply, they could maintain more even quality in all subject areas. If school districts could hire part-time teachers, they could draw upon the many in our population who enjoy teaching as a sideline but are unwilling to devote their entire career to the field.

Some progress in this direction is being made as part of the reform effort. Some colleges and universities are devising more flexible teacher education programs; some school systems are finding ways of bringing people into the schools on a part-time basis; and some special inducements to enter teaching are being given to those with a bent toward mathematics and science. But the opposition of teacher organizations to differentiated pay schedules and to less restrictive recruitment practices is likely to be intense. Also, many colleges of education are reluctant to see changes in teacher education requirements, especially when present requirements guarantee a stable supply of students in an otherwise shrinking market for higher education.

Not only is it politically difficult to reduce the restrictions on teacher supply, but it is possible that even more restrictions on supply will be imposed in the name of reform. Should this happen, reforms proposed under the rubric of enhancing teacher quality could ironically have quite the opposite effect. Compulsory national examinations for teachers are one example. Unless it can be shown that exam scores correlate with teacher effectiveness—and most studies show no such effect (Hanushek, 1981)—then such tests simply restrict the supply of potential teachers. The requirement that teachers take an additional year of college instruction is another attempt to restrict the supply of teachers. Inasmuch as a teacher loses a full year's salary by being held in school longer, such a requirement greatly increases the cost of becoming a teacher. Unless teacher salaries go up by an equivalent amount, the so-called reform will only make teaching a less attractive potential career.

Other attempts to restrict the supply of teachers include extensive in-service training requirements, rules that discourage re-entry into teaching if one has left the profession for several years, refusal to recognize teacher certificates from other states, and special training in order to earn certification in specific subject domains. As Gary Sykes (1983) has observed:

> To date, the response of policymakers to the decline of the teaching profession has been largely symbolic, emphasizing regulatory measures that misconstrue the problem. Mandating competency tests for prospective teachers and otherwise tightening licensing and certification requirements may screen out the least academically able teacher candidates, but such actions will not contribute to the more important task of attracting bright, committed young people to teaching, nor will they sustain them throughout a career in the classroom. (p. 24)

Some rules and requirements are certainly necessary. Some preparation for a teaching career undoubtedly enhances one's ability to work effectively in a classroom setting. But all additions to the already elaborate code of requirements governing teacher supply need to be examined in order to see whether the benefits of additional training outweigh the costs that come from restricting teacher supply.

Changing the Pupil/Teacher Ratio: The Computer Revolution

Apart from reducing the restrictions on teacher supply, we could improve teacher quality without increasing educational costs by increasing pupil–teacher ratios. To do so would, of course, reverse the historic tendency in American education. Over the past 50 years we have increased the number of teachers relative to the number of pupils with every passing decade. Since 1965 the ratio in elementary schools has dropped from 26 to 22 pupils per teacher (Peterson, 1983b, p. 47). There is reason to expect that, with continued emphasis on compensatory and special education, the ratio will remain low. But what if new technological developments make possible learning contexts where teachers do less in the way of direct instruction and provide instead a framework within which children teach themselves? The computer revolution may be reaching a point where in the next decade or so the machine does more than supplement the teacher—it may actually be able to act as a partial substitute.

At this point we have no way of knowing whether computers—like the printing press—will allow capital to substitute for labor in education as it has in so many other fields. In fact, experience with the first generation of computers has not been particularly promising.

Many have cast doubt on the ease with which schools deploy computers, the appropriateness with which they have initially been used, or the eagerness with which students will respond to these machines. Undoubtedly, many of the claims of the computer movement are as unwarranted and exaggerated as have been the claims of other pedagogical reformers. But if we look at the longer-run implications of computers in education and not simply at the immediate problems associated with their introduction, a number of considerations deserve emphasis:

1. The current capacities of computers in education are an imperfect measure of their potential. The cost of the basic hardware continues to fall rapidly, the capacity of computer chips continues to multiply, and the ability to exchange information among systems is accelerating exponentially.
2. Computer software for education remains in its infancy. As the capacity of hardware rapidly expands, imaginative applications making the computer a more effective teacher are inevitable.
3. Computerized instruction can be individualized to a degree impossible in the regular classroom. The extent to which computers can free students from classroom routines has only begun to be explored.
4. Computers offer perhaps one of the most significant opportunities to substitute capital for labor in education since the printed word replaced oral communication as the primary medium for transmitting ideas and information. If pupil–teacher ratios are increased, schools can pay teachers higher salaries without increasing overall educational costs. Higher quality personnel can be attracted to a

profession whose responsibilities would be more complex, whose income relative to other occupations would be higher, and whose prestige would be enhanced.

The processes by which these changes would occur are fairly predictable. Private schools and prestigious schools in high-income communities will begin experimentation with a more complete use of computer instruction. Real and imagined successes will be touted in colleges of education, in teacher conventions, and by manufacturers of computer software. New approaches will be encouraged by a special grant program financed by the federal government and mandated by state legislatures. Adoption will begin slowly, but once success stories are believed the innovation will rapidly spread outward from the early "lighthouse" schools.

Luddites will oppose the innovation, arguing that students can learn only from teachers, not from machines. Computers will be accused of isolating students from their peers and from adult authority. It will be said that they aggravate autistic tendencies and inhibit penmanship. Teachers' organizations will complain about rising pupil–teacher ratios, and inevitable computer breakdowns will create concern about the reliability of the new approaches to education. Most of all, policy analysts will demonstrate that organizational ineptitude and bureaucratic sluggishness impede the rate at which effective computerization is adopted. Yet an older generation uncomfortable with these new machines will gradually be replaced with a younger one more accepting of the new technology, and education will adapt itself to the revolution in information and communication that is transforming nearly every phase of American life.

These changes will occur well after 1990. However optimistic one might be about the longer term outlook, the near-run state of affairs is quite bleak. On the one hand, we have seen that educational costs must increase rapidly if the current enthusiasm for educational reform is to be translated into improved performance. On the other hand, the country's mood is in favor of fiscal retrenchment in the public sector.

FISCAL SOURCES OF SUPPORT FOR PUBLIC EDUCATION

The Federal Role

Nowhere is retrenchment as well entrenched as in Washington, D.C. To be sure, the federal government has never paid for more than 10% of the total cost of public elementary and secondary education, but in the first years of the Reagan administration that figure fell steadiliy so that by 1983 it was less than 7%. In the two areas where the federal role had become the most substantial—compensatory education and aid for the handicapped—the federal contribution in real dollar terms fell by 24% and 14%, respectively (Table 5).

Given the current concern with fiscal deficits, an enhanced federal role in education should not be anticipated in the foreseeable future. Three graphs illustrate how much greater are the deficits of the 1980s, compared with past deficits. Figure 3 shows that the real value of the gross federal debt changed hardly at all over the three decades after World War II. In 1981 the debt was no larger than it had been in 1947, though it had increased moderately from the level reached in 1974. Although annual deficits were incurred throughout this period, they were offset by inflation-caused declines in the real value of pre-existing debt. In short, the government was monetizing its debt (by devaluing its currency) as rapidly as it was adding to it. Only after 1981 does the real

TABLE 5: IMPACT OF BUDGET CHANGES IN MAJOR EDUCATION PROGRAMS DURING THE REAGAN ADMINISTRATION

Fiscal year	Appropriation (in thousands)	Percentage change from FY 1980	Percentage change adjusted for inflation[a]
Compensatory education for disadvantaged children			
1980	$3,215,593	——	——
1981	3,104,317	−3.5	−12.0
1982	3,033,969	−5.6	−20.6
1983	3,200,394	−0.5	−22.0
1984	3,480,000	+8.2	−19.7
1985 (administration request)	3,480,000	+8.2	−23.8
Education of the handicapped, state grant program			
1980	$ 874,500	——	——
1981	874,500	0	− 8.8
1982	931,008	+ 6.5	−10.4
1983	1,017,900	+16.4	− 8.8
1984	1,068,875	+22.2	− 9.3
1985 (administration request)	1,068,875	+22.2	−13.9

Source. Education Times, November 5, 1984 (cited in Evans, 1984).
[a]All amounts calculated in 1980 dollars, as estimated by Consumer Price Index.

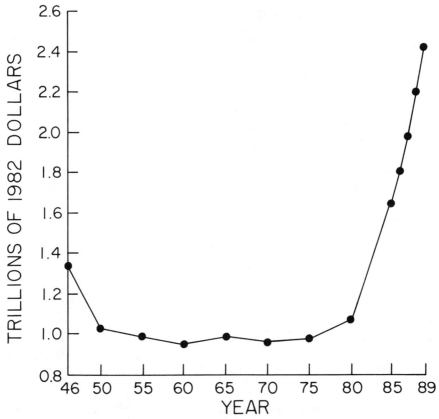

FIGURE 3:   Gross debt expressed in 1982 dollars. (*Source:* **Office of the President, 1984, p. 306; and Congressional Budget Office, 1984, p. 27**).

value of the debt begin to increase at a remarkable rate, increasing by 43% between 1981 and 1985 and expected to increase at a comparable rate in the future, unless current tax or expenditure policies are markedly revised.

The shift that occurred after 1981 appears even more dramatic when one examines in Figure 4 the changes in the size of the federal debt as a percentage of the nation's gross national product. Inasmuch as the economy grew steadily if unevenly throughout the postwar period, the debt, though remaining constant in real terms, declined sharply as a proportion of the United States economy. This decline averaged 7% per year in the decade immediately following the war, as the country substantially "repaid" its war debts. But even after 1955, debt as a percentage of GNP dropped rapidly; between 1955 and 1974 it fell on average 2% each year. After 1981 it began increasing 3.8% per year, and an

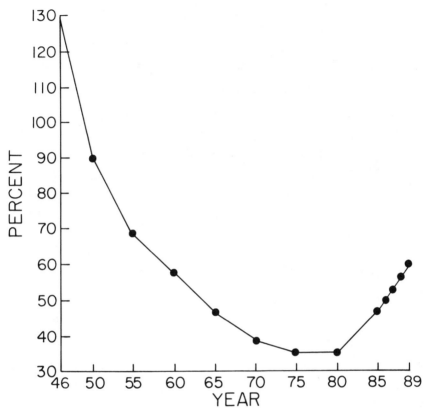

FIGURE 4:   Gross debt as a percentage of GNP. (*Source:* **Office of the President, 1984, pp. 230, 306; and Congressional Budget Office, 1984, pp. 12, 27).**

increase of roughly this same magnitude is expected with every passing year until the current deficit-producing political constellation comes to an end.

Deficits have been the consequence of a combination of tax reductions, defense expenditures, continued high costs of what are known as entitlement programs, and rising interest payments on the national debt. In addition, the president and the public remain opposed to major tax increases necessary to close the gap between revenues and expenditures. To keep the deficits from escalating further, discretionary programs, including those in education, have borne the brunt of the budget-cutter's knife. As can be seen in Table 6, discretionary programs in the federal budget, as a percentage of GNP, already declined by 1983 below the level they had reached in 1970 and by 1989, if projected plans of the Office of Management and Budget are executed, they will drop

TABLE 6: OUTLAYS FOR DOMESTIC PROGRAMS AS A PERCENTAGE OF GROSS NATIONAL PRODUCT, SELECTED FISCAL YEARS, 1962–89

Program	Actual				Projected		
	1962	1970	1980	1983	1985	1987	1989
Total	7.7	9.9	14.9	15.0	13.6	13.2	12.8
Payments to individuals	5.0	6.4	10.4	11.8	10.8	10.4	10.3
Social insurance	3.4	4.2	6.8	8.1	7.4	7.1	7.1
Social Security	2.6	3.1	4.6	5.3	4.9	4.7	4.6
Medicare	—	0.6	1.3	1.6	1.8	1.9	2.1
Unemployment	0.7	0.4	0.7	1.0	0.5	0.4	0.3
Other general retirement and disability	0.1	0.1	0.2	0.2	0.2	0.1	0.1
Means-tested payments	0.5	1.0	2.1	2.2	2.0	1.9	1.9
SSI, AFDC, and other income security	0.4	0.4	0.7	0.7	0.6	0.5	0.5
Medicaid	—	0.3	0.5	0.6	0.6	0.6	0.6
Nutrition and housing assistance	0.1	0.2	0.8	0.9	0.7	0.7	0.7
Student financial assistance	—	0.1	0.1	0.1	0.1	0.1	0.1
Other	1.1	1.2	1.5	1.5	1.4	1.4	1.3
Federal retirement	0.4	0.6	1.0	1.1	1.0	1.0	1.0
Income security for veterans	0.7	0.6	0.5	0.4	0.4	0.4	0.3
Other domestic programs	2.7	3.5	4.5	3.2	2.8	2.8	2.5
Science, space, energy, natural resources environment, and transportation	1.6	1.6	1.8	1.4	1.3	1.2	1.1
Agriculture	0.7	0.5	0.2	0.7	0.4	0.4	0.4
Community and regional development, education, training, employment, and social services	0.3	1.0	1.5	0.9	0.9	0.8	0.7
Veterans' benefits and services (less income security)	0.3	0.3	0.4	0.3	0.3	0.3	0.2
Other[a]	-0.2	0.1	0.6	-0.1	-0.1	0.1	0.1

[a] Includes commerce and housing credit, civilian agency pay raises, offsetting receipts, health (less Medicaid and Medicare), administration of justice and general government, and general purpose fiscal assistance.

Source. Rivlin, 1984, p. 46.

still further to 2.5% of GNP, less than what they were when Eisenhower was president.

Table 6 also shows that entitlement programs, especially those serving the needs of older Americans, such as Social Security and Medicare, have withstood the current tax-cutting mood more successfully than such discretionary programs as educational aid. Expenditures on social insurance programs as a percentage of GNP actually grew between 1980 and 1983 (from 6.8% to 8.1%), and even the president's budget does not project a decline in these programs to lower than their 1980 levels. By contrast, the discretionary programs, as a percentage of GNP, are to drop back to the levels of the Eisenhower years.

Part of the difference in the political treatment of these two types of programs has to do with their legislative status. Entitlement programs can be altered only by positive legislative action which requires that the entire network of subcommittee and committee institutions in Congress be navigated in order for cuts to be made. Cuts in discretionary programs can be made simply by blocking new appropriations. In addition, a politically minded president and Congress may be more responsive to a politically mobilized, actively voting, growing, predominantly white elderly population than to the needs of young people, whose social and political characteristics are quite different. There is little reason to expect education to escape the fate other discretionary programs are experiencing (Peterson & Rabe, 1983).

The State Role

Significantly, it is the state governments, not local school boards, that have assumed the fiscal responsibility Washington has abdicated. Continuing a historical trend evident over several decades, states, which in 1940 paid for less than one-third of the cost of education, now provide more than 48% (Table 7). By the end of the decade it is almost certain that the states will be paying for one-half of the cost of public education. It is also at the state level that one finds the most energetic efforts to promote educational reform, whether this means merit pay for teachers, competency tests for high school graduation, longer school years, or extended in-service training.

It can be argued that the shift in financial responsibility from Washington to state capitals will have little educational impact. If the country is willing to support its public schools, it can do so as easily through its state income and sales taxes as by means of federal income taxes. And local school boards can be regulated and subjected to mandates as easily by state as by federal legislation. Any improvements in school efficiency

TABLE 7: SOURCES OF PUBLIC-SCHOOL REVENUE AND THE PERCENTAGE SPENT ON PUBLIC ELEMENTARY- AND SECONDARY-SCHOOL CURRENT EXPENDITURES

	1929–30	1939–40	1949–50	1959–60	1969–70	1979–80	1982–83
Total revenue receipts (in billions)	$2.09	$2.26	$5.44	$14.75	$40.27	$96.90	$116.90
Percentage of revenue from:							
Federal government	.4%	1.8%	2.9%	4.4%	8.0%	9.8%	7.1%
State government	16.9	30.3	39.8	39.1	39.9	46.8	48.3
Local sources	82.7	68.0	57.3	56.5	52.1	43.4	44.6
Total %	100.0%	100.1%	100.0%	100.0%	100.0%	100.0%	100.0%
Total expenditures for all public schools (in billions)	$2.32	$2.34	$5.84	$15.61	$40.68	$96.00	$119.10
Percentage of total expenditures for elementary and secondary school current expenditures	79.6%	82.8%	80.3%	79.0%	84.1%	90.6%	90.8%

Source. National Center for Education Statistics, 1980b, 1981, 1982a, 1983.

are more likely to come from better classroom and building management than from any piece of federal or state legislation.

Whether or not educational equity will be as well served by a reduced federal role is another question. It may be argued that whereas strong federal intervention on behalf of minorities was needed two decades ago, federal withdrawal from this area today will have little effect on educational provision for disadvantaged groups. A series of judicial decisions, together with increasing minority group participation generated by such programs as the War on Poverty, have increased the level of political organization and sophistication among low-income groups so much that these groups are no longer in need of federal protection. For example, federal regulations require Chapter I, vocational education, and bilingual education programs to have local advisory councils, and these councils have become staunch defenders of these programs in many local communities. In addition, the school system contains educational specialists who have a vested interest in maintaining certain educational programs.

As persuasive as this argument may be with respect to bigger cities with politically effective, large minority-group populations, the political power of disadvantaged groups at the state and local level varies greatly. Recent court decisions have chipped away some of the equal protection doctrines that were laid down by the Supreme Court when Earl Warren was chief justice. And the major federal cuts in aid for disadvantaged and handicapped children have not been offset by major new programs at the state level directed at these populations. Two decades after the school finance movement sought to equalize resources among local school districts, the variation in per pupil expenditures among local school districts remains nearly as large as it was when this effort began.

According to a 1985 study, nearly all the equalization in educational finance that had occurred in the 1960s and 1970s has since attenuated. "We've lost almost all the ground we had gained," Alan Hickrod (Friendly, 1985) is reported to have concluded. Even in as reputedly progressive a state as Wisconsin, for example, schools in the top quintile of elementary schools spent more than $4,700 per pupil, while those in the lowest quintile spent less than $2,500. The pupil–staff ratio in the top quintile was 11 : 1, while in the bottom it was 16 : 1 (Cibulka, 1984).

The issue of educational equity is currently in abeyance, politically speaking, but there is every reason to believe that within a decade it will once again be a central concern. The proportion of school-age children who are Black, Hispanic, or Asian has increased and will increase steadily over the next decade, so that by 1990 nearly one in five will be of a minority group (Table 8).

At the same time regional shifts in population and income will

TABLE 8: ELEMENTARY- AND SECONDARY-SCHOOL-AGE
POPULATION OF THE UNITED STATES, BY RACE
AND WITH PROJECTIONS, 1965–90

| | Number in millions | | | | % |
	White	Black	Other	Total	Minority
5 to 13 years[a]					
1965	30.6	4.7	.4	35.7	14.3
1970	31.1	5.0	.5	36.6	15.0
1975	28.0	4.8	.6	33.4	16.2
1980	24.9	4.6	.7	30.2	17.5
1985[b]	23.8	4.5	.9	29.2	18.5
1990[b]	26.8	4.7	1.0	32.5	17.5
14 to 17 years[a]					
1965	12.3	1.7	.2	14.2	13.4
1970	13.6	2.1	.3	16.0	15.0
1975	14.3	2.3	.4	17.0	15.9
1980	13.1	2.3	.4	15.8	17.1
1985[b]	11.8	2.2	.4	14.4	18.1
1990[b]	10.3	2.1	.4	12.8	19.5
	Percent change				
5 to 13 years[a]					
1965–70	1.6	6.4	20.2[c]	2.5	
1970–75	−10.0	− 3.9	19.4[c]	− 8.7	
1975–80	−11.2	− 4.9	23.8[c]	− 9.7	
1980–85	− 4.5	− 2.8	20.0[c]	− 3.6	
1985–90	12.8	6.2	17.7[c]	11.9	
14 to 17 years[a]					
1965–70	11.0	20.8	33.6[c]	12.4	
1970–75	5.2	11.9	32.0[c]	6.4	
1975–80	− 8.4	− .7	19.0[c]	− 6.9	
1980–85	− 9.9	− 5.2	16.9[c]	− 8.7	
1985–90	−13.1	− 6.6	19.0[c]	−11.3	

[a]Estimates of July 1 of each year. Includes armed forces overseas.   [b]Census Series II projections.   [c]Based on unrounded numbers.
Source. National Center for Education Statistics, 1980a.

leave the older cities in northeastern and midwestern parts of the country with declining resources but increasing responsibilities for disadvantaged groups. In the past 30 years, these cities have dramatically changed their racial coloring. In the 20 largest cities of the Northeast and Midwest (hereafter referred to as the snowbelt cities) the white population fell by more than 2.5 million, or 13%, between 1960 and 1970 and by another 4 million, or 24.3%, by 1980.[3] The Black population in the same cities grew by 1.75 million (35.8%) in the first of these decades and by more than 200,000 (3%) in the most recent one. Reliable data on the size of the Hispanic population are more difficult to obtain, but Kasarda (1985), using the best quality data available, reports that in the four largest cities of these regions the Hispanic population grew by nearly 400,000, or by 26%. As a result of these changes, snowbelt cities have become homes for racial minorities; in the 20 largest, the white population in 1980 was but 53.8%. Clearly, the processes of urban decline have been accompanied by an equally profound process of racial succession.

That cities have become homes for Blacks means that they have also become the residence for many of society's most unfortunate. Although differences in the social and economic well-being of urban whites and Blacks are well known, their magnitude deserves emphasis. In the five largest metropolitan areas of the snowbelt—New York, Chicago, Detroit, Philadelphia, and Boston—Blacks consistently found themselves in 1980 to be at a great disadvantage. Their median family income was $13,299, while whites' was $24,194. The percentage of Blacks living below the poverty line was 29.6%; for whites the figure was only 8%. The Black unemployment rate was 9.4 percentage points higher than the white rate and the percentage of adult Blacks employed was 11.9 percentage points less than the percentage of adult whites employed. Nearly 52% of all Black, female-headed households have children under the age of 18, while less than 14% of comparable white households do. As Table 9 demonstrates, urban Blacks have less income, less education, and fewer employment opportunities. Their households are less likely to include an adult male and are more likely to live in rented quarters.

It is this poor, Black population which has replaced a white population that has increasingly chosen to live in suburbs, small towns, and the sunbelt. In 1980, 58% of all Blacks in the United States lived in central cities of metropolitan areas, compared with 25% of all whites. In the metropolitan areas of the snowbelt, 77% of Blacks live in the central city, but only 28% of whites do. Within the central city, too, Blacks and whites live in separate areas. Even after the passage of numerous civil rights laws, studies showed that central city housing was nearly as segregated in 1970 as it had been in 1960. A more recent study of Chi-

---

[3]The cities are New York City, Chicago, Philadelphia, Detroit, Baltimore, Indianapolis, Washington, Milwaukee, Cleveland, Columbus, Boston, St. Louis, Kansas City, Pittsburgh, Cincinnati, Minneapolis, Buffalo, Toledo, Newark, and St. Paul.

TABLE 9:   AVERAGE BLACK–WHITE DIFFERENCES
IN ECONOMIC AND SOCIAL WELL-BEING
IN THE 5 LARGEST METROPOLITAN AREAS
OF THE SNOWBELT (1980)

	White	Black	White/Black difference
Median family income	$24,194	$13,299	$10,895
Percentage of persons whose income is below poverty line	8.0	29.6	21.6
Percentage of adult population employed	58.3	46.4	11.9
Unemployment rate	6.4	15.4	9.0
Percentage of female-headed households with children under 18	13.9	51.7	37.8
Percentage completed high school	70.2	56.3	13.9
Percentage living in owner-occupied housing	60.8	36.3	24.5

Source. Chicago Urban League, 1983.

cago which used 1980 census information found that more than 85% of
the Black population of the city lived in precincts (areas that typically
include three to four city blocks) that were racially homogeneous with
90% or more Black (Election Data Services, 1981). Neighborhoods con-
taining both Blacks and whites are usually communities undergoing
processes of racial transition.

The Growth of the Nonpublic Sector

The combination of developments that I have portrayed—declining
teacher salaries relative to those in other industries, increasing percent-
ages of racial minorities especially in central cities, declining teacher
quality, increasing inequality in educational provision, an increase in
concern for problems of the elderly, an increasing concern about educational quality among a prosperous upper middle class—could well be
taken as signs that the system of public school education, as it has
developed over the past 150 years, will become split into two unequal
parts. The secular decline in the percentage of students attending nonpublic schools evident in the 1960s and early 1970s has been reversed,
and official Department of Education statistics predict growth of the
private sector through the 1980s (see Table 10). If prosperous, two-
earner, middle-class families decide to use their additional income for
private education, public schools will become increasingly identified as
schools for the disadvantaged.

Three decades ago, school officials in big cities talked about establishing racial quotas that kept the minority percentage in neighborhood

TABLE 10: ENROLLMENTS IN PUBLIC AND PRIVATE SCHOOLS,
BY LEVEL, 1965–1981 WITH PROJECTIONS, 1985–1990

By Level and Control of School	Year					
	1965	1970	1975	1980	1985	1990
		(in thousands)				
Public						
K–8	30,563	32,577	30,487	27,674	26,951	30,244
9–12	11,610	13,332	14,304	13,313	12,215	11,023
Total	42,173	45,909	44,791	40,987	39,350	41,276
Private						
K–8	4,900	4,052	3,700	3,623	3,600	4,000
9–12	1,400	1,311	1,300	1,339	1,400	1,400
Total	6,300	5,363	5,000	4,962	5,000	5,400

Private as a % of Public	Year					
	1965	1970	1975	1980	1985	1990
K–8	16.0%	12.4%	12.1%	13.1%	13.4%	13.2%
9–12	12.1	9.8	9.1	10.1	11.5	12.7
Total %	14.9	11.7	11.2	12.1	12.8	13.1

Source. U.S. Bureau of the Census, 1983, p. 140.

schools at no more than 25%. To go higher than that figure would risk the danger of reaching a tipping point that would trigger a white exodus. By 1990 the public schools in the United States might be approaching just such a tipping point. Declines in school resources and teacher quality could reinforce these tendencies. What is now a modest trend could become a stampede to private education, especially if tax credits, tuition vouchers, or other fiscal support were available to families choosing private education.

This scenario seems more plausible than it did even 2 years ago. If the national mood continues to swing in a conservative direction, if the antitax mood evident in Figure 5 prevails, if the Republican victories in presidential elections are accompanied by comparable trends in party identification and congressional seats—and there are some signs that this is beginning to happen—then the structure of the American educational system could significantly change in the dying years of the 20th century. Public schools may become much more like the charity schools from which they evolved; private schools may assume a broader function than providing education for religious minorities and a narrow social elite.

Yet these conclusions should not be reached without considering countertrends. Americans remain as committed to public education as

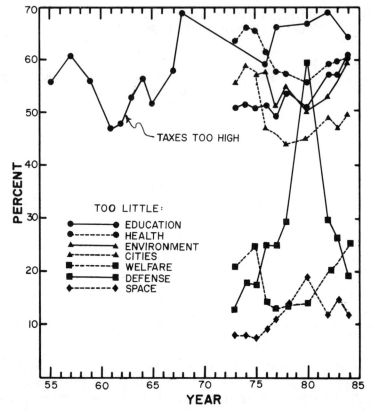

FIGURE 5:   Public Opinion on Federal Tax and Expenditure Policy, 1955–
1984

Source: Tom W. Smith, *A Compendium of Trends on General Social Survey Questions,* NORC Report No.
129, (NORC, 1980) and survey data from the General Social Survey in the NORC archives.

they ever have been. The percentage of the American public saying that
more money should be spent on education climbed steadily in the 1980s,
and schools today have more public support than any other governmental program (see Figure 5). The movements in favor of tuition vouchers
and tax credits were unable to gain much headway during the Reagan
administration and, with talk of budget deficits and efforts to eliminate
tax expenditures, they seem likely to encounter equally high hurdles in
the future. Few issues unite public school interest groups so tightly, and
few generate as intense a commitment to political action, as does the
debate over aid to nonpublic schools. And without some form of tax
subsidy, it is difficult to see how large segments of the population could
pay the large tuitions that the increasingly expensive private schools will
need to charge. All the factors driving up the cost of public education

that were discussed at the beginning of this chapter are also increasing the cost of private schools. At the college level these increasing costs have left the private colleges and universities with ever smaller proportions of the college-bound population. A substantial trend in the opposite direction at lower levels of the educational system seems quite unlikely.

THE RENEWED ENTHUSIASM FOR THE PUBLIC SCHOOL IN THE SOUTH

In order to expand on this optimistic note, it is worth considering the case of public education in the South, for it is in these states that interest in educational renewal has been most apparent. Tennessee has developed a new career-ladder program, which allows teachers to move to higher salaries, provided they agree to an evaluation process. Florida has mandated merit pay, stricter graduation requirements, and a longer school day. North Carolina and Arkansas have both extended the school day and the school year. Georgia and Mississippi have developed a college loan program with a forgiveness clause designed to attract teachers in subject areas such as mathematics and science. And South Carolina has established centers devoted to enhancing "teaching excellence" in colleges throughout the state.

There is a danger in exaggerating the degree of reform activity, of course. Much of what passes for change and innovation is little more than a symbolic gesture, token experiment, or minor adaptation of long established practice. One cannot expect major strides forward as a result of each and every one of the more than 200 commissions and study groups appointed in the wake of the National Commission's (1983) report. Much of what has happened probably would have occurred even had there been no commission reports. And much that has happened may be too limited in focus or too poorly funded or too inappropriately designed to have a major impact. In Florida, for example, a number of the changes originally proposed have been held up due to a shortfall in revenue. One can expect a new wave of implementation studies in the next few years showing that the reforms of the 1980s had little or no more effect than did some of the Great Society reforms of the 1960s.

But even with these qualifications, it must be recognized that the distinctive efforts of the southern states are worth emphasizing. For it is in the South that many states are committing their money to the reform effort. Not only are states talking reform; they seem to be willing to pay for it. Arkansas, South Carolina, and Tennessee have all raised their sales taxes in order to help pay for increased educational costs. Virginia and Georgia have committed substantial sums to pay for increased teacher salaries. Altogether, southern states increased their 1983–84 ed-

TABLE 11:   SEVEN OF THE 10 STATES
             WHICH INCREASED
             APPROPRIATIONS THE
             MOST FOR ELEMENTARY
             AND SECONDARY
             EDUCATION FOR
             1983–1984 ARE FROM
             THE SOUTH

	% Increase
1. South Carolina	33.3%
2. Texas	24.5
3. Tennessee	22.8
4. North Carolina	18.4
5. Alabama	18.3
6. Arkansas	17.5
7. Maryland	17.5
8. Wyoming	16.2
9. Idaho	15.3
10. California	14.5

Source. National Conference of State Legislatures, 1984.

ucational appropriations by 16.1%, while in the United States as a whole the increases were limited to but 9.8% (National Conference of State Legislatures, 1984). And the seven states which increased their appropriations the most—South Carolina, Texas, Tennessee, North Carolina, Alabama, Arkansas, and Maryland—are located south of the Mason-Dixon line (Table 11).

What accounts for this unusual receptiveness by the southern states to the National Commission's (1983) recommendations? Part of the answer is simply that the South was especially in need of reform. As one well-known political leader from Iowa recently observed, unlike the South, "we didn't need to reform—we already had the best schools in the country." In this regard, it must be said that southern schools have traditionally ranked low on many measures of educational performance. What's more, the South did not improve its ranking on these measures in the decade before the National Commission reported (Table 12).

Consider expenditures per pupil for example. Not only did the South trail the nation by 23% in 1972, but its gain over the next decade barely exceeded the national average—6.7% for the South, compared with 4.6% for the U.S. as a whole (National Conference of State Legislatures, 1984). As a percentage of personal income, the educational expenditures in the South actually fell further behind over the course of the decade, increasing only 1.1% in the South and 1.6% in the nation as a whole (Office of Planning, 1984). Teacher salaries in the South were but

TABLE 12:   AMERICAN COLLEGE
TESTING PROGRAM (ACT)
AND SCHOLASTIC
ACHIEVEMENT TEST (SAT)
SCORES HAVE DROPPED AS
MUCH IN THE SOUTH AS IN
THE UNITED STATES, BUT
GRADUATION RATES HAVE
DROPPED LESS

	1972	1982	Change
ACT Scores			
South	17.9	16.9	−1.0
United States	19.1	18.4	−0.7
SAT Scores			
South	881	848	−33
United States	937	893	−44

Percentage			
Graduation Rates			
South[a]	68.4	67.9	−0.5
United States	77.2	72.8	−4.4

[a]Georgia is not included.
Source. Office of Planning, 1984.

83% of the national average in 1972, and in real terms they dropped almost as much in the South as elsewhere over the next 10 years. Achievement test scores in the South were less than the national average in 1972, and they too fell in the South almost as fast as they did in other parts of the nation. And graduation rates, although they fell less than in the rest of the country, were still nearly 5% below the U.S. average (Table 12).

The South, in short, had done little to catch up in the decade before the National Commission (1983) reported. Why should it make strenuous efforts to do so in 1983? The answer, I think, is that the report triggered a reaction that was beginning to happen in any case. The South is the fastest growing, economically most dynamic region in the country. Past and projected population growth is greater in the South than elsewhere. The South grew by 20% in the 10 years before 1980, compared with 11% for the rest of the nation; from 1980 to 1990, the South is projected to grow by 16%, compared with 10% for the country as a whole (U.S. Bureau of the Census, 1983, pp. 14–15).

Employment gains in the South have outpaced those of the rest of the nation; nonagricultural employment grew by 28% between 1972 and 1980 in the South but only 19% in the rest of the nation (U.S. Bureau of

Labor Statistics, 1983). Also, expansion of wholesale and retail trade is greater in the South (U.S. Bureau of the Census, 1983, pp. 804, 808). Increases in per capita income have been 15.2% in the South, compared with 6.6% nationwide. The number in poverty declined by 7% between 1972 and 1982 in the South, while it actually increased nationwide. At the same time, the educational level of adults rose more rapidly in the South than in the country as a whole (U.S. Department of Education, 1984a). On almost every social and economic indicator, then, the South showed strong gains between 1972 and 1982, relative to the nation as a whole.

But similar gains have not been made in education. In this sphere the South's positions relative to the country as a whole changed hardly at all. The National Commission (1983) report thus fell onto fertile ground. To mix metaphors, southern schools were looking for a spark that would ignite the dry kindling that had gradually accumulated. It is only a slight exaggeration to say that if there had not been a national commission, the South would have had to invent one. The southern economy requires a higher level of skills, and a better educated southern public expects and is willing to pay for higher quality schools. It seems that the economic change had to occur before the political effort to reform the schools could become effective.

CONCLUSIONS

These changes in the South remind us that the educational scenario set forth at the beginning of this chapter is by no means inevitable. It is true that the costs of education continue to escalate, public willingness to pay for these costs seem to be waning, schools are becoming increasingly a place for minority students, an aging population seems more interested in social security than in investment in human capital, and private education is enjoying a renaissance. But public schools are still likely to adapt to the necessities of the late 20th and 21st centuries. The public supports increased financial support for schools to a greater extent than a decade ago, the costs of private education could very well escalate beyond the capacities of all but the very well to do, the opposition to tax credits and tuition vouchers remains intense, and public schools may be able to turn technological progress to their advantage. Eighty years ago, schools were still fragile institutions that could be formed and reformed by aggressive political action. Modern schools are too complex and too entrenched in a multitude of social, political, and governmental relationships to be quickly transformed.

The hope, as well as the bane, of public education may be its combination of inertia and adaptation. Though frustrating to the reformer in search of either greater efficiency or more social justice, this combination may be necessary to preserve an institutional fabric in periods of social, economic, and political change.

REFERENCES

Chicago Urban League. (1983, November). *A perspective on the socio-economic status of Chicago-area blacks.* Chicago: Author.

Cibulka, J. G. (1984, Fall). School finance trends in Wisconsin. In J. G. Cibulka, *Research and Opinion* (Vol. 1, pp. 1–4). Milwaukee, WI: University of Wisconsin, Urban Research Center.

Congressional Budget Office. (1984). *Baseline budget projections for fiscal years 1985–1989.* Washington, DC: U.S. Government Printing Office.

Darling–Hammond, L. (1984). *Beyond the commission reports: The coming crisis in teaching.* Santa Monica, CA: Rand.

Election Data Services. (1981). *Analysis of redistricting plan.* Washington, DC: Author.

Evans, A. (1984). *An overview and analysis of Reagan administration education policies.* Washington, DC: Congressional Research Service.

Friendly, J. (1985, February 19). The disparity of resources. *New York Times,* p. C1.

Hanushek, E. A. (1981). Throwing money at schools. *Journal of Policy Analysis & Management, 1*(1), 19–41.

Kasarda, J. (1985). Urban structural transformation and minority opportunity. In P. E. Peterson (Ed.), *The new urban reality.* Washington, DC: Brookings.

National Center for Education Statistics. (1980a). *The condition of education.* Washington, DC: U.S. Government Printing Office.

National Center for Education Statistics. (1980b). *Digest of education statistics.* Washington, DC: U.S. Government Printing Office.

National Center for Education Statistics. (1981). *Digest of education statistics.* Washington, DC: U.S. Government Printing Office.

National Center for Education Statistics. (1982a). *Digest of education statistics.* Washington, DC: U.S. Government Printing Office.

National Center for Education Statistics. (1982b). *Projections of education statistics to 1990–91* (Vol. 1). Washington, DC: U.S. Government Printing Office.

National Center for Education Statistics. (1983). *Digest of education statistics.* Washington, DC: U.S. Government Printing Office.

National Center for Education Statistics. (1984). *Digest of education statistics, 1983–84.* Washington, DC: U.S. Government Printing Office.

National Commission on Excellence in Education. (1983, April). *A nation at risk: The imperative for educational reform.* Washington, DC: U.S. Government Printing Office.

National Conference of State Legislatures. (1984). *State budget actions in 1984.* Denver: Author.

National Education Association. (1983). *Estimates of schools statistics; 1982–83.* Washington, DC: U.S. Government Printing Office.

National Education Association. (1984). *Estimates of schools statistics.* West Haven, CT: Author.

Office of Planning, Budget, and Evaluation. (1984). *State Education Statistics.* Washington, DC: U.S. Department of Education.

Office of the President. (1984, February). *Economic report of the President.* Washington, DC: U.S. Government Printing Office.

Perry, G. (1985). [Projected gross national product]. Unpublished data.

Peterson, P. E. (1983a, Winter). Did the educational commissions say anything? *Brookings Review,* 3–11

Peterson, P. E. (1983b). Background paper, in Twentieth Century Fund, *Making the grade.* Report of the Task Force on Federal Elementary and Secondary Education Policy.

Peterson, P. E., & Rabe, B. G. (1983, Spring). The role of interest groups in the formation of educational policy: Past practice and future trends. *Teachers College Record, 84,* 725–727.

Rivlin, A. (1984). *Economic choices 1984.* Washington, DC: Brookings.

Sykes, G. (1983, May 4). Incentives, not tests, are needed to restructure the teaching profession. *Education Week,* p. 24.

U.S. Bureau of the Census. (1972, February). Population estimates and projections. *Current Population Reports,* Series P–25, No. 476.

U.S. Bureau of the Census. (1983). *Statistical abstract of the United States: 1984* (104th ed.). Washington, DC: U.S. Government Printing Office.

U.S. Bureau of Labor Statistics. (1983). *Employment and earnings.* Washington, DC: Author.

U.S. Department of Education. (1984a). *State Education Statistics.* Washington, DC: Author.

U.S. Department of Education. (1984b). *The nation responds: Recent efforts to improve education.* Washington, DC: U.S. Government Printing Office.

THREE

THE PREPARATION AND RETENTION OF TEACHERS

DONALD J. STEDMAN

INTRODUCTION

For the past several years, I have spent most of every workday (and not just a few nights) immersed in the problems and opportunities present-ed by a faltering public school system in North Carolina. My major focus has been the role the university in general, and the professional educa-tion of teachers in particular, can play in improving the public schools. Professional education is today burdened by a sometimes tedious public opinion and a steady parade of educational seers and do-gooders who often manage to obscure the issues and retard real progress.

It has been at once stimulating and frustrating. Traditions weigh us down. An army of free consultants beats us about the ears. National and state reports abound. And there are too many sources of policy that are either irresponsible or not responsible at all. However, I still believe that the most important task before the university and society is to renew and strengthen the public schools. The schools of the country are, in-deed, its future in miniature.

Nearly everyone agrees that an important part of school reform will be improved ways of training and retraining teachers. In this chap-ter, I examine three aspects of teacher preparation and retention. First, I will discuss recent actions taken in North Carolina to improve educa-tion, some of which address the preparation and retention issue. Sec-ond, the proposition will be considered that the most compelling mag-net for bright students and competent teachers is a sound educational experience (a strong and relevant professional education and access to continuing professional education). I believe that a sound educational experience is a significant offset to marginal salaries and conditions of work. In this regard, I recommend a model for teacher preparation that represents key features that need to be addressed to assure the preparation of educated teachers and to establish an activity in the university that will provide the link to public schools and the educational community generally. Third, seven policies are recommended that I believe to be essential to a strong college of education and to effective and productive teacher preparation programs if competent students and teachers are to be produced.

RECENT ACTIONS TAKEN TO IMPROVE NORTH CAROLINA SCHOOLS AND TEACHERS

Recent improvements in the schools range from significant increases in teacher salaries and the structure of salaries to broad-gauged reforms such as the Basic Education Program which has been partly funded by the North Carolina General Assembly. This program provides for a common core of knowledge and skills for all high school graduates; when implemented, it will require (among other things) the hiring of a substantial number of additional teachers.

Some impressive advances have been made in North Carolina to improve education and teaching mostly under the initiatives taken during Governor James Hunt's administration (1977–84). The university is doing its share. A few recent contributions may be listed. It is important to note that groundwork for these activities was laid in part by two significant recent programs. First, the Teacher Education Review Program (TERP; University of North Carolina, 1977a, b, c, 1979, 1981) was a comprehensive review and evaluation of all teacher preparation degree programs on the 15 campuses of the university that prepare teachers. The objectives included not only an evaluation of the effectiveness of these programs but also a review of their structure, scope, and methods, and the development of measures to assure their continued improvement over the ensuing years. The recommendations of the TERP report made a significant impact on these 15 programs, and implementation of those recommendations is ongoing.

Second, the Quality Assurance Program (Liaison Committee, 1981) was a systematic, multidimensional approach to strengthening and assuring quality in teacher preparation and professional certification in North Carolina. Undertaken jointly by the Board of Governors of the University and the state Board of Education, the Quality Assurance Program is now being implemented through pilot programs across the state. Various features being implemented include procedures for evaluating students' general knowledge prior to admission to a teacher evaluation program, close supervision of the student teaching experience jointly by the university and schools, and an educational support system for teachers in their initial certification period.

Since the completion of TERP and the Quality Assurance Program, the university has undertaken four new initiatives to improve the quality of public instruction:

1. *The Mathematics and Science Education Center Network.* This network is comprised of a statewide consortium of nine universities and the North Carolina School of Science and Mathematics. Its major goal is to address the serious shortage of math and science teachers and to improve the overall level of math and science teaching in the public schools. This is a collaborative project, involving the public schools at all levels, and is fast becoming a national model for school–college partnerships on a statewide scale.

2. *The Principals' Executive Program.* Offered through the Institute of Government at the University of North Carolina at Chapel Hill, this is a statewide leadership and management development program for public school principals in North Carolina. The program provides short-term, intensive training for principals nominated by their superintendents and is offered at no cost to schools or principals.

3. *Rural Education Institutes.* These Institutes have been established at Western Carolina University and East Carolina University to improve our understanding of the special needs of teachers and schools in rural areas and to provide training and technical assistance to improve rural school systems.

4. *Summer Residential Programs in Math and Science.* Designed for high school students, these programs have been established under the leadership of the North Carolina School of Science and Mathematics on the campuses of five constituent institutions of the University of North Carolina (Appalachian State University, East Carolina University, Western Carolina University, North Carolina Central University, and UNC–Charlotte). These 5-week programs will serve more than 600 juniors and seniors each summer in math, science, and computer sciences enrichment programs. Programs will be offered without cost to students or their families.

In addition to these four major activities designed to improve public education and teacher training, North Carolina may soon have a significant reform in the Basic Education Program (with major improvements in teacher–student ratios) and some form of a career development plan for teachers and administrators.

All of these activities are important and each is a piece of the total puzzle that must be solved in order to change the landscape of education in North Carolina. Each will contribute something to the improvement of education, teaching, and schooling.

Even so, there are many factors affecting the teaching profession and public schools that lie outside the area that can be directly manipulated or shaped by the university. Certainly the advice of university faculty exerts some leverage on policymakers, but the university can be most effective by improving the nature and quality of the professional education experience. Salaries of teachers should be higher but legislatures and school boards will decide on that, partly based on what they think they can afford. Performance-based pay schemes, career ladder programs, teacher–student ratios, teacher aide and staff patterns, and other such issues will be determined by administrators, school boards, and politicians. Nevertheless, we have to take them seriously since they affect teacher preparation.

The North Carolina Career Development Plan

An important proposal that has emerged from the education reform activities in North Carolina is the career development plan for teachers (see Figure 1). This plan has its origins in a prior plan developed in the Charlotte–Mecklenburg district and includes elements of the approaches of other states as well. It is very promising as a highly structured career ladder designed to attract, reward, and retain effective teachers in a program of continuing professional education and performance evaluation. It is currently being pilot tested in 16 school systems in North Carolina.

A fair assessment of this proposed plan would reveal some important strengths and weaknesses. On the plus side:

1. The emergence of the plan signals the readiness of a critical occupation to take charge of itself and become an organized profession.
2. The plan is the first attempt to create a career path for teachers within an orderly system of progression and incentives which combines seniority or experience, level of education, proficiency, and continuing professional development.
3. Once in place the plan would provide important information about teachers that could be used to inform and improve preservice teacher education programs and guide the construction of continuing education programs.
4. If the plan succeeds, it can help restore the confidence of the legislature and school boards in the teaching profession and forge a stronger link between schools and colleges.

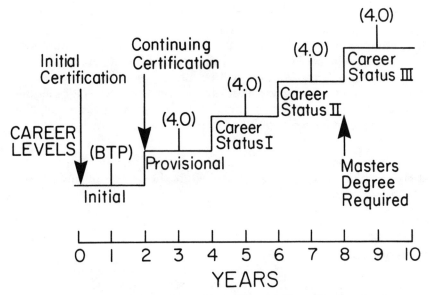

FIGURE 1: North Carolina Career Development Plan: Five levels of differentiated professional roles, requirements, and salary schedules (BTP = participation in the Beginning Teacher Program; 4.0 = 4 continuing education units).

5. The plan provides a more uniform system of evaluation of teachers than is currently available.

On the negative side:

1. The plan includes incentives for good teachers to leave the classroom. For a teacher career development scheme, this feature is a serious flaw.
2. The validity of teacher performance measures may not yet be sufficient to allow them to function as a central element in an expensive, statewide, comprehensive plan for career development. (We should not stall implementation of pilot programs, however, since they are an important part of the process required for developing and evaluating such measures for use throughout the state.)
3. The career development plan is not a merit pay plan. Teaching effectiveness is a necessary but not a sufficient condition for advancement in this scheme.
4. The current format for implementing the plan is complicated. There are several ill-defined critical features, for example "continuing edu-

cation units," and the role of the university in relation to the plan is, as yet, unclear.

5. Perhaps most troublesome is the specter of quotas for the number of teachers who could occupy any one rung of the career ladder at any given time. Because funds will be limited, not all eligible teachers will be able to progress along the career path as rapidly as they would like. Some method of managing and costing out the pipeline will have to be developed and applied.

Nevertheless, the basic concept is a good one and the plan will almost certainly add to the attractiveness of the profession and assist in retention of "good" teachers.

A Special Note: School-based Career Development Organizations for Teachers

The emergence of organized career development organizations in public schools should signal an opportunity for new arrangements for the continuing professional education activities of colleges of education. But three points should be made about this new development.

First, advanced educational programs created for teachers and administrators should originate from career development organizations associated with the schools and be financed by them. Colleges of education will require expanded staffing to relate effectively to these organizations, but there should be a strong collaborative effort here that allows schools to set their staff development priorities in direct relation to weaknesses in public school curricula as reflected by student achievement at the local level (see Chapter 8). The educational programs offered by universities for career development should represent a range of credit and noncredit activities, but there should be no noncredit activities or credit-for-experience allowed toward continuing certification for teachers or administrators.

Second, these organizations should be used to establish what Cooley and Bickel (1986) would call "decision-oriented educational research" programs, using computerized data files for continual monitoring and inprovement of school functioning. This approach would provide not only direct aid to schools in a variety of important administrative, curricular, and policy areas, but would also offer research opportunities for teachers, administrators, and college of education faculty and graduate students.

Third, career development organizations should provide an opportunity to evaluate alternative certification programs, working with colleges of education to help reduce the inappropriate "irregular" certification and "endorsement" actions that now exist to meet rising demands for teachers in critical areas.

In short, I am making a strong plea for continuation and strengthening of the bonds that have developed and continue to thrive between and among colleges of education and the public schools. It is difficult work but I believe it is our best hope for developing sound professional education practices and maintaining a pool of effective teachers and administrators.

Another Special Note: Performance-based (Merit) Pay

Recent reports and education reform measures have placed great reliance on performance-based pay for teachers. These measures are designed to reward the more competent and effective teachers and to attract and retain more and better people to the profession. This approach has great appeal and constitutes a fairness-in-reward system that would be a significant advance over simple across-the-board increases typical of salary improvement measures up until now. Every effort should be made to insert this approach into the incentive systems for public schools as a part of a larger mix of strategies which focus on improved conditions of work. School boards and educators should realize, however, that there are strong head winds against performance-based pay schemes, some of which originate from unlikely sources. Let me list some of these:

1. Teacher associations and unions do not believe there are valid teacher performance evaluations available that can be applied fairly.
2. Minorities fear the possibility of quotas for the number of teachers that would be rewarded and that they would not be included.
3. The scarcity of funds at the state and local levels may keep merit increases too low to be attractive.
4. Legislators, county commissioners, and school board members are wary of any open-ended budget category such as merit pay.
5. Many teachers think of themselves as being part of a "helping profession." As a result, they will not compete with peers for tangible rewards or emphasize differences among themselves. Teachers often view themselves as members of an "underdog" group and they want to stay linked together, not singled out.
6. Using the analogy of university faculty, merit pay increases is inappropriate in the public school setting. The analogy breaks down because five important conditions present in the university are not present in the public schools:
   a. Public-school teachers are not recommended by their peers for initial employment.

b.   The public school curriculum is less flexible than the university curriculum.
c.   Nonacademic duties are not required of university faculty as part of their duties.
d.   Education at the K–12 level is mandatory. All students must be taught and some teachers get better students than others. Thus, how will it be possible to compare the effectiveness of teachers with students of differing abilities, motivations, and background?
e.   Faculty may be assigned and reassigned from one school to another in a school system. Moreover, teachers are often assigned to classes for which they are not prepared or in subject matter areas in which they may have "endorsement" but little education or training. These procedures are, to say the least, infrequent in the university and assignment to other departments or universities by some administrative authority is not possible.
7.   Many administrators see a merit pay system as more complicated than the problem and "don't want to mess with it."

These are serious forces acting against effective implementation of performance-based pay plans and they should give reformers some pause.

One Last Note: Irregular Certification

No other profession has as many legitimate routes to licensing as public school teaching. In some states, there are as many as seven routes, ranging from transcript course review to the new and dubious practice of endorsement to the "regular" full-scale state approved preparation program. The rising demand for teachers, particularly in math and science, is leading to a loosening of standards that no other profession would tolerate. If states are serious about the quality of teachers and teaching, irregular certification procedures will be—and should be—discontinued.

NEW MODELS AS ATTRACTIONS TO STUDENTS AND TEACHERS

It is interesting to note that while national, state, and professional organization reports, including the University of North Carolina TERP report in 1978, call for reform, revision and innovative action in the area of teacher preparation programs, few new models have emerged. Even fewer model programs have actually produced graduates whose work could be evaluated and compared with current or traditional programs. The Quality Assurance Program model, and benchmark testing models generally, offer opportunities for revision and creativity. However, little has happened in North Carolina or elsewhere to take advantage of these options. There is a timidity and a lethargy in professional education in the university that is not found in other professional schools and which does not seem to vary by type or mission of the university. In fact, I would assert that the colleges of education in research universities are the least aroused of all and in a very real sense are forfeiting their responsibility to lead other institutions toward effective reform in teacher education.

What has yet to take place may be the most important reform of all—the reform of the process whereby teachers are educated for a difficult but rewarding professional career. Colleges of education are in the cross-hairs as never before and they must change to meet the significant reforms that are already being implemented in the public schools. Those colleges that do not change will wither on the vine, withdrawing into pseudoresearch organizations or highly specialized schools for administrators that nobody will need.

A handful of what may be significant reforms are taking place around the country. The few that seem promising to me are the Pro-Teach program at the University of Florida at Gainesville, the 5-year baccalaureate and certification program at the University of Kansas, the dual degree program at Kenyon College associated with Teachers College at Columbia University, and the SCAT program at the University of South Florida in Tampa. Others that have gained some popularity appear to me to be only simple rearrangements of the same old deck chairs. The ones I mentioned specifically should be watched carefully and we should learn from their experiences. These programs seem to have at least four features in common:

1. They require or provide a sound educational program *prior* to professional training.
2. They constitute a well-orgainzed professional training program carried out *in close association* with the public schools.
3. They require a *well-educated and current faculty* capable of conducting and translating research.
4. They have achieved a solid *university financial base* from which to operate and regularly evaluate the program.

Building on the exciting innovations offered by these adventuresome programs, I would like to offer the following modest proposal for teacher training.

A Professional Teacher Education Model

Over the years, I have come to favor the baccalaureate degree as the minimum preparation and the best requirement for admission to a professional teacher education program. In other words, I prefer the graduate school of education, most desirably for all teacher preparation but *absolutely* for preparing teachers for the junior and senior high school levels. Now, I realize that as a practical matter, we cannot simply wipe out all undergraduate teacher education programs, nor should we. But for the major university, for the research university, for the university that seriously wants to apply its vast range of faculty resources and research capability, I think the graduate school of education is the only way to go.

I do not refer here to simple emulation of the Harvard or Teachers College or any other graduate college arrangement. Those models are nearly obsolete. I am proposing a new model that will provide not only preservice teacher education programs but also in-service programs for experienced teachers re-entering the profession or for other professionals seeking lateral entry to the profession.

There are several basic features of the model program (Figure 2) that require explanation:

1. It is a 2-year graduate program leading to the master's degree in education. These are 2 calendar years, including summer work between the 2 academic years and prior to employment as a teacher. The majority of the training is conducted in close association *with* and *in* one or more public schools.
2. Entry to the graduate program may be gained through any undergraduate program or a special, preprofessional undergraduate program that emphasizes the behavioral and social sciences and some guided experience in the schools.
3. Core courses and experiences in the graduate program would include:
   - history, philosophy, and sociology of education,
   - learning and child development,
   - computer and technology applications,
   - diagnostic teaching and testing,
   - classroom research methods and research utilization,
   - parent counseling and behavior management.
4. Temporary initial certification would be awarded upon completion of the first year of the 2-year graduate program.
5. The master's degree (M.Ed.) and a conditional 3-year certificate would be awarded upon completion of the second year of the 2-year graduate program.

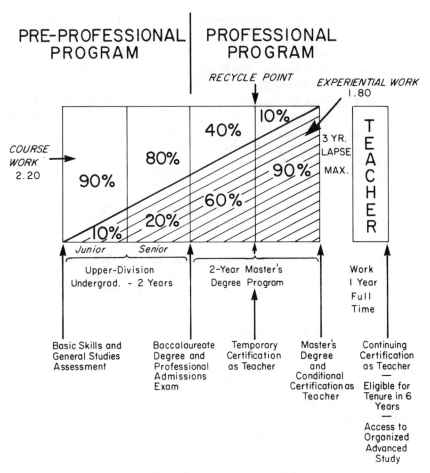

FIGURE 2:   A professional teacher education model.

6. Scholars would earn half-salary (of base salary) for the first year, and three-quarters salary for the second year of the program.
7. Continuing certification would be earned upon completion of the first full year of work beyond the 2-year graduate program. The tenure decision would be made upon completion of the fourth year of the subsequent 5-year contract.
8. Teachers previously certified, but who for 3 successive years had not been employed full time as a teacher, would be required to recycle through the second year of the 2-year graduate program.
9. Lateral entry programs would consist of completion of the 2-year graduate program.
10. The ratio of coursework to in-school experience during Year 1 would be 40%–60% and shift in Year 2 to 10%–90%.

Additional features and requirements of the proposed model remain for development and debate. The program would preclude the need for "irregular" certification of all kinds and the primary responsibility for recommending all teacher certification would reside in such university-based programs.

This proposed professional teacher education program model is not necessarily the last word. It is a beginning and it does contain the basic features required to provide for both in-service and preservice education needs. Colleges of education should be encouraged to adopt this or similar approaches.

POLICIES ESSENTIAL TO THE BUILDING OF STRONG TEACHER EDUCATION PROGRAMS

If we are to build and maintain strong teacher education programs and colleges of education, then some important policies must be developed and followed. I would recommend at least these seven.

Resistance to Demand Pressures

One of the greatest threats to quality education, especially teacher education, is the tendency for universities and licensing agencies to lower standards to meet surging market demands. The biggest test before us is to see whether we will resist the temptation as the new demand emerges. In North Carolina, for example, new legislation may require nearly 13,000 additional teachers to meet the proposed student–teacher ratios. We must establish and maintain high standards of admission and retention in teacher education even in the face of these new demands.

Disentanglement from Credentialing

We need to disentangle professional education from the credentials process. North Carolina's career development program, for example, would require a master's degree to move up the ladder. This is an example of entanglement and it is a mistake. An advanced degree should be worth more money, but it should not be a requirement for career advancement.

Second, we need to examine carefully the extent to which our education degree programs may have been built upon or have eroded down to the minimum standards required for certifying a graduate to be a teacher. An academic degree program should constitute much more than the base curriculum required for training students in certain areas of competence.

Revitalization of Education Faculty

We need to initiate a serious and long-term program directed toward revitalization of education faculties. This will require re-education and updating as well as the provision of research skills to energize scholarly activity and to improve teaching.

Further, there is a need for teacher-training institutions to provide incentives for good teaching and for effective work with the public schools. Such incentives should include greater impact of those currently marginal activities on promotion and tenure decisions. Young faculty members know or soon learn that exemplary teaching and public service do not pay off at promotion time. This is a particular problem in the research universities and a growing concern in the comprehensive universities.

There is a need to improve the graduate education of people who aspire to membership on faculties of colleges of education. Particular attention should be paid to teaching skills.

Colleges of education need to work harder to create research opportunities for faculty members and to develop programs of organized research activities in which both faculty members and graduate students can engage. There is a general need to restore confidence to education faculty and to provide more cohesion and create more enthusiasm in college of education activities.

Public School Linkage

We need to establish linkages with the public schools to reform professional education and to re-establish a research base which is relevant to our professional education curriculum. Too often, the questions posed in educational research are trivial or irrelevant to the central issues of education.

Interdisciplinary Linkage

We need to re-establish linkages with the other disciplines in the university, including the behavioral and biological sciences, law, religious studies, fine arts and letters, the humanities, and science and mathematics to assure a sound educational program and to expand interdisciplinary research in pursuit of improved teaching. Professional education is a university-wide enterprise and professional educators require a well-rounded education. This will require joint appointments for faculty and it will encourage interdisciplinary curriculum development.

Disproportional Support for Schools of Education

We need to gain the support of the university administration to achieve the financial and psychological base required to establish sound professional education programs. For some time to come, colleges of education will require a disproportionately larger share of university budget support in relation to their enrollments. The reforms and revisions in education over the past decade have created serious financial problems for many colleges of education. These problems cannot be remedied through ordinary means and the only real source of balanced support is from the university itself. If a university is unwilling or unable to provide disproportional support, then it should consider getting out of the teacher education business.

"Stick to the Knitting"

One of the most important lessons provided in Peters and Waterman's *In Search of Excellence* (1982) is the admonition to organizations to "stick to their knitting." That is, to do what they know how to do best, to concentrate on it, to be the best, and to be satisfied with that. Some colleges of education have violated this stricture. Faculty members deal themselves into areas for which they have no education, training, or experience, or worse, they let themselves be assigned to teach or do research in areas that are foreign to them. Colleges initiate new programs of study, directed toward student markets or funding opportunities, for which they are poorly organized and staffed and for which there is little ardor or inclination to make a serious investment or contribution. This is a serious mistake and, over time, blurs the identity and destabilizes the operations of a professional school. The mission drifts. Faculty forget why they are there. Administrators begin to become authoritarian to get their faculty to respond. Serious scholars go underground and young faculty, sensing aimlessness, leave.

Further, programs and departments emerge inside the college that poach on dwindling faculty resources by expanding programs that produce graduates who neither seek nor desire employment in or near the public schools. Universities and colleges of education cannot afford to support duplicate psychology departments, to concentrate efforts on programs that populate the staffs of human services organizations or prepare large numbers of graduates for private practice. Such colleges do not attract students to teaching and they repel students who do enroll only to find too little support for their aspirations to teach or to work in the schools.

Finally, I would reassert two strong values that undergird the arguments on behalf of reforming schools of education. First, contrary to Warren Corbin's (1985) assertions, I believe that it is *essential that universities be the primary base* for the initial preparation of teachers. If, as Secretary of Education William Bennett asserts, we are in a "trivialization mode," then we compound the problem by preparing teachers who may be trained but who are uneducated. Teaching is not a performing art. Only the university can guarantee an educated teacher corps.

Second, the university cannot prepare teachers without a *strong, authentic, collaborative relationship* with the public education system. The *vitality* of the university is a prime source of continuing renewal for the public schools. The *reality* of the schools provides fuel for the research and educational core of the universities' teacher preparation efforts.

If there is a fundamental network of policy, it lies in these two values. Neither value is motivated by a need for control or a need for altruism. They serve the best interests of the children we seek to educate. And only the educated are free.

REFERENCES

Cooley, W. W., & Bickel, W. E. (1986). *Decision-oriented educational research.* Boston: Kluwer-Nijhoff.

Corbin, W. (1985, January 23). Universities should get out of the business of teaching teachers. *Chronical of Higher Education.*

Liaison Committee. (1981). *Quality Assurance Program: Liaison Committee report.* Chapel Hill, NC: Author.

Peters, T. J., & Waterman, R. H. (1982). *In search of excellence: Lessons from America's best-run companies.* New York: Harper & Row.

University of North Carolina. (1977a). *The education and training of teachers and other educational personnel in The University of North Carolina: Report 1.* Chapel Hill: University of North Carolina, Teacher Education Review Program.

University of North Carolina. (1977b). *The education and training of teachers and other educational personnel in The University of North Carolina: Report 2.* Chapel Hill: University of North Carolina, Teacher Education Review Program.

University of North Carolina. (1977c). *The education and training of teachers and other educational personnel in The University of North Carolina: Report 3.* Chapel Hill: University of North Carolina, Teacher Education Review Program.

University of North Carolina. (1979). *The education and training of teachers and other educational personnel in The University of North Carolina: Report 4.* Chapel Hill: University of North Carolina, Teacher Education Review Program.

University of North Carolina. (1981). *The education and training of teachers and other educational personnel in The University of North Carolina: Report 5, Final Report.* Chapel Hill: The University of North Carolina, Teacher Education Review Program.

FOUR

THE DRIVER OF THE CLASSROOM: THE TEACHER AND SCHOOL IMPROVEMENT

ERNEST R. HOUSE and STEPHEN D. LAPAN

> Educational change depends on what teachers do and think—it's as simple and as complex as that. (Fullan, 1982, p. 107).

The view of professional knowledge that has shaped our efforts at professional improvement is what some have labeled the model of technical rationality (Schön, 1983). According to this view professional practice consists of instrumental problem solving made rigorous by the application of scientific theory and scientific method.

Professional practice, it is believed, rests upon a body of scientific knowledge which is applied to practical problems. Professional knowledge is scientific, specialized, and standardized. Professionals apply general principles and standard techniques to concrete problems. Hence, professional knowledge consists of three components: an underlying discipline or basic science; an engineering component that derives standard procedures for the discipline; and skills with which the professional actually supplies services to the client.

This conception of professional knowledge has been institutionalized in the structure of our professional training, epitomized by the medical school. The early years of professional training are spent learning the fundamental sciences and the later years learning to apply the basic principles, culminating in clinical work. The teacher-training curriculum has tried to emulate this pattern, beginning with the foundations of education, psychology, and the discipline to be taught, and culminating in practice teaching.

To validate the knowledge base of the profession requires the application of scientific method. Researchers discover and validate the general principles, and practitioners apply these principles in a concrete setting. "Real" knowledge resides in the principles and techniques of the basic and applied sciences. The rest is application (Schön, 1983). So the development of professional knowledge necessitates the separation of research and practice.

At its most rigorous, validation consists of scientific experiments. Within the current logic of scientific inquiry we rely upon crucial experiments to choose among competing theories and to determine which techniques of treatment are most effective. Through careful experiments we discover general cause-and-effect relationships which can then be transmitted to practitioners, incorporated into newly developed techniques and materials, and generally made the basis of professional practice. Enlightened professional practice entails mapping these cause-and-effect relationships onto practical problems, thereby finding the best means to our given ends. For example, if we want to teach disadvantaged children to read, we construct selectively varied approaches, compare these approaches with one another, and decide which approach is best, as in the Follow Through Experiment.

Professional improvement then occurs through producing new knowledge and techniques, testing them, and inducing practitioners to use them. This model of professional improvement is based upon the premise that researchers can discover general cause-and-effect relationships, causal laws as it were, and that these relationships can be applied in concrete professional settings by well-trained professionals. Professional improvement requires an investment in the discovery of general principles and their conversion into a form that is usable in the professional setting, in the classroom for those of us in education. This is the orthodox view. How well does it hold up in education?

LEARNING TO TEACH

Let us imagine a situation in which a person is learning to teach for the first time, say a beginning teacher is faced with teaching her first class, an introductory educational psychology course, to undergraduates. How does she proceed? Does she review the research literature in search of causal regularities between teaching and learning, for example, the relationship between positive reinforcement and learning curves? After all, this is the content she will be teaching.

Such a prospect seems highly unlikely. A far likelier scenario is that over the years the new teacher has had teachers that she thought were particularly effective or ineffective. She tries to remember what they did that worked with classes in which she was a student, as well as what didn't work very well. Based upon her own experiences in the classroom as a student, she has notions of cause-and-effect relationships, of what works and what doesn't. Some of those ideas may well be mistaken but she holds them nonetheless.

From this repertoire of ideas and techniques, she selects notions around which to organize her classes initially. Some cause-and-effect relationships she thinks might be effective she either cannot do or they do not fit her overall style. For example, she decides that small-group work, although effective when used by some teachers at some times, doesn't really fit with her own nascent style of teaching. She is more directive and would like to be more in control of the students' attention. Her belief is based upon her own experiences as a student in which small groups seemed hazy and unfocused. She decides to direct class discussion herself, using the class as a whole. In addition, she remembers that she never liked teachers who assigned work but graded it tardily. She vows to return the students' graded papers the following class period. The students will accept rigorous grading, she reasons, if they perceive it as quick and fair.

How many of these considerations will there be? Ten? Fifty? No doubt it depends on the person and the situation. There will be many. What they have in common is that most will be based upon the new teacher's actual experience as a student participating in former classes. A student is a participant rather than merely an observer. But even all this is preparatory to learning to teach–trying out these ideas in the classroom. One can be a passenger on a car trip and learn something about where one has been, but when one is the driver the learning is more intense and permanent. Both are cases of doing something, but driving is a far more active role and the driver learns far more. The new teacher is now the driver in the classroom and what she has learned tentatively will be validated or invalidated in the course of her actions in the classroom.

As the new teacher begins to teach, the general considerations of how to act (Should she be highly organized? Authoritative? Flexible? Well dressed?) give way to more specific considerations of exactly what to do (Should she lecture? Lead group discussions? Show movies?). The easiest thing for her to do is to lecture, to tell facts and stories, and she does this first. She is certain of her ability to control the class through her knowledge and less certain of her ability to interact with students or lead a discussion. So she lectures initially.

As her confidence grows, she adds to her teaching repertoire. Although she has never liked small groups as a student, she finds that if she makes the group task small enough and specific enough, the students can stay focused. She finds that the students really love the small groups but still her small-group experience as a student was not positive and she does not fully trust small-group work in spite of her students' reaction.

As she gradually tries out new things she sometimes encounters difficult problems. For example, she cannot seem to teach moral development properly. In her first classes she presents Kohlberg's and Gilligan's theories of moral development but somehow the ideas "bounce off" the students. The lessons don't "work," and by not working, she means that the students cannot discuss the ideas in class, cannot talk about the subject, and have no conception of morality even though they can answer the short items on her tests. Perhaps the students do not have enough background.

The next semester she assigns extra readings on the topic. The lessons still do not work. She talks to colleagues, wondering what to try next. In her third semester she tries a different approach. She begins the topic by presenting the students with two moral problems, one in which a Black is rejected by a sorority because of her race. She has the students discuss these two situations in small groups, answering questions she has prepared for them, then discusses the situations with the whole group.

For the next class she has the students read Kohlberg's theory to see how the students' specific discussions fit Kohlberg's hierarchy. The students are appalled to find themselves operating at the lower levels of moral development. They are upset, ask questions, become engaged. In the third and final class, she has the students fit the examples to Gilligan's theory. Now the students have ideas, a vocabulary, and most importantly, can talk about the topic. They *want* to talk about it. As further proof of success, some students choose moral development as a topic for their term papers, which none had ever done before. Even though the students do no better on her tests than before, the teacher is now satisfied that the lessons work.

Although the new teacher experiments, she changes only one thing at a time. She will try a new textbook, but nothing else new. She will change the assignments, but nothing else. Often she has no idea how a change will work; she must always assess its success in practice. By trying out only one new thing at a time, she not only simplifies her assessment but also remains in control, assured that her class will still be a good one, even if the new idea doesn't work well.

The teacher is learning cause-and-effect relationships through direct participation, through participating first as a student and then as the teacher. This direct experience is gained mostly by participating and acting rather than by passively observing, and this direct personal experience is so intense and powerful that it shapes what the teacher will do and try to do throughout her career. After a few years her learning rate will decline because she will feel she has mastered her environment. Her teaching repertoire will be largely formed. After 4 or 5 years she may become rather fixed in her practice.

One may well wonder if this is the proper way for the teacher to proceed. Perhaps we have here an ineffective teacher who has learned the wrong things. In fact, this is an actual case and during her first semester of teaching this teacher was placed upon the university list of excellent teachers, which is determined by comparing her scores with other classes in the university on a student response instrument. By her second semester, she was awarded a "star" on the list, which meant that her scores were among the top 10% of excellent teachers.

She has learned to teach by having something in mind, trying it out, and judging its success or failure. The determination of whether the lesson works is based largely upon first-hand experience, and through those experiences the teacher develops a personal set of cause-and-effect relationships about teaching. These are singular, causal claims and not dependent upon universal laws or regularities which assert universal correlations of events. Rather they are based upon personal experience. They may well be mistaken but mostly they are not. The teacher can develop a reasonable set of cause-and-effect relationships to guide her through the day, just as most of us manage to drive our cars to work, feed ourselves, and conduct our daily affairs. All this is not ordinarily a problem, except perhaps when the car won't start, because causality is not the problem that we think it to be. Causal inference guides our lives every day, which is not to say that either our lives or the teacher's training cannot be improved. It is to say that most of what we do is rational and makes good sense.

The teacher learns to teach not through observing her own actions or other people's actions as a spectator, but through performing certain actions. The direct experience of acting is the basis of the cause-and-effect relationships she learns. She does not infer the essential cause-and-effect relationships from repetition or regularity or universal causal laws. One can ride as a passenger in a car, witness the passing scene, yet not be able to retrace the routes one has traveled. However, if one is the driver of the car there is an intentionality to one's action, perhaps a responsibility, that makes it highly likely one has learned the route. In addition, the driver with more experience anticipates likely occurrences that the inexperienced passenger cannot grasp. One can learn to teach in a few semesters by performing the teacher role.

PRACTITIONER KNOWLEDGE

This illustration of learning to teach contrasts sharply to our view of professional knowledge gained through research-based techniques. The teacher discovers cause-and-effect relationships based upon what she has directly experienced in the past and the situation she now faces. No doubt her formal training also has a discernible influence upon what she does in the classroom but her own experience dominates the way she teaches. For better or for worse, what the teacher learns from her direct experience has primacy.

It is also the case, we think, that most trainers of teachers operate somewhat the same way as teachers, even though the dominant model of professional preparation demands a scientifically based practice. In fact, teacher trainers depend upon their personal experiences, course guidelines, and textbooks just as teachers do. They are teachers and problem-solve through their experience.

Teachers think differently than people who are not teachers, a fact much underappreciated by the rest of us and misunderstood when it is appreciated. Schön (1983) contends that professional knowledge in general consists of a tacit knowing-in-action. That is, professionals can recognize certain phenomena, such as families of symptoms of a particular disease in the case of physicians, without being able to give a complete or accurate description of what these symptoms are. Faced with a concrete situation, professionals are able to make judgments of quality in their area of expertise without being able to state the criteria which they use. They can demonstrate particular skills without being able to state the rules or procedures by which they do so. Professionals are also able to describe deviations from the norm in their area of expertise without necessarily being able to describe the norm itself. In short, they can spontaneously perform tasks which they are unaware of having learned or be able to express. Sometimes they accomplish this through tacit knowing; a common example of this is that one can ride a bicycle with ease but would have an impossible time specifying the principles and procedures by which one did so. Not all the professional's knowledge is tacit, however. Much is also based upon explicit knowledge learned in training.

The professional has a repertoire of examples, images, understandings, and actions that he or she brings to bear in a concrete setting (Schön, 1983). Professional knowledge is organized into loose domains. For example, an architect's knowledge domains may include use of the building, siting, building elements, organization of space, form, structure, cost, and scale. Each of these domains includes a complex of examples, images, and actions that are often used metaphorically to frame or reframe the practical problem at hand. Within the professional's knowledge structure some domains have priority over others. One architect may give priority to form, another to cost. Professionals themselves may not be aware of the knowledge they possess.

The professional engages the particular situation at hand, drawing upon this complex assortment of knowledge, perhaps making deliberate moves to try out this or that, to experiment when a problem arises. Then he or she evaluates the moves by a more or less finely tuned appreciative system which judges in reference to the categories of the domains, the moves already made and the new possibilities opened up. Virtuosity in professional performance consists of being able to respond to the situation at hand and spin out webs of great complexity, each web of moves in turn subjected to multiple evaluations (Schön, 1983).

The overall structure of professional thinking is not one of simply applying standard techniques, but rather one of approaching a problem as a unique case, attending to the particularities of the concrete situation, looking at the situation in several different ways, framing and reframing the situation, making moves that might work in the situation, and evaluating the consequent moves by reference to the professional's appreciative system. Although the professional's action repertoire may be influenced by formal training, actions are derived more from direct experience than by the application of fundamental principles. This is especially true in the professions not based on physical science.

The question remains as to what constitutes the teacher's professional knowledge. We may presume that the teacher has knowledge of the subject matter that she teaches and that this is organized into various domains, but what beyond that? It is significant of our attitudes toward teachers that our information about how they actually think about instruction is skimpy: We act as if it doesn't matter that much.

Some research on how teachers think about the instructional process has been done (Shavelson & Stern, 1981). For example, in planning instruction teachers focus upon the *activities* the students engage in during the lesson, the *content*, which most frequently is decided by which textbook to use, the *materials* the students see and manipulate, the *goals* for instruction, and the *student*, particularly the student's abilities, needs, and interests. Finally, there is the *social community*, which includes the sense of groupness, as well as the grouping of the students for instructional purposes. The teacher creates instructional tasks by drawing upon these domains. Exactly how these domains are utilized or what they consist of is unknown.

Apparently, teachers' concern with the content is not with the structure of the subject matter itself but with selecting content for constructing tasks for the students to perform and teachers' concern about students in planning is focused early in the year when they are getting to know the students. The activities that teachers develop control the pacing and timing of the instruction.

These instructional tasks, perhaps in the form of mental scripts or images in the teacher's mind, serve as a mental plan for carrying out classroom instruction, and once begun these tasks are ordinarily carried out in the classroom for good or for ill. The teacher strives to keep the activity flowing and the students engaged in it, monitoring the classroom routine to see that the activity is proceeding as planned. By monitoring student reactions, such as lack of involvement or behavior problems, teachers can judge when a lesson is successful. If the lesson is awry, they decide whether to intervene immediately or to change the lesson later. Sometimes the clues indicating whether the lesson is within an acceptable tolerance are subtle.

These categories or domains of teacher planning are embarrassingly familiar to us, yet at the same time we cannot describe them in great detail or say how they work. They are reflected in the example of the beginning teacher that we described earlier. She planned certain activities for the students and expected the students to become involved. When the students did not discuss the content the way she wanted, the instructional task was rearranged, first by including different content, then by devising different activities for the students to engage in. To determine how well the lessons were working, she observed the involvement of students, particularly whether they could talk about moral development, rather than their performance on her tests, which did not vary that much. Fundamentally our knowledge of how teachers conceive their tasks is limited.

EXPERIMENTING

The beginning teacher did try out new activities and content to see what would work, especially when she encountered what she defined as a lack of success, in a sense conducting her own experiment to find a better approach. Schön (1983) has distinguished between the kinds of experiments that practitioners engage in and the types of experiments researchers conduct. The practitioner comes to an understanding of his or her environment by trying to change it, by making "moves" to change the situation and then assessing the consequences of these moves. In deciding what move to make, the practitioner draws upon her repertoire of examples, images, and actions, the repertoire itself being based upon the practitioner's entire experience. The teacher sees the current situation as more or less like something in her repertoire and, based upon that similarity, makes a new move to change the situation at hand. But the move-testing experiment of the practitioner is quite different from the hypothesis-testing experiment of the researcher.

The researcher wants to test alternative hypotheses about a phenomenon and the logic of the experiment is that of eliminating rival hypotheses so that one is left with the most likely candidate. If we are testing an educational technique or program, we look for an effect of the program, and with the aid of the appropriate experimental design, eliminate potential rival causes for the effect, such as the possibility that maturation or improper measurement or regression to the mean accounted for the effect that we observed. The logic of these experiments is elaborated in splendid detail in Campbell and Stanley (1963) and Cook and Campbell (1979). If we are conducting an evaluation of an educational program, we have the double task of first making certain that no factor other than the program itself caused the effect and, second, comparing the size of the effect, often a test score, with the effect of another competitive program to determine which is better. First, we must eliminate the potential rivals for cause, then make the comparison with the other program.

The scientific experiment itself must be objective, controlled, and conducted at a distance so as to eliminate potential biases. Conditions of practice seldom lend themselves to such controls. Not many school districts will allow a researcher to assign students randomly to an experimental program. There is also the possibility of bias from the researcher wanting the new program to succeed. Hence, research is separated from practice and the researcher from the practitioner. Above all, the scientific experiment must be reproducible so that its veracity can be checked by other researchers. What we call internal validity depends upon this reproducibility, and this in turn means that the program be sufficiently specified so it can be reproduced and the procedures of the study be specified so that they can be reproduced. Presumably the results of the study can be reproduced as well.

In this way it is expected that the findings of the scientific experiment will be generalizable to the practitioner's work. If one finds that a program is effective in one setting, one will find it effective in a similar setting; the only problem is to specify the proper qualifying conditions. Like causes produce like effects. Reproducibility is the key concept underlying this particular conception of the scientific experiment. It is expected that the experiment will discover causal regularities, causal laws which obtain elsewhere. The utility of the experiment for professional practice depends upon the idea that the causal regularity will apply elsewhere.

Now the move-testing experiment of the professional practitioner differs substantially from this model of the scientific experiment (Schön, 1983). The practitioner makes a move to produce an intended change and that move is affirmed when it produces what was intended. The questions for the practitioner are, "Do you get what you intended?" and "Do you like what you get?" It is often the case that the practitioner will not only get what was intended but considerably more besides, which may be either good or bad. To return to our example of the beginning teacher, the teacher sees that she has a problem teaching moral development and from her repertoire of experience she constructs a different set of activities for the students to engage in. The activities produce what she wanted, which was student involvement and the ability to talk about the concept of moral development. Before that she tried other activities, such as providing more background material, which did not work. The move-testing process is not self-confirming.

Whereas the researcher tries to make the hypothesis or findings conform to the world, the practitioner tried to make the world conform to her intentions. The practitioner tries to transform the world into something that she likes better. By contrast, the researcher tries to understand the world and would be severely chastised if caught trying to change the world to obtain the results desired. Ideally the researcher changes the hypothesis to fit the world, whereas the practitioner makes moves to change the phenomena to fit the hypothesis. Of course, this is an oversimplification. The researcher actually changes pieces of the world to make the hypothesis fit and the practitioner changes her image of the world as to what will work.

In fact, many people would be reluctant to call what the practitioner does an experiment at all. The practitioner can hardly afford to be objective, impartial, and distanced from what she is doing. On the contrary, the beginning teacher is vitally concerned that the situation turn out as she wants it to. Nor can she conduct a controlled experiment. The practitioner is in the situation and is learning by doing, not by observing. If she is wrong, some consequences are immediate and unpleasant. Furthermore, the practitioner has a great advantage over the researcher: the domain of inquiry is the unique situation at hand. The teacher knows the students in her classroom, knows the material she works with. Her knowledge of that particular situation is far deeper than the researcher's can possibly be. She does not have to discover what will work in other classes but only what will work in her class alone. Reproducibility is not the key concept. In fact, when professionals lose their perception of the situations as unique cases, they also lose their effectiveness and their interest.

So if she lacks the scientist's objectivity, she has far more detailed knowledge of the domain of inquiry and a different task at hand. The teacher's focus can be on what actions to take that will make a difference in this particular setting for her. Insofar as one believes that cause-and-effect relationships are complex matters involving a great number of particular factors, the teacher's knowledge of the particular situation puts her in a far better position to perceive cause and effect in the classroom than a more objective but distant researcher.

Whether one wants to label this exploratory behavior an experiment or not, the teacher does acquire a set of cause-and-effect relationships that are embodied in her performance and actions rather than verbalized in explicit statements. She has derived these cause-and-effect relationships from her own direct experience rather than from theory or from someone else's experience. Furthermore, this direct experience is gained by participation rather than observation, either participation as a student or as a teacher. And she will have constructed this causal knowledge herself, through her own reasoning processes.

It is our contention that causal knowledge gained in this fashion has primacy for the practitioner when it comes to her professional practice. What she learns as the driver of the classroom will shape how she teaches the rest of her life. What she learns may well be wrong; she may have reasoned improperly or have not been witness to long-term consequences of her actions. But most of the time she will be correct. Given the constraints of her teaching environment, she will draw reasonable conclusions most of the time. Teachers are rational people, that is to say, causally inferring people, just like researchers, most of the time.

IMPROVING TEACHING THROUGH RESEARCH

Given this view of the teacher in action, what are we to say about school improvement? First, nothing that has been said suggests that teaching and schools cannot or should not be improved. Even though teachers are far more rational and effective than many believe (given the constraints of their situation) does not mean that improvement is unnecessary or undesirable. After 4 or 5 years of teaching, teachers often become set in their ways and less flexible than they once were. This is no doubt partly a result of having mastered their craft to a considerable degree. But routine, boredom, and inflexibility become problems in the careers of many teachers. Change is necessary, as in any profession, even for the best teachers. Second, if change occurs through individual teacher inference, it is likely to be very gradual. Schools are very conservative institutions and if change depends on each teacher readjusting his or her thinking to new conditions, changes will occur slowly. Furthermore, only change strategies that affect teacher thinking are likely to be very effective.

Let us turn now to specific strategies for school improvement, beginning with the dominant model of professional improvement, but with an important caution in mind: The strategies for improvement discussed here all involve research as an important component. It may well be that substantial school improvement could dispense with research altogether. So these are research-based strategies only.

1. *Technical Rationality.* The idea that we can discover a principle or technique that works in one place and simply apply it in another is a deceptive one. If we may be so bold, we believe it is based upon a defective conception of causality. The argument for that is far longer than this chapter and we have attempted it elsewhere (House, Mathison, & McTaggart, 1985). The essential idea is that our current, orthodox theory of causation, called the regularity theory, asserts that we can never discern causation directly but can only know causation through repetition of events, regular succession, and correlation. Once we discover a causal regularity or law, it will be repeated in other settings, if we only take care to specify the accompanying necessary conditions. Hence, although correctly discerning causation is a difficult problem, the transfer of principles and techniques from one setting to another is really not difficult. Like causes produce like effects.

This model sometimes works reasonably well in physically based professions such as medicine, although even here there are difficulties. Individuals' susceptibilities to various drugs vary tremendously, for example. And when one enters a medical specialty such as psychiatry, the certainty of like causes producing like effects evaporates quickly. In professions like education this technical transfer model does not work well at all. For example, in the Follow Through experiment the variation in effects between sites of the same programs was nearly as great as the variation between the programs themselves. If like causes produce like effects, the same program should produce similar results. But they often do not. There are several ways of explaining this. One explanation is that there are so many influential factors in these cause-and-effect relationships that we cannot sort them all out by our simple experiments. Cronbach (1982) takes this view, asserting that the interactions among variables are stronger than the main effects.

We encountered this phenomenon in another form when we evaluated the Illinois demonstration centers for gifted youth (House, Kerins, & Steele, 1972). Teachers would visit these demonstration centers, observe excellent teaching but when they returned home they said that factors in their home setting prevented them from implementing the techniques they had seen. They could discern factors in their own situation, perhaps in themselves, that prevented the implementation of the model programs. Some people might say this shows their lethargy and inertia. We say that it demonstrates their perceptiveness.

Now we do not think we should stop trying to discover new principles and techniques altogether. New curricula and models of teaching serve as guideposts to what is possible, even when they are not implemented. For example, the BSCS high school biology curriculum has had its greatest impact not in being implemented in toto but in influencing writers of high school biology textbooks to include materials that they never would have dreamed of a few decades ago. What we cannot expect is that teachers will adopt these principles and techniques in anything like the fashion their developers envision. Teachers already have a strong working knowledge of their classroom and any changes must be mediated through that. The technical rationality or technical transfer model is not a particularly effective strategy for changing the schools.

2. *Study and Prescribe.* A related but different strategy is to study what teachers do and how they think and make judgments about the classroom, then prescribe ways teachers might improve. This of course presumes that we know how to improve what they are doing but has the advantage at least of actually finding out what they are doing and thinking first.

Shavelson and Stern (1981), who have summarized such research as exists on teacher judgments and decisions, have suggested the construction of a taxonomy of critical teacher decisions. For example, research shows that teachers group students by reading ability without seriously considering other possibilities. Researchers might try to map out the consequences of such a decision and suggest other information that might lead to a better decision or better consequences. For the most part teachers are not in a position to know the long-range effects of their teaching. Empirical research might help. We are quite a long way from being able to construct such a decision taxonomy and Shavelson and Stern recommend that research on teaching focus on how various factors influence teachers' thoughts about classroom processes.

3. *Practitioners as Exemplars.* Another strategy for improvement is to admit that practitioners know more about practice than researchers and not only to study practitioners but also to use the best as exemplars. Scriven (1985) has argued that we need a practical science in education rather than a theoretical one. Educational researchers should abandon attempts to discover underlying principles and should take the discipline of evaluation as the paradigm for all educational research.

Scriven's formula is to identify a number of practitioners who are outstandingly successful at the task in question, identify the distinctive features of their approach (possibly but not necessarily by comparison with unsuccessful practitioners), then teach new or unsuccessful practitioners the "winning ways." Scriven's approach assumes that the best practitioners have learned how to teach successfully and know far more than the most knowledgeable researchers. The researchers' task is to abstract this knowledge from their practice and teach it to others. This approach assumes that good practice is abstractable and teachable in terms of techniques but that the problems to be addressed should be defined by practitioners rather than researchers.

One question that arises with Scriven's strategy is whether good teaching is abstractable and generalizable in this way. If teachers learn through doing, must they also relearn through doing as well? Are the cause-and-effect relationships simple enough to be taught in this manner? We don't know. Watching exemplary teachers in the Illinois demonstration centers was not sufficient to improve teaching but intensive follow-up in the visiting teacher's own classroom did have significant results. Again this meant dealing with the particular concrete realities of the teacher who was changing.

4. *Vicarious Experience.* Yet another strategy is to accept the idea that practitioners know what they are doing and that they learn primarily from experience. Stake (1985) has suggested that researchers conduct studies that will provide *vicarious* experience to teachers in such a way that the new experience will combine easily with the old. The role of the researcher would be to aid practitioners in reaching new experiential understandings, which Stake calls "naturalistic generalization," a concept similar to the experience-based reasoning of practitioners that we have portrayed. The main difference is that we have emphasized direct participation as the basis for practice rather than vicarious experience.

The naturalistic researcher presents "portrayals of actual teaching and learning problems, witnessing of observers who understand the reality of the classroom, words of the people involved." These new data provide readers with vicarious experiences which interact with existing naturalistic generalizations from previous experience. The research study should serve the subjective experience of the teacher. Presumably the vicarious experience leads to naturalistic generalizations on the part of the practitioner and these in turn lead to internal conviction and action.

The difference between this approach and the earlier one of studying teacher thinking is the difference between reading a novel and a textbook. In the naturalistic study the classroom is portrayed in its full complexity and the teacher must make use of it, absorb it somehow. The researcher conducts the study but the teacher must draw the conclusions for his or her practice, albeit in a complex indirect way, as in reading a novel.

One of the questions with this approach is whether vicarious experience is powerful enough to interact with prior direct experience. Naturalistic case studies have been used successfully to inform readers distant from the scene, such as higher level policymakers who have no first-hand experience about a program or setting. Whether it is powerful enough to interact with direct experience is unclear. Does reading a novel change one's life?

5. *Action Research.* The most radical strategy in this progression is to turn the research itself over to the practitioners altogether, with perhaps some help from researchers. The practitioners would operate either as individuals or a group to define what their problems are and to study them in their own school. Researchers might assist in this process but the teachers would be in control.

The idea of action research originated with Kurt Lewin and acquired a bad reputation in the 1950s when it seemed to consist of teaching teachers positive research methodology such as elementary statistics and expecting them to produce studies. Needless to say, the studies that were produced lacked rigor by the standards of researchers. However, research by teachers does not have to be a weak version of that done by researchers.

If one conceives the basis of teaching as the personal cause-and-effect relationships that individual teachers derive from their own direct experience, particularly their participation as the driver of the classroom, then it makes good sense to test these inferences against standards and data beyond oneself. The research methods we have devised are really not very useful for this purpose. What would be useful would be to engage one's colleagues in checking one's inferences, engaging at the same level of detail and particularity as the teacher's knowledge. One can imagine procedures by which this would be accomplished. The focus then would be very much on the particular subjective world of the teacher.

We state this strategy hypothetically because there is very little of this type of practitioner reflection going on at this time in the United States. In a study of a medium-sized school district in Illinois, McTaggart (1985) found only 3 of approximately 900 teachers doing anything like this. There has been more action research in both England (Elliott, 1980) and Australia (McTaggart, 1985). The external accountability pressures in American education currently work against this type of reflective practice.

6. *Change in Conditions.* In this chapter we have concentrated upon only one aspect of educational change—the teacher's mental framework, especially the causal inferences that he or she draws about what works in the classroom. We believe that this aspect is a vital key to understanding educational change, and one very much underappreciated and misunderstood. However, there are many other

aspects to educational change that we group here under the catchall category of changing the conditions of teaching. Teachers draw their inferences from the circumstances they find themselves in, and it is possible to change their thinking by changing the structural circumstances in which they teach.

Two of the best reference books in this regard are Dan Lortie's *School Teacher* (1975), the best single study of teachers, and Michael Fullan's *The Meaning of Educational Change* (1982), the best summary of the research on the change process. Lortie shows that teaching is an overwhelmingly personal, individual experience. The teacher is in the classroom with his or her students, expects little help from the outside, even from other teachers, and strongly resents any interference in the classroom. Other teachers refrain from offering advice or even making comments. This isolation and privatization is built into the very cellular structure of the school and institutionalized in the norms of the teachers themselves. One of the strongest rules for teachers is, "Don't interfere in another teacher's class." Bridging this isolation and privatization of teaching would result in immense change, no doubt in ways not fully predictable.

Fullan notes that the degree of successful change is strongly related to how much teachers interact with one another. Frequent communication, mutual support, and personal contact are essential to spreading new ideas and dealing with problems that often arise when one attempts something different. It is precisely this supportive colleagial interaction which is lacking in teaching. If we could do so, this is the condition of teaching that we would change first.

In summary, what we have contended in this chapter is that teachers learn to teach primarily through direct experience and participation, first as a student then as a beginning teacher. From direct experience the teacher draws cause-and-effect inferences as to what works and doesn't work. This knowledge is personal and particular to the actual situation, and much of it is tacit: The teacher knows how to do things he or she cannot explain. This knowledge has primacy when it comes to actually teaching classes and shapes what the teacher does throughout his or her career. Any strategy for improving education must work through the basic fact that the teacher is the driver of the classroom.

REFERENCES

Campbell, D. T., & Stanley, J. E. (1963). *Experimental and quasi-experimental designs for research*. Chicago: Rand McNally.

Cook, T. D., & Campbell, D. T. (1979). *Quasi-experimentation.* Boston: Houghton Mifflin.

Cronbach, L. S. (1982). *Designing evaluations of education and social programs.* San Francisco: Jossey–Bass.

Elliott, J. (1980). Implications of classroom research for professional development. In E. Hoyle & J. Megasry (Eds.), *World yearbook of education.* London: Kogan Page.

Fullan, M. (1982). *The meaning of educational change.* New York: Teachers College Press.

House, E. R., Kerins, T., & Steele, J. M. (1972). A test of the research and development model of change. *Educational Administration Quarterly, 8*(1), 1–14.

House, E. R., Mathison, S., & McTaggart, R. (1985). *Validity and its advocates.* Champaign-Urbana: University of Illinois at Champaign-Urbana, Center for Instructional Research and Curriculum Evaluation.

Lortie, D. C. (1975). *School Teacher.* Chicago: University of Chicago Press.

McTaggart, R. (1985). *Conditions for action research.* Unpublished doctoral thesis, University of Illinois, Champaign–Urbana, IL.

Schön, D. C. (1983). *The reflective practitioner.* New York: Basic Books.

Scriven, M. (1985). Evaluation as a paradigm for educational research. In E. R. House (Ed.), *New directions for educational evaluation.* Lewes, England: Falmer Press.

Shavelson, R. J., & Stern, P. (1981). Research on teachers' pedagogical thoughts, judgments, decisions, and behavior. *Review of Educational Research, 51*(47), 455–498.

Stake, R. E. (1985). An evolutionary view of program improvement. In E. R. House (Ed.), *New directions for educational evaluation.* Lewes, England: Falmer Press.

Part Two

Diversity and Equity

FIVE

EFFECTIVE SCHOOLS OR EFFECTIVE STUDENTS: DEALING WITH DIVERSITY[1]

JOYCE L. EPSTEIN

Thinking about effective schools, I am reminded of some schools I once studied in maximum security prisons. One warden complained about the students' achievement: "We have a good school here," he said, "but we get the wrong kind of students." The prison may have had an effective school. There was strong leadership, an emphasis on basic skills, frequent testing, and high expectations for success—all characteristics of theoretically effective schools. But the prison school was not effective for its students. As in many places, the administrators and teachers expected the students to fit the school.

Not all schools are like that prison's school. For many students, schools are highly successful, liberating places. But for many other students, schools as they are currently organized are not effective. Many students are neither supported nor challenged by their schools' instructional and social programs.

The recent surge of reports and books on school reform (Boyer, 1983; Goodlad, 1983; National Commission on Excellence in Education, 1983; Sizer, 1984; Twentieth Century Fund Task Force, 1983), and the popular "effective schools literature" (Edmonds, 1979a,b; Purkey & Smith, 1983; Weber, 1971), have focused attention on school improvement at the federal, state, and local levels (Children's Defense Fund,

---

[1]The author thanks John Hollifield, Bruce Wilson, participants at the Colloquium Series on Public Education Policy for the 1990s, Bush Institute for Child and Family Policy, University of North Carolina, Chapel Hill, April 1985, and the editors of this volume for helpful comments and suggestions on earlier drafts of this paper.

1985; Education Week, 1985; Olson, 1986). But the suggested reforms and the resulting swift actions from states and school districts have missed some important aspects of effective education. The most glaring omission is the lack of adequate attention to students.

The effective schools movement requires an auxiliary "effective students movement." There are three reasons for this. First, there has been too much emphasis on the practices of teachers and principals and too little on the impact of those practices on the outcomes of schooling for different groups of students. A focus on students would recognize the wide and important diversity in students' abilities, needs, and interests in any year in school, and the increasing diversity in students' skills and learning histories as they proceed from elementary through middle and high school.

Second, there has been too much attention to universal tenets for effective schools and not enough to the manipulable or alterable structures in schools and classrooms. More attention to learning environments would allow teachers and principals to organize programs that are responsive to more students and that build specific academic and social skills, attitudes, and behaviors.

Third, there has been too little attention to the contributions needed from research and evaluation to increase understanding of the effects on diverse students of particular organizational designs and teaching practices. Schools need new measures of processes and outcomes in addition to achievement tests in order to monitor how their programs, teaching, and administrative practices affect the opportunities, experiences, achievements, attitudes, and social development of different groups of students. And, they need to use the information they collect to continue to improve their programs for effective students.

It is not mere semantics to redirect attention from effective schools to effective students. The goal to develop more effective students is different from the goal to make an effective school. It is possible and even common to have effective teachers who "cover" their subjects well, but whose classes are filled with ineffective students. Effective schools may have students who, on average, score at some acceptable level on achievement tests. But averages are often deceptive, hiding large numbers of students who are being ignored, pushed back, or pushed out of the school. Effective students are enthusiastic about learning and learn how to use resources in and out of school to assist their own progress. This chapter examines the three issues that could move discussions of effective schools toward attention to effective students: student diversity, alterable school and classroom environments, and comprehensive research and measurement models.

RECOGNIZING STUDENT DIVERSITY

Discussions of effective schools must include questions about effective students. For which students are the schools already successful? For which students are schools ineffective? Should the programs, schedules, methods of instruction, and climate in schools be changed for some or all students? How will educators know what to change and when to stop changing programs? How can schools deal with the differences among students at each grade level and across grade levels in order to improve all students' success and positive attitudes toward school and learning?

Schools are reasonably successful with most students who are at or above grade level, especially if the students are motivated to learn and have decided to attend college. For these students there is an easy fit between the schools' and students' goals for education. These effective students learn how to learn, are rewarded and recognized for their achievements, and are included in school life.

Schools are acceptable—not really "effective"—for most students who are average in academic skills, reasonably well-behaved, socially competent, and who have the general goal of completing high school and moving on to work, military service, or some postsecondary education. For these students, there is a loose but troubling fit between the instructional program and the students' needs, abilities, and often formless goals. Elementary, middle, and high schools serve these students without distinction, and the students respond without excitement. The students are rarely rewarded or punished for their academic progress, and most of them stand on the periphery of school life.

Schools are unsuccessful and unappealing places for most students who are below average in academic skills, failing one or more subjects, socially immature or isolated, or without clear goals for life after high school. For these students there is a poor fit and few connections between the schools' programs and the students' needs. Neither the academic nor the social organization of the school is designed to help these students define or attain success. The students receive few rewards and many punishing evaluations, and are largely excluded from school life. This is true at all levels of schooling but becomes especially important in high school, where little remedial instruction is offered in ways that could re-establish poor students as effective learners.

These three main groups are further diversified because students in each category may be stronger or weaker in one subject or another, with good or poor attitudes about school, learning, and themselves. Thus, some high-achieving students may be apathetic about some subjects; some average students may have sincere interest in learning and high rates of participation in activities; and some below-average students may have high self-esteem and dogged perseverance. Other combinations of academic skills, social skills, and personal characteristics define the scope of student diversity that exists in all schools, often unheeded, and almost always unmeasured.

For unsuccessful or unmotivated students there have always been two alternatives: change the students or change the schools. Usually, educators try to *change the students* to make them fit the established programs of the schools. In this approach, unsuccessful students are directed, implored, or punished to become more like successful students. The teachers' programs and practices remain unchanged. For a few students this strategy works. Marginal students who "buckle down" may pass their courses and develop better work habits and more positive attitudes about learning. But most students who are barely passing or clearly failing need more than an order to shape up or ship out. In 1982, for example, 34%, 48%, and 60% of U.S. white, Black, and Hispanic students, respectively, had not graduated from high school by age 19 (National Center for Educational Statistics, 1985). Large numbers of students—almost 40% of the age cohort of 18- and 19-year-olds—did not succeed in schools as they are typically organized.

The alternative approach for correcting the lack of fit between schools and unmotivated or unsuccessful students is to *change the schools*. Changes in school and classroom organizations can be made to help more students master prerequisite skills, basic requirements, and higher-order skills, to reward all students for the progress they make, and to enable all students to participate in the academic and social life of the school. There are several sociological, psychological, and anthropological perspectives on the importance of alterable variables in schools and classrooms, including Bloom (1980), Boocock (1979), Carroll (1963), Doyle (1985), Gump (1980), Hamilton (1983), McPartland, Epstein, Karweit, and Slavin (1976), and Minuchin (1977). The theory is that by changing the schools—by creating, implementing, testing, and improving new organizational designs—more students will become effective learners. This literature is largely untamed, with different terms and emphases used in the various perspectives. In the next sections, we suggest some connections between dimensions of organizational structure and student performance that may help educators deal with diversity and promote more effective students.

RECOGNIZING ALTERABLE SCHOOL AND CLASSROOM STRUCTURES

The basic building blocks of school and classroom organizations are the task, authority, reward, grouping, evaluation, and time (TARGET) structures.[2] These six broad, manipulable structures form a framework that can help systematize and clarify the many perspectives and long lists of suggested school reforms that have inundated educators.

Task structure (T) concerns what students are asked to learn and what assignments they are given to do. It includes the content and sequence of the curriculum, the design of classwork and homework, the level of difficulty of the work, and the materials required to complete assignments. These alterable characteristics of the task structure may be varied to accommodate student diversity. Teachers can give every student the same work or give different assignments to groups or individuals, concentrate on the printed or spoken word or the visual or performing arts, use one text or a variety of materials that include one or many levels of difficulty or perspectives on a topic. Tasks can proceed from grades 1 to 12 in a logical, sequential, and cumulative curriculum or can be repetitive or disjointed. Tasks can be designed that have meaning and importance to some or all students. New knowledge can be obtained from lectures by teachers and recitations by students, project or group work by students, or paper- or computer-based seatwork by students. The work may be limited to basic skills or go beyond the basics to higher-order thinking skills and creative work. The tasks may vary in the degree of independence or dependence required for completion, with some assignments conducted by individuals, in pairs, teams, or small or large groups. Variations in the sequence, scope, design, difficulty, variety, meaning, media, passivity, and interdependence of tasks affect whether activities and arrangements are challenging, enjoyable, and appropriate for students and whether students can learn academic or other important skills from the tasks. (For other perspectives and studies on task structures see Bidwell, 1972; Bossert, 1979; Cohen, 1980a; DeVries & Edwards, 1973; Doyle, 1983; Dreeben, 1968; Rosenholtz & Rosenholtz, 1981; Slavin, 1984; Tammivaara, 1982.)

Most educators believe that tasks should be appropriate and challenging for students, according to their prior levels of ability and read-

---

[2]Research on alterable structures in schools and classrooms and their effects on academic and nonacademic outcomes for students has been conducted for many years by the social scientists of the School Organization Program of the Johns Hopkins Center for Social Organization of Schools (now the Center for Research on Elementary and Middle Schools). This approach represents the Hopkins Center's "school" of sociology of education. Key researchers at the center have studied different TARGET variables over the years, including Karl Alexander, Henry Jay Becker, Jomills Braddock, David DeVries, Keith Edwards, Doris Entwisle, Joyce Epstein, Denise Gottfredson, Gary Gottfredson, Nancy Karweit, James McPartland, Edward McDill, Nancy Madden, and Robert Slavin. See references to their work.

iness. But to assure maximum progress in learning over a school year, teachers need to measure and work from the students' starting places, with an understanding of all aspects of the task structure. If the task structure is ignored, teachers may have to accept the fact that their instruction—too easy for some and too advanced for others—is not producing many effective students.

Authority structure (A) concerns the kind and frequency of participation that occurs in academic and other programs in school, including the distribution of decision making among administrators, teachers, students, parents, and others in the school community. Participation and decision-making opportunities are alterable features of the authority structure that vary considerably from school to school, and among classrooms within schools. In some settings, authority is exercised only by the teacher; in other settings, teachers and students share responsibilities for making choices, giving directions, monitoring work, setting and enforcing rules, establishing and offering rewards, and evaluating student success and teacher quality. In some schools and classrooms, parents, businesses, and others in the community are included in ways that alter the typical structure of school authority. Variations in the structure of authority in schools make students more active or passive learners, more confident investors in their learning, and in this way, affect student attitudes and achievements.

Students may be "active" in responding to questions (as in direct-instruction teaching practices) but this is a limited part of learning. A broader definition of students as active learners includes participation with teachers in selecting topics for study and discussion, in deciding how long to work to master skills before being evaluated, when to continue with deeper study of a topic, when to ask for help to understand difficult concepts, and many other decisions. Like adult workers, students may be more effective when they feel some control over their own activities and progress. (For several perspectives and studies on aspects of the authority structure see deCharms, 1976; Eckstein & Gurr, 1975; Epstein, 1981; Epstein & McPartland, 1979; Metz, 1978; Minuchin, 1977; Schonfeld, 1971; Spady, 1974; Tjosvold, 1978; Wang & Stiles, 1976.)

One of the most popular emphases in the reform literature has been to call for more active learning by students and less lecturing by teachers (Boyer, 1983; Goodlad, 1983; Sizer, 1984). This goal requires teachers to give students a greater share in decisions and more responsibility for learning. Teachers and administrators can design and test methods to increase active thinking, questioning, opportunities for choice, self-direction, and leadership by all students in a class. If the authority structure is ignored, teachers will include some students and ignore others as active participants in learning, producing only a few effective students.

Reward structure (R) concerns the procedures and practices used to motivate and recognize students for their progress and achievement in school. Schools and teachers can officially reward few or many students for few or many behaviors, achievements, or talents. Tangible and intangible rewards that are more or less valued by the students may be issued for relative or absolute accomplishments, with more or less public attention. Variations in the purposes, types, criteria, publicity, and distributions of rewards may dramatically affect how students feel about themselves as learners compared with others.

Rewards define what the system, school, and teachers consider important, and influence whether and how students invest their time to learn. Schools may reward individuals for earning top grades, contributing to group goals, or making good progress, or other achievements and behaviors. These different emphases promote different investments from students. And, the goals of a school require different investments from the teachers, too. For example, if schools value students helping each other, then teachers need to recognize and encourage cooperation in classrooms as well as in extracurricular activities and sports. (For a variety of perspectives and studies on reward structures, see Ames & Ames, 1984; DeVries & Edwards, 1973; McPartland & McDill, 1977; Michaels, 1977; Nicholls, 1984; Slavin, 1983.)

All teachers know that students need some recognition for good work in order to become committed to more advanced learning. But in most schools, few students receive official recognition and rewards. Teachers can design and test procedures that appropriately, equitably, and widely acknowledge all students for their efforts and for their actual progress in learning (Beady, Slavin, & Fennessey, 1981; Slavin, 1980). It would help for teachers and students to know where the student started (history), what the student was striving for (plans, goals), and what was accomplished (outcomes), in order to reward improvement fairly. These facts are clear, for example, when records are set in competitive sports, or when students keep track of their "personal best" accomplishments. But of the three elements of evaluation—history, plans, and outcomes—only outcomes regulate the reward structure in most subjects in most schools. If the reward structure is ignored, teachers may find that their distributions of grades, honors, and other awards support and boost the energies of some students, while the same practices alienate and destroy the energies of others.

Grouping structure (G) concerns the way student diversity is distributed. Grouping practices determine how students who are similar or different on particular dimensions (e.g. sex, race, SES, ability, goals, or interests) are brought together or kept apart in schools and in classrooms for instruction and for social activities. Grouping practices determine which students are taught together by the teacher, whether, how, and when group memberships can change, which students interact and become acquaintances or friends, and how and why students influence each others' behaviors, attitudes, and ideas. (Other perspectives and studies of the effects of grouping on students are found in Barr & Dreeben, 1983; Cohen, 1980b; Epstein, 1985, 1986b; Epstein & Karweit, 1983; Evertson, Sanford, & Emmer, 1981; Hallinan, 1976; Hallinan & Sørensen, 1985; Hamilton, 1983; Haskins, Walden, & Ramey, 1983; Heyns, 1974; Oakes, 1985; Peterson, Wilkinson, & Hallinan, 1984; Rosenbaum, 1980; Rowan & Miracle, 1983).

The grouping structure involves the placement of students in instructional groups or tracks. Teachers have been said to treat instructional groups differently—giving more time, opportunities for creativity, more work and more personal attention to brighter students, or more encouragement but less work and less interesting assignments to slower students. The group or track to which a student is assigned can dramatically affect the tasks, opportunities for participation, rewards, and evaluations they experience in school. Grouping also concerns the degree of flexibility for students to change track or group memberships. In some schools and classrooms, rigid grouping or tracking, or restrictive prerequisites for joining groups prevents students from changing status from one year to the next, regardless of the students' efforts and accomplishments. In other settings, flexible grouping helps students set goals and plan actions needed to improve their academic status and to change their academic and social peer groups (Epstein, 1985). Finally, teachers' designs for group activities determine the breadth of social exchanges that are possible or encouraged among students. If the grouping structure is ignored, teachers may be reducing student effectiveness by limiting the curriculum, closing students' options for improvement, and by restricting the number and diversity of contacts made with other students. There are strong connections between the grouping and task structures in how students are put to work as individuals, or in homogeneous or heterogeneous pairs, teams, or small or large groups.

Evaluation structure (E) concerns the standards that are set for student learning and behavior, the procedures for monitoring and judging the attainment of those standards, and the methods for providing information about performance for needed improvement. These standards and judgments may lead to rewards or punishments, and so the evaluation structure is closely linked to the reward structure.

Teachers' evaluations of students' academic, social, or personal skills may be public, private, or personal. Judgments may be based on comparative or individual standards. Teachers may make frequent or infrequent evaluations, based on subjective or objective criteria. Reports may be explicit or concealed, offering students much or little useful information about their current status and about ways to maintain or improve their status. These characteristics of the evaluation structure—standards, monitoring, and reporting procedures—may have different effects on student motivation and learning. (For other perspectives and studies of the structure of evaluation or studies of effects on students, see Bloom, 1980; Entwisle & Hayduk, 1982; Gottfredson, Hybl, Gottfredson, & Casteneda, 1986; McPartland, 1987; Natriello & Dornbusch, 1984; Stipek, 1984; Weiner, 1979.)

Public evaluation is open for others to hear. Many evaluations in school are made in front of classmates during lessons, in other school settings, and in front of other teachers or administrators. Private evaluations are between the teacher and student, principal and student, or student and student in conversations, formal conferences, or in comments written on students' papers, but without other audiences. Personal or intrinsic evaluations are conducted by students in accordance with their own goals. Students may internalize teachers' or parents' values or goals about schooling, but personal evaluations are conducted by monitoring the quality of one's work, setting personal goals, and directing one's own actions to improve or maintain standards.

An effective evaluation structure—with important, challenging, yet attainable standards, fair and clear procedures for monitoring progress, and explicit and frequent information about progress—should lead students to a higher level of understanding about their own effort, abilities, and improvement. An ineffective structure can embarrass or confuse students and misdirect their efforts for improvement, by withholding information on what and how to improve, or by setting standards too high to attain. If the evaluation structure is ignored, teachers should know that many students will experience failure, disappointment, or alienation in school.

Time structure (T) concerns the schedules set for students' work on tasks. If the time allocated is too short, or if the pace of instruction is too fast, only a few students will finish the work and qualify for rewards. If too much time is allocated or the pace is too slow, useful time will be wasted and school work will be boring for many students. Time for learning is alterable; it can be arranged and changed to accommodate few or many students' rates for learning. (For different perspectives and studies on the structure of time see Arlin, 1979, 1984; Bloom, 1976; Carroll, 1963; Fisher, Berliner, Filby, Marliave, Cahern, & Dishaw, 1980; Karweit, 1981, 1985; Stallings, 1980.)

There are important connections between the time and task structures (e.g., the design of assignments within fixed time periods); time and authority structures (e.g., options for self-directed activities if the students finish work ahead of time); time and grouping structures (e.g., time allocated for different instructional groups, time per pupil in each group, and the order of teacher's attention to various instructional groups); and time and evaluation structures (e.g., restrictions and opportunities to meet standards for mastery and assessment). For example, students are expected to learn or master material in a defined period of time. In some settings, if they finish early, students may not go on to new or advanced material beyond the lesson, unit, or grade level. In other settings, students are permitted to move as quickly as they can through an endless set of skills in and beyond their current grade level. And, Doyle (1985) notes that flexibility in time allocations may make a class look poorly managed by the teacher, but may, in fact, result in better learning by more students.

Teachers can allocate more or less time in and out of class for students to complete their work. They can limit interruptions and non-instructional activities during class time. Although schedules are currently set to establish *time for teaching* (e.g. a six- or seven-period day), an effective students movement would direct attention to the variation in *time for learning* needed by students with different prerequisite skills. If they ignore the structure of time, teachers deny differences in students' learning rates and will reduce the number of effective students in their classes.

Summary: TARGET Structures as Alterable Variables

Sizer (1984) suggests that students in school are too docile, compliant, and without initiative. But outside the classroom, students are neither docile nor compliant. Therefore, their behavior and attitudes in school must have something to do with how the class is organized and what students are required or permitted to do. This includes how tasks are designed (T), whether and how authority allows students to participate (A), why and when they are recognized and rewarded (R), how they are grouped to interact with others (G), how they are evaluated and given information and opportunities to improve (E), and how their different requirements for time to work are respected (T). We consider next how the TARGET structures can be changed within and across grade levels in order to meet the demands of student development and diversity.

LINKING THE TARGET STRUCTURES TO STUDENT DEVELOPMENT

Schools can organize these key, manipulable structures in ways that are developmentally responsive to students' diverse abilities and needs

(Lipsitz, 1984). Child and adolescent development research documents students' increasing independence and responsibility, accuracy in self-assessments, accumulated knowledge, understanding of abstract concepts, resolution of conflicts, and appreciation of the strengths of others. These skills can be strengthened when schools organize, monitor, and continually change the TARGET structures at each grade level and, as needed, within grade level, so that learning opportunities are developmentally appropriate for the students.

Task (T) Structures and Student Development. In addition to basic skills, students need to build problem-solving skills, analytical thinking, planning, and critical and creative-thinking skills. As they mature, students need to identify and develop individual talents and specialties by going beyond basic skills in some areas of interest. Schools can meet developmental demands for knowledge and thinking skills by sequencing academic and extracurricular tasks to challenge all students increasingly to think, plan, study, and create.

In many schools, students at all grade levels and subjects are assigned boring, repetitive, or disjunctive textbook and workbook assignments. The tasks are not designed to capture students' interests, encourage creativity, generate commitment to deeper study, or build on new capabilities of older students. Because all schools seek to improve student achievement, teachers need to pay special attention to the structure of tasks to provide the appropriate levels of instruction for all students, change the quality of tasks to become increasingly abstract and challenging, and create supportive remediation and review programs for students at risk of failing.

Authority (A) Structures and Student Development. With age, all students need more opportunities to develop responsibility, independence, and self-direction. Students need to develop leadership skills and the ability to recognize and respond to effective leadership. Eccles and her associates (Eccles, Midgley, & Adler, 1984) found that in many junior high schools there is an unmet need for increasing autonomy. Contrary to the expected developmental patterns, young children are often given more choice and opportunities for self-direction than older students. When authority structures are not responsive to student growth and changing needs, student attitudes toward school and toward teachers become increasingly less positive (Epstein, 1981, 1983).

Most schools take the initiative for learning out of the students' hands, placing the authority for decisions about learning under the teachers' total control or offering responsibilities to a few student leaders. In many schools, *active teaching* is given more consideration than *active learning.* The common fear is that increasing the students' share in decisions that affect them will reduce the teacher's authority. Other schools have demonstrated, however, that increasing participation by students, parents, businesses or others in the school community, can *increase* the teacher's professional status by creating a more complex role for the teacher as a manager of many educational resources to promote effective learning for all students (Epstein, 1986a). Teachers and administrators can examine how authority is distributed in their schools, and how to increase incrementally and sequentially shared teacher–student decision making about school goals, programs, scheduling, courses, and other policies that affect students to match the development and need for increasing independence—not only for the brightest students, but for all.

Reward (R) Structures and Student Development. As students mature they must develop strong self-confidence and clear self-concepts of their abilities as students and as citizens. They begin to understand their own strengths and weaknesses, how they compare with other students, and how to invest their time in school subjects or nonschool subjects. Schools can meet students' needs for increased self-confidence and recharge their motivation to learn by focusing rewards on change and improvment as well as excellence, and by increasing students' understanding of the intrinsic rewards in learning.

Most reward systems in schools have little influence on most students' behavior, achievement, and motivation because rewards are distributed to relatively few students, the same students over the years, and for relatively few accomplishments (e.g., sports and high achievement). Because most rewards are made for the highest, the most, and the best (and not for the greatest gains, the most change, or the newest directions), students who start out lower than other students rarely reach positions worthy of acclaim. By rewarding incremental progress, schools could help more students develop an appreciation of their abilities as learners. Because older students are more diverse in their interests and abilities, it is important for schools to increase the degree to which students are recognized and rewarded for multiple talents and skills.

Older students need to continue to receive official, extrinsic rewards for their progress and achievements, but also need opportunities to build their intrinsic motivation to learn and to feel personal satisfaction from learning. Teachers and administrators can review the distribution of rewards to students at each grade level to consider whether changes in types, reasons, and distributions of rewards are needed to meet the needs of younger and older students.

Grouping (G) Structures and Student Development. As students mature, peers increase their influence on behavior. Students need to build new social skills that increase their tolerance, acceptance, understanding, and appreciation of people who are different from themselves. They must develop abilities to cooperate and resolve conflicts with those whose opinions differ from their own, and decide whether and when to accept or reject peer influence. Over the school years, students' social and academic peer group relations are critical for developing character, personal ethics, and social values.

Few schools systematically organize programs to build students' social contacts and social skills. Most schools leave it up to the students to succeed or fail socially and to make contact with more or fewer students outside their own classes or curricular tracks. Yet, school grouping structures affect which students interact, become friends and influence each other (Epstein & Karweit, 1983). In middle and high schools, teachers and administrators can provide important opportunities for students to broaden their contacts and interactions with others. Also, flexibility of membership in groups and tracks and accompanying programs that help students change and succeed in new groups can influence students' investments in learning and their selection of influential peers and friends (Epstein, 1983, 1986b). Schools can examine their philosophy and design of grouping practices to consider how to structure positive peer group experiences and opportunities for diverse social contacts at each grade level.

Evaluation (E) Structures and Student Development. The evaluation structure can be developmentally responsive to students' increasing abilities to understand the causal connections between their plans, actions, and results in learning. Young children do not usually pay attention to the causes of their performance, nor do they analyze how to improve their work (Harter, 1978). The school's evaluation structure— the form, content, frequency, and pertinence of messages—can assist students to develop skills in self-evaluation and correction. Students increasingly can benefit from information from teachers involving the reasons for judgments and ratings of their schoolwork and opportunities to correct and improve their status. Unfair or unclear evaluations may create critical gaps in students' abilities to execute school assignments successfully, even if the students were initially motivated to learn. Teachers and administrators can increase the extent to which older children are involved and responsible for setting standards and judging their own progress on schoolwork and learning, and planning improvements—thus, linking authority and evelution structures.

The evaluation process measures performance. Too often, however, students are evaluated after a specific skill has been "taught" (by the teacher) and not necessarily after it has been "learned" (by the student). This distinction may be critical for developing more effective students. Individualized programs (e.g., SRA reading, Team Assisted Individualization—TAI math, and others) permit students to help decide when they are ready to be evaluated in order to move on to new and more difficult skills. This type of evaluation may produce fairer estimates of student success or failure, and greater understanding by students of their potential and progress in learning.

Time (T) Structures and Student Development.   As students develop, they increase their attention spans for learning and increase their capacities to study topics in depth. As important, older students who are slow learners often need more time to master difficult material than they did when they were younger and the material was easier (Arlin, 1984). In the upper elementary, middle, and high school grades, then, teachers may need more flexible scheduling policies both to give students time to work longer to master required skills and time to delve deeper into topics that interest them. Presently, the most flexible schedules are in preschools, primary grades, and colleges. Yet, there may be more need for flexibility in learning time in middle and high schools to preserve the potential for students to master basic skills and prerequisite skills for postsecondary education and work.

As students develop, they become more diverse in their styles and rates of learning. Schools can design assignments and tests, and structure learning time to respect the increasing differences in students' learning rates. Speed, or finishing within a fixed time frame, is not always the most important criterion for gaining or demonstrating knowledge.

Summary: TARGET Structures and Student Development

As students change, their educating and socializing environments need to change with them. If this does not occur, students are likely to be at a disadvantage on important outcomes of schooling (Epstein, 1984). Because students develop at different rates, schools need to be alert, responsive, and flexible in the design, conduct, and revision of programs for promoting effective student behavior. Student apathy, failure, and dropping out may be due in large part to inappropriate tasks, lack of participation, unresponsive reward structures, restrictive grouping, irrelevant evaluations, inadequate time for learning, and other weaknesses in the TARGET structures. But these structures can be designed and revised over time to help teachers organize education that is appropriate for the changing characteristics of students across the school years. We recognize, then, not only the cumulative nature of learning and the changing characteristics of individuals, but also the changing designs of school and classroom organizations.

RECOGNIZING THE NEED FOR RESEARCH AND EVALUATION

In the previous sections we presented two perspectives: Students are diverse; and, school structures are manipulable and can be responsive to student differences and development. These facts about students and their schools should encourage researchers and educators to take a comprehensive approach in monitoring student characteristics and initial skills, school environments, instructional processes, and many student outcomes. Only through programmatic research and on-site school evaluations will educators know whether changes they make in programs and practices are being implemented as planned, and whether their programs have positive or negative effects on some or all students.

All schools need not—indeed, cannot and should not—follow the same plan for improvement. Initial assessments of students' cognitive, social, and personal characteristics, school programs, problems, and underlying structures for organizing instruction, will help determine the degree of diversity among students and what each school needs to do to improve programs for its population of students.

For example, some schools may already have flexible grouping or tracking policies and programs that encourage and advise students with poor academic status how to move and improve. Other schools with fixed tracking may need to examine their grouping structure to see if it is responsive to the diversity and desires of the student population. This would involve an initial assessment of the school's grouping practices at all grade levels, an account of changes or desired changes in student placements over a school year, and the kinds of intergroup contacts that are encouraged or discouraged among students. Or, as another example, schools with students who have poor attitudes about schoolwork and learning may need to devise and test revisions in their reward structures to recapture the enthusiasm and energies of unmotivated students. This activity requires an initial assessment of student attitudes and an account of the kinds, conditions, and distributions of rewards over at least one school term. Changes in the reward structure would need to be planned, implemented, and measured, and changes in student attitudes would be monitored. As a third example, schools with younger or older students may need different plans to revise authority and decision-making structures, with middle and high schools designing ways to give students more opportunities each year to develop independence and to improve student–teacher relations. This activity requires initial and later assessments of the types of decisions teachers and students share, and initial and later measures of student participation, independence, problem-solving skills, and attitudes toward teachers.

One common way to identify effective schools has been to examine the relationship between the school SES and achievement at the school or grade level (Brookover & Lezotte, 1979). A school has been considered effective if the typical, strong, positive relationship between family socioeconomic status and student achievement declines sharply or disappears, presumably because of school programs and teacher practices. If, however, the focus of attention were on effective students, more sophisticated analyses would be necessary, based on individual level measures of student socioeconomic status, achievement test scores, other kinds of achievements and other outcome measures, as well as school and classroom characteristics, including the nature of the TARGET structures in teaching practice. Few schools or districts and few researchers measure all of these factors adequately in their studies of school improvement.

Even simple studies of effective students require analyses of the effect of SES on achievement before *and* after particular effective schools practices are put in place. This approach would, at least, document whether the effect of SES on achievement changed due to the improvement plan. Researchers could be more specific about the effects of particular organizational strategies on different groups of students by analyzing outcomes by grade level, classroom, and subject; and by race, sex, SES, and starting abilities of students. Because the impact of SES on achievement may not be quickly eliminated even under the best school improvement programs, it is important also to study the independent effects of particular school practices on achievement and other outcomes after SES is accounted for. Thus, better studies of effective students would examine the SES/achievement relationship over time and the school environment/achievement relationship over time for important subgroups of students.

Just as there is diversity among students and diversity in the design of school and classroom structures, there is diversity in research and evaluation methods that can contribute to an effective students movement. A comprehensive approach to understanding how different students succeed in differently organized programs would include the use of qualitative and quantitative methods. In an effective students movement, information would be needed from broad surveys with analyses of cross-sectional and longitudinal data, from incisive observational studies of students in differently structured classroom contexts, from field experiments that test clear contrasts in TARGET structures for their effects on students, and from self-study analyses and improvement plans conducted by the school administrators and classroom teachers.

Although it is quite likely that the reorganization of TARGET structures helps schools deal with diversity and promote more effective students, schools should not initiate improvement programs unless they plan to monitor and evaluate the teachers' practices and the effects on students of particular changes in TARGET structures. This should involve teachers and administrators as evaluators and cooperative projects with school district, state department, or university researchers.

LINKING THE TARGET STRUCTURES TO STUDENT OUTCOMES

One key problem for research and evaluation is identifying, selecting, or developing measures of school and classroom structures and measures of specific outcomes that characterize effective students. Table 1 shows how each TARGET structure is linked, theoretically, to different outcomes that are characteristic of effective students. For example, the task structure (T) and its components are linked to numerous outcomes of knowledge and competence. If the task structure is ineffective, the students will not be engaged in creative and challenging work at the appropriate level of difficulty, and, as a result will not complete as many assignments, will not accumulate as much knowledge, and will not be prepared to make ambitious and informed long-term goals.[3]

An effective authority structure (A) that offers students opportunities for decisions about their classwork may build students' positive attitudes toward teachers, self-confidence, and reduce behavior problems in school (Epstein, 1981, 1983; Epstein & McPartland, 1979). The authority structure and its components are linked especially to outcomes that measure independent or dependent behaviors.

Table 1 suggests that aspects of the reward structure (R) may especially affect students' confidence or doubt about their work and themselves as students, and may influence students to invest their time in school activities if they know that someone will frequently appreciate and acknowledge their efforts.

The grouping structure (G) may especially boost or limit students' social skills, social responsibility, and may influence the balance of conformity and individuality behaviors.

---

[3]In another paper, we argue that each structure may be linked to particular, mediating motivational forces, which in turn affect these outcomes (Epstein, in press).

TABLE 1: THEORETICAL LINKS BETWEEN TARGET STRUCTURES AND EFFECTIVE STUDENT BEHAVIORS

Main TARGET structure	Needed measures of effective students
TASKS (T) at appropriate levels of difficulty, including the academic curriculum of basic and advanced skills and extracurricular activities. Tasks that challenge thinking. Novelty and variety in tasks. Changes in tasks for new levels of ability.	New knowledge; knowing how to learn; mastery of curriculum; completion of classroom and homework assignments; attitudes about schoolwork and homework; development of special interests, talents, advanced skills; persistence in subjects, taking additional courses in a field. Other competence/incompetence outcomes.
AUTHORITY (A) that emphasizes active learning by students and shared decision making by teachers and students. Opportunities for choice and self-direction. Change in rate and type of participation according to age and new abilities.	Participation in class and in extracurricular activities; choosing topics of interest for deeper study; positive attitudes toward teachers; wise use of counsel and knowledgeable use of "the system"; initiative in leadership and problem-solving activities. Other independence/dependence outcomes.
REWARDS (R) that recognize the daily or periodic progress by all students, as well as excellence in many skills and talents. Change in rewards to meet new values and new abilities.	Positive self concept; feelings of self-worth and awareness of progress; commitment to improving schoolwork; positive attitudes toward school and learning; awareness of behavior and actions valued by others; willingness to invest time and effort in tasks. Other confidence/doubt outcomes.
GROUPING (G) that encourages interaction among students with same and different abilities and backgrounds. Flexible grouping or tracking to permit students to improve status. Grouping patterns that change as peer relations change.	Positive attitudes toward peers; tolerance, acceptance, and appreciation of group and individual differences; diversity of contacts; selection of friends and best friends; cooperaton, moral commitment, social responsibility; negotiation, compromise, sharing, and other interpersonal skills. Other conformity/individuality/character skills.
EVALUATIONS (E) that establish clear standards and fair procedures for judging success in school skills. Informative messages, for improvement. Standards, monitoring, and information systems that change with student abilities.	Improvement and awareness of progress; internalized standards; ability to compare self and others; fairness in judgments of self and others; plans and actions for improvement; setting future goals. Other measures of understanding/misunderstanding personal skills and progress.
TIME (T) that recognizes and respects diversity in rates of learning, and provides opportunities for intensive study in subjects of interest. Flexible scheduling of courses and assignments. Change in time restrictions to match level of task difficulty and students' levels of ability.	Rates of completion of classwork and homework; understanding and working at one's fastest pace for progress in learning; improved skills in scheduling school work, homework, study, and test taking; development of expertise in one or more topics or subjects. Other completion/quitting outcomes.

The evaluation structure (E) should promote students' self-awareness and sense of certainty about their skills and increase their ability to predict the level of effort needed to reach the standards that they and their teachers set. Uncertainty about how to improve may create barriers to action and reduce students' ability and willingness to invest productively in learning.

Time structures (T) that deal with the diversity in students' rates of learning may be especially important for improving the rates of completion of assignments; for building skills in scheduling time for schoolwork, homework, and study; for planning time use during tests and quizzes; and for influencing other outcomes that measure completion vs. quitting behaviors.

Although specific, strong connections between structures and outcomes are suggested in Table 1, we can also see that the structures and outcomes are interconnected. For example, completing homework requires *tasks* at an appropriate level of difficulty, adequate *time*, and appropriate and valued *rewards*. Some schools include homework as 10%–25% of a course grade to recognize officially the importance of completing the work. Homework also is a self-directed, *participatory activity* in which students control the time they spend on an assignment, and homework may be part of a teacher's parent involvement program, with the parent assuming some of the teacher's *authority* to monitor and assist learning. And, homework can involve *group* projects, peer review, coaching and study groups, and other pair, team, or group assignments. A research and evaluation approach to studying effective students would increase an understanding of the interconnections among the TARGET structures and their separate and combined effects on different student outcomes.

Although some research supports the connections suggested in the table, studies are sorely needed at all grade levels and for diverse groups of students to document or to revise these assumptions. We need to build a collection of tests, survey, and observational instruments to help researchers and educators study the extent and importance of the hypothesized connections between different TARGET structures and particular student outcomes.

THE SOCIAL ORGANIZATION OF REMEDIATION

In this section, we examine patterns of diversity in students' skills, and discuss how research and evaluation of the manipulable TARGET structures can help schools deal with diversity through *the social organization of remediation*.

Identifying Patterns of Diversity.   What do educators do with diversity among students? Eliminate or reduce it? Maintain it? Increase it?
Differences between groups can be reduced or eliminated by limiting the
advancement of capable students or by increasing the advancement of
slower students, as shown in Figure 1. Differences between groups can
be increased by limiting the advancement of slower students or by increasing the advancement of brighter students, as shown in Figure 2.

The two figures show patterns that can occur under different instructional approaches as schools work toward their main goal of helping all students master required skills. Some methods of instruction are
designed, in theory, to *reduce diversity* as shown in Figure 1, where the
slope indicating improvement is steeper for less capable students. These
include whole class instruction, mastery learning, remedial instruction,
and instructional emphasis on minimum competency testing (Block &
Burns, 1976; Brophy, 1983). These approaches mainly attend to the
needs of average or slower students. They may restrict the progress of
brighter students if they hold all students to the same basic curriculum,
limit projects or advanced work, or use available financial resources for
materials or staff to correct students' learning deficiencies.

Some methods of instruction are designed to *increase diversity* as
shown in Figure 2, with a steeper slope showing improvement for the

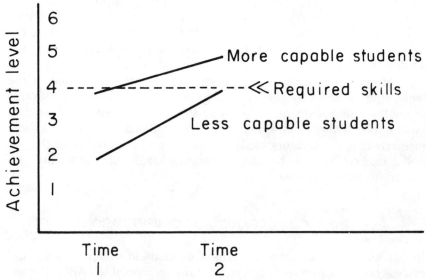

FIGURE 1:   **Decreasing diversity by enhancing progress of initially less
capable students.**

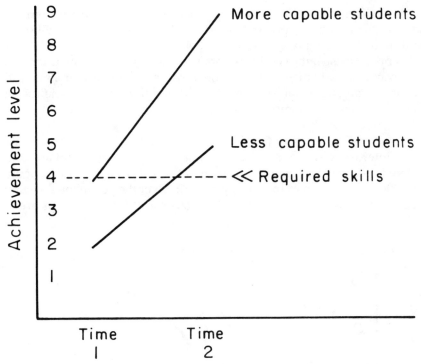

FIGURE 2: Increasing diversity by enhancing progress of initially more capable students.

more capable students. These instructional approaches include individualized instruction, homogeneous grouping, gifted and talented programs, and advanced placement courses. These approaches encourage students to learn at their fastest, personal paces. They are often instituted to respond to the needs of brighter students, although, in theory, all students could benefit. The progress of slower students may be restricted or reduced if these programs use financial or staff resources that would otherwise be used for remedial instruction.

Schools may choose to minimize or eliminate differences in achievement in some subjects and increase diversity in other subjects. For example, schools may purposely organize programs so that all students have equal exposure and mastery of basic skills in elementary school science or middle school civics, sex education, nutrition, or other courses on social responsibility or personal health and safety, or in courses that require or benefit from social interaction (e.g., middle school physical education, high school history, psychology, or mass media). At the same time, schools may organize other programs to increase diversity in skills in math, science, literature, or creative writing to meet the needs and prevent boredom of advanced students who, by middle or junior high school, may be 4 or more years ahead of other students in these subjects. Educators may use a variety of instructional approaches to organize and monitor purposely a mixture of standard, advanced, and remedial courses to provide students with experiences in heterogeneous and homogeneous classes.

Increasing Diversity Over Time.   The patterns of diversity become more interesting when more students or more years in school are considered, as shown in Figure 3. The hypothetical students in this figure are at least 2 years apart in skills by grade 2. Over the years, the diversity in students' skills increases so that by grade 4, the three groups are at

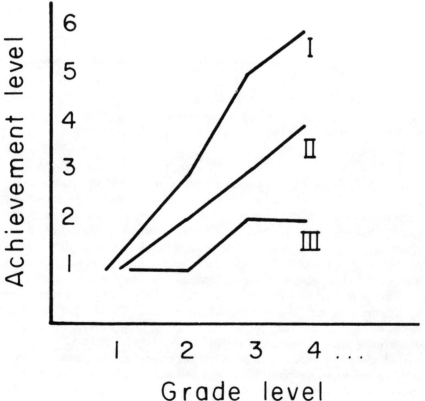

FIGURE 3:   Hypothetical progress of three students or groups of students over 4 years.

least 4 years apart in skills. This accentuation of differences is a common pattern across the grades throughout the school years.

Figure 3 raises many questions about the diversity of students' skills, especially about students who do not master the required skills at their grade level: Do students who are 2 years behind grade level in reading, for example, need to make 1 year of reading progress or 2? Is it feasible to expect double speed in learning by these students to erase the disadvantage? Will students retained in grade 3, for example, also need 2 years to learn the skills required in grade 4? Do students need differently structured assignments, methods of instruction, rewards, grouping, evaluation, and time in order to learn skills that were not learned the first time? Can instructional approaches and materials be doubly or triply efficient to boost the skills of slow or failing students? Are students failures if they need more time to learn or is the school failing the students?

In part, the patterns shown in Figure 3 are accentuated when teachers ignore the diversity needed in the task structure (T) and make standard, daily assignments, knowing that many students in a group or class will fail or do poorly. The patterns are reinforced when only some students are encouraged to participate (A) or receive rewards (R). The patterns are all but fixed when effective remedial instruction is not provided to students who fall behind in their skills. Students in Group II in Figure 3 may have less effective instruction than students in Group I. Students in Group III may have less effective instruction and may hold less positive attitudes about school or receive less support for school from their family. Thus poor or inappropriate instruction from the teacher, little or no social support, and low personal commitment or interest in learning may each reduce achievement over time. Groups II and III in Figure 3 may look like *less effective students* but the reasons for their slow progress may be due, in part, to the school's organization of instruction and social support for students who are slower learners.

Figure 4 shows four common patterns of progress of students who started out only slightly dissimilar. For this discussion, Time 1 (T1) could be September and Time 2 (T2) could be June of one school year, or entry and exit from elementary, middle, or high school, or any important start and end periods for student growth or change. Panel A shows that some students (line a) make rapid progress, and others (line b) proceed at much slower rates, although learning occurs for all students over time. In this case, students who fall behind do not make up lost ground and, consequently, fall further behind the others. In some cases, the discrepancy between lines a and b widens to a point where slower students are making little or no progess, and are at high risk of failing subjects or dropping out of school. These high-risk students usually receive little or

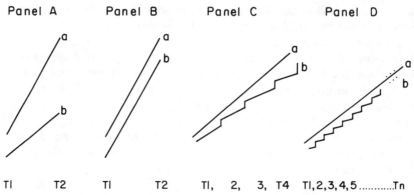

Panel A   Panel B   Panel C   Panel D

TI   T2   TI   T2   TI, 2, 3, T4   TI,2,3,4,5..........Tn

FIGURE 4:   Patterns of progress and rates of remediation for students over
time.

no academic assistance or social support for improvement, in part because they are often absent or truant for large portions of time, or because remedial instruction is not offered, or if available, is not effective
or socially acceptable.

Panel B shows equal rates of progress for students originally at
different starting points. This is a common pattern when students are
placed in two or more groups for instruction that proceed lockstep
through highly specified curricula. For example, a slower reading group
may read the same books as the faster group, but later in the year. The
less able and more able groups make about a year's progress in a year's
time, but those who start out lower and proceed slower never fully catch
up to the others. Or, in high schools, students in less demanding curricular tracks take required courses (e.g., biology), but do not learn the
same amount of information as students in regular or honors tracks.
Some schools consider equal growth or gains (represented by the *equal
slopes* of the lines) as important and as acceptable as equal scores. Other
schools view this pattern as one that reflects a lack of adequate attention
to average or slower students and keeps them locked in low-status
programs.

Panels C and D show two of many possible remediation models to
reduce discrepancies in student learning in some skills or some subjects.
Panel C shows a periodic remediation schedule, for example, at grades
3, 5, 8, and 10 for students who need to master basic skills in order to be
promoted to upper elementary, middle school, high school (Frank,
1984). These correction periods or "gates" may require the retention of
students for one full year, or may be accomplished with other strategies
such as half-year remediation programs, after-school programs, Satur-

day schools, or summer schools for students who need assistance in mastering the skills required for the next level of schooling.

Panel D shows a continuous correction plan. This plan may include daily corrective instruction, biweekly coaching classes, weekly Saturday schools, daily or weekly parent involvement in learning activities at home, weekly peer tutoring, annual summer school, or combinations of these or other practices to give more assistance, time, and support to students who miss key skills, fail tests, or are at risk of failing courses or grade levels. The rate of remedial instruction may vary as in Panels C and D, according to the teachers' organization of the task, evaluation, and time structures.

Patterns C and D were documented by Arlin (1984) in his studies of mastery learning. Slower students who were given extra time to learn did master the required skills, but continued to need extra time to learn and longer periods of extra time with each passing grade. Thus, flexible time structures that supported learning academic skills helped students learn, but did not make them faster, or "equal" learners.

Student diversity and the need for remedial instruction are problems at all levels of schooling. Even if remedial instruction were highly successful in the first 6 years of elementary school, new discrepancies and increased diversity in academic skills and social and emotional development would require attention in the middle and high school grades. Indeed, remediation can best be understood as a continuous problem for students and a continuous process for schools, with students coming in and out of remedial classes and other special programs designed to assist learning. Even the brightest students attend some high school coaching classes to clarify confusing lessons; and sometimes the slowest students will make rapid progress in regular or remedial classes if the teacher's organization of the TARGET structures is appropriate and supportive.

Dealing with Diversity with a Social Organization of Remediation. Instruction in academic skills is only part of an effective remedial program. The other needed component is the *social organization of remediation*. By the "social organization of remediation," I mean the academic and social support systems for students who need more time or different methods or extra encouragement to learn required skills. This may be accomplished when the TARGET structures are responsive to levels of student ability and development.

It is no more odd for students to need 5 years to finish high school, than it is for students to take 5 or 6 years to finish college or graduate school. It is not strange that some students need 18 months to complete algebra successfully, while others finish the work in 9 months or less. The academic and social structures of schools are not presently designed to accommodate and support students who do not complete the prescribed work in the prescribed time. Indeed, where adjustments have been made, schools tend to reduce the amount or complexity of work required to fit the prescribed time, instead of allowing longer time to complete the prescribed work.

Students who fall behind or fail at any grade level experience humiliation and reduced self-esteem. Most remediation programs stigmatize the very students who are most in need of social and academic support and make it even more difficult for these students to learn. Private schools may make more flexible arrangements to support students who repeat grades or extend the number of years in school to complete academic requirements (Persell, personal communication).

Educators know that students learn when they are interested in the work, feel challenged, apply energy, succeed, receive rewards or personal satisfaction for their efforts, and when they can discuss new ideas and knowledge with teachers, peers, and parents. These factors are part of the social organization of remediation that must support slower students the same way they presently encourage successful students. Changing the TARGET structures would include providing appropriate levels of instruction and materials (tasks); including students in decisions about their academic programs and progress, and encouraging active rather than passive learning and high participation in class (authority); recognizing student effort and improvement (reward); promoting opportunities for positive interaction among many groups of students, and helping students move out of remedial groups into regular classes (grouping); providing clear information on how to improve to reach set standards (evaluation) and creating ample time to complete work so that participation and rewards are possible (time). Now, teachers establish these conditions in the learning environment for some students (especially brighter students) although they are important for all students (especially average and slower students). These organizational features are needed to build the interest, motivation, energy, follow-through, and enjoyment that all students need in order to learn.

Research on the effects on students of contrasting models of remedial instruction are few and limited to the early elementary grades. McPartland and Crain (1987) call for studies on the types, timing, methods of instruction, coordination with classroom instruction, duration, costs, and effects of different models for remediation to redress problems created when schools set more rigorous standards for promotion and graduation. In this chapter we emphasize the need for research and development of *the social organization of remediation*—studies not only on the design of the task structure to correct academic deficiencies, but also on the other TARGET structures that contribute to the overall quality of life in school.

SUPPORT FOR AN EFFECTIVE STUDENT MOVEMENT?

We have discussed three important aspects of an effective student movement to supplement the popular emphasis on effective schools— student diversity, the alterable quality of key variables to improve school and classroom programs and practices, and the need for research and evaluation to measure the effects of school improvements on many student outcomes and to understand successful designs for remedial instruction to deal with diversity. Support for an effective student movement comes from two perspectives in the current literature. First, we examine the early and later studies of effective schools to suggest that an initial emphasis on effective students was shifted and weakened. Second, we look at the difference between "effective schools" and "school effects" studies to suggest that there is a tradition in research and evaluation that emphasizes effective students.

Initial vs. Later Studies of Effective Schools. Weber (1971), the "father" of the effective schools movement, began his work with more attention to students than those who followed him (e.g., Edmonds, 1979a,b). Weber examined the organization of a single subject (reading) to identify effective teacher practices and student behaviors and outcomes. He noted the need for additional reading personnel to make the teaching of reading more effective, individualization in reading to make learning more effective, and careful evaluation of students' reading progress to detect and solve specific reading problems.

"Careful" evaluation of student progress (Weber) was transformed to "frequent" evaluation of student progress in later lists of effective practices. As a result, attention shifted from information on how to improve *student* experiences and assignments to how to improve *teachers'* management and accountability. The focus on "frequent" evaluation has resulted in an overemphasis on testing to document school effectiveness and an underutilization of test results to guide the students' instructional programs or their own understanding of skills and needed improvements.

The emphasis was switched from the students' "pleasure in learning" (Weber), to a "safe and orderly" atmosphere conducive to learning controlled by teaching and administrative decisions. This change dramatically reversed the emphasis from the students' attitudes and motivations to teachers' rules and patterns of control and punishment. It takes hard work to go beyond a safe and orderly climate to develop a creative climate that is challenging, supportive, and enjoyable for all students. Creating such a climate requires an understanding of how the manipulable structures of school organization can be changed to offer opportunities and experiences to students who start out with different attitudes and achievements. Using the TARGET structures, a supportive environment may require a reward structure that recognizes and motivates all students for the progress they make regardless of their starting point. A challenging environment may be built on an authority structure that provides opportunities for teachers and students to participate in academic and curricular decisions that affect them. A challenging and supportive environment may require a task structure that takes students from wherever they start to increasingly advanced levels of learning, and an evaluation structure that sets clear incremental standards that can be understood by students as stepping stones to overall goals.

Although Weber emphasized "strong reading skills," later work emphasized "basic skill acquisition." This well-meaning extension from one subject to all subjects had an unintended result—attention was directed away from the measurement of well-specified reading skills for each student to the measurement of poorly specified minimum competencies for the school as a whole. When Weber's approach was generalized from the classroom to the school level by later researchers, synthesists, and education evangelists, the subject-specific content of Weber's work was replaced by a too-general, too-simple prescription for school improvement. Not enough attention was given to differences in grade levels, subjects, or diversity within populations of students. The redirection may account for the common complaint from educators that the effective schools literature is too vague to guide daily educational practice. Despite the good intentions of the researchers and the remarkable impact of this work on practitioners, it may be that more useful results will occur in the future with the reinstatement of Weber's original emphasis on practices for promoting effective students.

Effective Schools vs. School Effects Studies.   Even before the effective schools movement became popular, educational researchers conducted school effects or school productivity studies to build a knowledge base about the importance of particular variations in school and classroom environments for specific student outcomes (see studies by Alexander & Cook, 1982; Anderson, 1970; Averch et al., 1974; Brookover et al., 1979; Coleman et al., 1966; Coleman, Hoffer, & Kilgore, 1982; Epstein & McPartland, 1979; McDill & Rigsby, 1973; McPartland & Epstein, 1977; Moos & David, 1981; Murnane, 1975; Rutter, Maughan, Mortimore, & Ouston, 1979; Summers & Wolfe, 1977.)

The distinction between *effective schools* and *school effects* studies is important because the research questions and purposes of the two types of studies differ. Effective schools studies aim to identify successful, existing practices in schools *within* the present range of variation. School effects studies aim to identify or design new and improved practices to *extend* the present range of variation in useful educational approaches. The difference in approaches and purposes can be understood by comparing the way research questions might be phrased in the two types of studies.

An *effective schools* study question would ask:

> What methods of teaching are used in schools where students have higher than expected achievement test scores or greater than expected gains in test scores, given the socioeconomic status of the families of the students in the school?

Schools would be selected and labeled effective that showed higher than expected achievement scores for 2 or 3 years in a row, or, that showed equal growth in scores for students from less educated and better educated families. A researcher would list and describe practices used in the effective schools that might account for the gains by students. The researcher might conduct additional studies to compare the first list of effective practices with new observations or reports from other schools identified as effective. In most studies of this sort, the focus is on student achievement test scores at the school level or grade level, especially of children from economically disadvantaged families. Little or no attention is given to classroom level measures of students, or measures of teachers' practices or the organization of TARGET structures in specific subjects.

A *school effects* study question would ask:

> Which of two or more differently organized math (or English, or other) classes (e.g., specifically different ability grouping, decision making, and reward structures) has significant, positive effects on the students' math (or other) achievement, attitudes, and other outcomes?

> Or: Which of two or more differently organized schools (e.g., different tracking and grouping, participation, and time schedules) affects students' graduation rates, participation in activities, race relations, self-esteem, and other attitudes and achievements?

Methods and approaches would be labeled effective if, in those classes or schools, students or identifiable subgroups of students showed significantly higher gains in achievement, attitudes, or other outcomes, compared with students in typical or control classes or schools.

Both kinds of questions are useful, but each yields different information for school improvement. Effective schools questions help identify currently effective schools, and may help educators disseminate information on some useful teaching and administrative practices. School-effects questions test specific practices or new designs for their effects on students' academic and affective outcomes. Results from school effects studies can change or improve the way math or other subjects are taught or the way schools and classrooms are organized to benefit student learning and development in ways that are different from existing practices.

There are a few examples of new approaches that developed from school effects studies at the Johns Hopkins Center for Social Organization of Schools. For example, studies of the effects on students of differently designed task-and-reward structures (e.g., DeVries & Edwards, 1973) resulted in new classroom processes to organize student learning in teams, including Student Team Learning (DeVries et al. 1980; Slavin, 1983) and Team-Assisted-Individualization (Slavin, Madden, & Leavey, in press). Basic research on the effects on students and parents of teachers' practices of parent involvement (Becker & Epstein, 1982; Epstein 1986a) informed the development of the Teachers Involve Parents in Schoolwork (TIPS) process (Epstein, 1986c) to help teachers revise the classroom authority structure to organize parent involvement for more effective students. Neither of these processes would have emerged from effective school studies as they are typically conceived.

It would be useful to combine effective schools and school effects approaches to study student diversity and to promote more effective students. From 5 to 20 practices are identified as necessary for effective schools from different research studies and syntheses (Purkey & Smith, 1983), but information is not available on which elements at which grade level are more important than others for teachers' and students' effectiveness (Firestone & Herriott, 1982). It would be possible and profitable to use the effective schools literature as the basis for a series of school effects studies on how contrasting organizations of instruction influence the academic and social development of students.

For example, the effective schools literature asserts that teachers should have high expectations for their students. This admirable goal must be translated into manageable practices based on the alterable structures that teachers can change in their classrooms—e.g., measures would be needed of the students' starting abilities to define the diversity of skills and to establish realistic expectations for improvement. Teachers would need to select or design and assign appropriate tasks; offer valued rewards to all students; involve students in evaluations of their progress, and so on. School effects studies of the results of different designs of the TARGET structures to set and to meet realistically high expectations for all students would be more helpful to practitioners than the simple call for "high expectations."

As another example, effective schools studies assert the virtue of a "businesslike" atmosphere in the classroom. Teachers can organize productive, businesslike environments in many different ways. One strategy involving the authority structure may increase students' *dependence* on the teacher for directions whereas a contrasting strategy may increase students' *independence* in their learning activities. One businesslike environment may require students to compete against their peers for a few rewards, whereas a second approach may encourage students to cooperate with their peers for many available rewards. Thus, school effects studies on different strategies to create businesslike atmospheres could assess the impact of contrasting organizational designs on the class climate and on several student outcomes. These studies would be more helpful to practitioners than the simple call or untested ideas for "businesslike" classrooms.

Recent reports by national commissions and educational commentators offer many suggestions for school improvement, but little evidence on the effects of particular reforms on students. For example, one sensible sounding suggestion to raise graduation requirements may mean either *better* educated students (National Commission on Excellence in Education, 1983) or *fewer* educated students, if students are forced or dropped out of school (McDill, Natriello, & Pallas, 1985). Similarly, the recommendation that all students take the same academically oriented program in high school (Adler, 1982) minimizes the importance of student diversity and obscures the need for attention to the organization of remedial instruction at the elementary and secondary levels.

Other suggested reforms are similarly based on insightful but unscientific analyses. One suggestion is to give students the same teacher for high school math and science to reduce the number of different students that teachers must teach, and the number of different teachers that students must get to know (Sizer, 1984). On this topic, educators should be calling for school effects studies with control or contrasting classes to determine how this practice affects student attachment to adults, satisfaction with school, and knowledge in subjects taught by one vs. two experts (McPartland, 1987).

The effective schools literature is a reminder of the textbook lessons used to train teachers and administrators (Bickel, 1983). The educational reform literature is ideological and inconclusive, with an unending list of possible improvements. There have been few demands for pilot tests, experiments, research, or evaluation on the effects on students of particular reform strategies. These would be needed for schools to make informed judgments about whether to accept or reject specific suggestions. A scientific approach to improving schools would require programmatic and longitudinal school effects research and evaluation to produce cumulative knowledge on the importance for teachers and students of particular school and classroom practices (Rowan, 1985).

If teachers and administrators had reliable information about how the organization of different, alterable school and classroom structures affected students' basic skills, higher-order thinking, social maturity, and other aspects of learning and development, they could purposely select—mix and match—particular organizational forms to reach academic and other goals. In so doing, they would be deciding how to organize their schools for more effective students.

SUMMARY: FOCUS ON EFFECTIVE STUDENTS

Effective schools must be defined, ultimately, in terms of effective students. Despite the fact that the effective schools movement has generated much optimism about improving schools, there has been too little attention to defining programs for developing more effective students. There has been an overemphasis on teachers' and principals' behaviors and a lack of attention to the diversity in students' achievement and development, or the meaning of that diversity for school organization, classroom practice, and educational evaluations. Seeley (1981) reminds us that the product of education—learning—is not produced by schools, but by students with the help of schools, parents, peers, and many other forces and resources in the community. He criticizes efforts to expand the delivery of education services without changing the relationships among schools, teachers, students, families, peers, and communities.

Delivery of instruction refers to the knowledge and skills of effective *teachers*, but important relationships in school contexts refer to the development of effective *students*. These relationships can change and improve if educators understand the manipulable structures in schools and classrooms that create opportunities and experiences that help students learn. Of course, there must be both effective teachers and effective students in our schools. But this obvious fact has not been so clear when the attention has been so overwhelmingly on the teacher (Hawley, 1985) and so little on the diverse students in school and classroom contexts (Bossert, 1985; Stallings, 1985).

In addition to knowing that they can improve schools in general, educators must have a working knowledge of the manipulable aspects of school and classroom organization that determine how students are asked to conduct their learning. Through key structures, such as the task, authority, reward, grouping, evaluation and time (TARGET) structures, school environments may promote or destroy students' achievements, positive attitudes toward school, independence, self-direction, and social skills. Presently, these structures are organized in most schools to meet the needs of the bright, successful students. But, they must be made responsive for students who are currently unsuccessful. The goal is for the social organization of advanced, regular, and remedial instruction to support and challenge all students, making school as important, enjoyable, and useful for those who need more time or different methods to learn as for those who learn more quickly.

A research-and-evaluation approach to school improvement is required to study, monitor, and revise the features of school and classroom organizations for positive effects on student learning and development. We need useful measures and diverse methods for studying school and classroom environments, student characteristics, and multiple outcomes to determine whether and when programs and practices are promoting effective students.

If we continue to study, measure, and create policies about how teachers teach, we will surely make advances in more effective teaching. This may be accomplished without attention to differences in approaches required by students at different grade levels, in different subjects, and with different learning histories. If we begin to study, measure, and create policies about how all students learn and how different outcomes are influenced by basic, manipulable structures in school and classroom organization, we will begin to make progress in understanding effective students.

REFERENCES

Adler, M. J. (1982). *The paideia proposal*. New York: Macmillan.

Alexander, K. L., & Cook, M. A. (1982). Curriculum and coursework: A surprise ending to a familiar story. *American Sociological Review, 47*, 627–640.

Ames, C., & Ames, R. (1984). Systems of student and teacher motivation: Toward a qualitative definition. *Journal of Educational Psychology, 1984, 76*, 535–556.

Anderson, G. J. (1970). Effects of classroom social climate in individual learning. *American Educational Research Journal, 7*, 135–152.

Arlin, M. (1979). Teacher transitions can disrupt time flow in classrooms. *American Educational Research Journal, 16*, 42–56.

————. (1984). Time variability on mastery learning. *American Educational Research Journal, 21*, 103–120.

Averch, H. A., Carroll, S. J., Donaldson, T. S., Kiesling, H. J., & Pincus, J. (1974). *How effective is schooling? A critical review of research*. Englewood Cliffs, NJ: Educational Technology Publications.

Barr, R., & Dreeben, R. (1983). *How schools work*. Chicago: University of Chicago Press.

Beady, C., Slavin, R., & Fennessey, G. (1981). Alternative student evaluation structures and a focused schedule of instruction in an inner city junior high school. *Journal of Educational Psychology, 73,* 518–523.

Becker, H. J., & Epstein, J. L. (1982). Parent involvement: A study of teacher practices. *Elementary School Journal, 83* (November), 85–102.

Bickel, W. E. (1983). Effective schools: Knowledge, dissemination, inquiry. *Educational Researcher, 12*(4), 3–5.

Bidwell, C. E. (1972). Schooling and socialization for moral commitment. *Interchange, 3,* 1–27.

Block, J. H., & Bruns, R. B. (1976). Mastery learning. In L. S. Shulman (Ed.), *Review of research in education,* (Vol. 4). Itasca, IL: Peacock.

Bloom, B. S. (1976). *Human characteristics and school learning.* New York: McGraw– Hill.

Bloom, B. S. (1980). The new direction in educational research: Alterable variables. *Phi Delta Kappan, 62,* 382–385.

Boocock, S. (1979). The social organization of the classroom. *Annual Review of Sociology, 4,* 1–28.

Bossert, S. T. (1979). *Tasks and social relationships in classrooms.* New York: Cambridge University Press.

Bossert, S. T. (1985). Effective elementary schools. In R. M. Kyle (Ed.), *Reaching for Excellence: An Effective Schools Sourcebook.* Washington, DC: U.S. Government Printing Office.

Boyer, E. L. (1983). *High school.* New York: Harper & Row.

Brookover, W., Beady, C., Hood, P., Schweitzer, Z., & Wisenbaker, J. (1979). *School social systems and student achievement.* New York: Praeger.

Brookover, W. B., & Lezotte, L. (1979). *Changes in school characteristics coincident with changes in student achievement.* East Lansing, MI: Institute for Research in Teaching, Michigan State University.

Brophy, J. E. (1983). Classroom organization and management. *Elementary School Journal, 83,* 265–285.

Carroll, J. B. (1963). A model for school learning. *Teachers College Record, 64,* 723–733.

Children's Defense Fund. (1985, February). *Survey of state education reforms.* Washington, DC: Education Division, CDF.

Cohen, E. G. (1980a). *A multi-ability approach to the integrated classroom.* Paper presented at the annual meeting of the American Psychological Association, Montreal.

Cohen, E. G. (1980b). Design and redesign of the desegregated school: Problems of status, power, and conflict. In W. Stephen & J. Feagin (Eds.), *Desegregation: Past, present, and future.* New York: Plenum Press.

Coleman, J. S., Campbell, E. Q., Hobson, C. J., McPartland, J., Mood, A., Weinfeld, F. D., & York, R. L. (1966). *Equality of educational opportunity.* Washington, DC: U.S. Government Printing Office.

Coleman, J. S., Hoffer, T., & Kilgore, S. (1982). *High school achievement.* New York: Basic Books.

deCharms, R. (1976). *Enhancing motivation: Change in the classroom.* New York: Longman.

DeVries, D. L., & Edwards, K. (1973). Learning games and student teams: Their effects on classroom process. *American Journal of Educational Research, 10,* 307–318.

DeVries, D. L., Slavin, R. E., Fennessey, G. M., Edwards, K. J., & Lombardo, M. M. (1980). *Teams-Games-Tournament: The team learning approach.* Englewood Cliffs, NJ: Educational Technology Publications.

Doyle, W. (1983). Academic work. *Review of Educational Research, 2,* 159–199.

Doyle, W. (1985). Effective secondary classroom practices. In R. M. Kyle (Ed.), *Reaching for Excellence: An Effective Schools Sourcebook.* Washington, DC: U.S. Government Printing Office.

Dreeben, R. (1968). *On what is learned in school.* Reading, MA: Addison–Wesley.

Eccles, J., Midgley, C., & Adler, T. F. (1984). Grade-related changes in the school environment: Effects on apparent motivation. In M. L. Maehr (Ed.), *Advances in Motivation and Achievement.* Greenwich, CT: JAI Press.

Eckstein, H., & Gurr, T. R. (1975). *Patterns of authority: A structural basis for political inquiry.* New York: Wiley.

Edmonds, R. R. (1979a). Some schools work and more schools can. *Social Policy, 9,* 28–32.

———. (1979b). Effective schools for the urban poor. *Educational Leadership, 37*(October), 15–24.

Education Week. (1985). Changing course: A 50-state survey of reform measures. 4(20), February 6.

Entwisle, D., & Hayduk, L. (1982). *Early schooling: Cognitive and affective outcomes.* Baltimore: Johns Hopkins University Press.

Epstein, J. L. (1981). *The quality of school life.* Lexington, MA: Lexington Books.

Epstein, J. L. (1983). Longitudinal effects of person–family–school interactions on student outcomes. In A. Kerckhoff (Ed.), *Research in sociology of education and socialization (Vol. 4).* Greenwich, CT: JAI Press.

Epstein, J. L. (1984). A longitudinal study of school and family effects on student development. In S. A. Mednick & M. Harway (Eds.), *Handbook of longitudinal research.* New York: Praeger.

Epstein, J. L. (1985). After the bus arrives: Resegregation in desegregated schools. *Journal of Social Issues, 41*(3), 23–44.

Epstein, J. L. (1986a). Parents' reactions to teacher practices of parent involvement. *Elementary School Journal, 86,* 277–294.

Epstein, J. L. (1986b). Friendship selection: Developmental and environmental influences. In E. Muller & C. Cooper (Eds.), *Process and outcome in peer relationships,* New York: Academic Press.

Epstein, J. L. (1986c). *Teachers' manual: Teachers Involve Parents in Schoolwork (TIPS).* Parent Involvement Report P–62. Baltimore: Center for Research on Elementary and Middle Schools.

Epstein, J. L. (in press). Family influence and student motivation. In C. Ames & R. Ames (Eds.), *Research on Motivation in Education* (Vol. 3). Orlando, FL: Academic Press.

Epstein, J. L., & Karweit, N. (1983). *Friends in school.* New York: Academic Press.

Epstein, J. L., & McPartland, J. M. (1979). Authority structures. In H. J. Walberg (Ed.), *Educational environments and effects.* Berkeley, CA: McCutcheon.

Evertson, C. M., Sanford, J., & Emmer, E. (1981). Effects of class heterogeneity in junior high school. *American Educational Research Journal, 18,* 219–232.

Firestone, W. A., & Herriott, R. E. (1982). Prescriptions for effective elementary schools don't fit secondary schools. *Educational Leadership, 40* (December), 51–53.

Fisher, C., Berliner, D., Filby, N., Marliave, R., Cahern, L., & Dishaw, M.

(1980). Teaching behaviors, academic learning time, and student achievement: An overview. In C. Denham & A. Lieberman (Eds.), *Time to learn.* Washington, DC: National Institute of Education.

Frank, C. (1984). Equity for all students: The New York City Promotional Gates Program. *Educational Leadership, 41*(8), 62–65.

Goodlad, J. I. (1983). *A place called school.* New York: McGraw–Hill.

Gottfredson, D. C., Hybl, L. G., Gottfredson, G. D., & Casteneda, R. P. (1986). *School climate assessment instruments: A review.* Report 363. Baltimore: Johns Hopkins University Center for Social Organization of Schools.

Gump, P. (1980). The school as a social situation. *Annual Review of Psychology, 31,* 553–582.

Hallinan, M. (1976). Friendship patterns in open and traditional classrooms. *Sociology of Education, 49,* 254–264.

Hallinan, M. T., & Sørensen, A. B. (1985). Ability grouping and student friendships. *American Educational Research Journal, 22,* 485–499.

Hamilton, S. F. (1983). The social side of schooling: Ecological studies of classrooms and schools. *Elementary School Journal, 83,* 313–334.

Harter, S. (1978). Effective motivation reconsidered: Toward a developmental model. *Human Development, 21,* 34–64.

Haskins, R., Walden, T., & Ramey, C. T. (1983). Teacher and student behavior in high and low ability groups. *Journal of Educational Psychology, 75,* 865–876.

Hawley, W. D. (1985). False premises, false promises: The mythical character of public discourse about education. *Phi Delta Kappan, 67* (November), 183–187.

Heyns, B. (1974). Social selection and stratification within schools. *American Journal of Sociology, 79,* 1434–1451.

Karweit, N. (1981). Time in school. In A. Kerckhoff (Ed.), *Research in sociology of education and socialization* (Vol. 2). Greenwich, CT: JAI Press.

Karweit, N. (1985). Should we lengthen the school term? *Educational Researcher, 14*(6), 9–15.

Lipsitz, J. (1984). *Successful schools for young adolescents.* New Brunswick, NJ: Transaction Books.

McDill, E. L., Natriello, G., & Pallas, A. M. (1985). Raising standards and retaining students: The impact of the reform recommendations on potential dropouts. *Review of Educational Research, 55,* 415–432.

McDill, E. L., & Rigsby, L. (1973). *Structure and process in secondary schools: The academic impact of educational climates.* Baltimore: Johns Hopkins University Press.

McPartland, J. M. (1987). Changing testing and grading practices to improve student motivation and teacher–student relationships. Paper presented at the annual meeting of the American Educational Research Association, Washington, DC.

McPartland, J. M. (1987). Balancing high quality subject-matter instruction with positive teacher–student relations in the middle grades. Paper presented at the annual meeting of the American Educational Research Association, Washington, DC.

McPartland, J. M., & Crain, R. L. (1987). Evaluating the trade-offs in student outcomes from alternative school organization policies. In M. Hallinan (Ed.), *Social organization of schools.* New York: Plenum.

McPartland, J. M., & Epstein, J. L. (1977). Open schools and achievement:

Extended tests of a hypothesis of no relationship. *Sociology of Education, 42,* 133–144.

McPartland, J., Epstein, J., Karweit, N., & Slavin, R. (1976). *Productivity of schools: Conceptual and methodological framework for research.* Report 218. Baltimore: Johns Hopkins University Center for Social Organization of Schools.

McPartland, J. M., & McDill, E. L. (1977). Research on crime in schools. In J. M. McPartland & E. L. McDill (Eds.), *Violence in schools: Perspectives, programs and positions.* Lexington, MA: D. C. Heath.

Metz, M. H. (1978). *Classrooms and corridors: The crisis of authority in desegregated secondary schools.* Berkeley: University of California Press.

Michaels, J. W. (1977). Classroom reward structures and academic performance. *Review of Educational Research, 47*(1), 87–98.

Minuchin, P. P. (1977). *The middle years of childhood.* Monterey, CA: Brooks/Cole.

Moos, R. H., & David, T. (1981). Evaluating and changing classroom settings. In J. L. Epstein (Ed.), *The quality of school life.* Lexington, MA: Lexington Books.

Murnane, R. J. (1975). *The impact of school resources on the learning of inner city children.* Cambridge, MA: Ballinger.

National Center for Education Statistics. (1985). *Conditions of education.* Washington, DC: Government Printing Office.

National Commission on Excellence in Education. (1983). *A nation at risk.* Washington, DC: U.S. Government Printing Office.

Natriello, G., & Dornbusch, S. M. (1984). *Teacher evaluative standards and student effort.* New York: Longman.

Nicholls, J. L. (1984). Conceptions of ability and coherent motivation. In R. Ames & C. Ames, *Research in motivation and education* (Vol. 1). Orlando, FL: Academic Press.

Oakes, J. (1985). *Keeping track: How schools structure inequality.* New Haven, CN: Yale University Press.

Olson, L. (1986). Effective schools. *Education Week,* January 15.

Peterson, P. L., Wilkinson, L. C., & Hallinan, M. T. (1984). *The social context of instruction: Group organization and group process.* New York: Academic Press.

Purkey, S. C., & Smith, M. S. (1983). Effective schools: A review. *Elementary School Journal, 83,* 427–452.

Rosenbaum, J. (1980). Social implication of educational groups. *Review of Research in Education, 8,* 361–401.

Rosenholtz, S. J., & Rosenholtz, S. H. (1981). Classroom organization and the perception of ability. *Sociology of Education, 54,* 172–190.

Rowan, B. (1985). The assessment of school effectiveness. In R. M. Kyle (Ed.), *Reaching for Excellence: An Effective Schools Sourcebook.* Washington, DC: U.S. Government Printing Office.

Rowan, B., & Miracle, A. (1983). Systems of ability grouping and the stratification of achievement. *Sociology of Education, 56,* 133–144.

Rutter, M., Maughan, B., Mortimore, P., & Ouston, J. (1979). *Fifteen thousand hours: Secondary schools and their effects on children.* Cambridge, MA: Harvard University Press.

Schonfeld, W. R. (1971). *Youth and authority in France: A study of secondary schools.* Beverly Hills, CA: Sage Professional Papers in Comparative Politics.

Seeley, D. S. (1981). *Education through partnership: Mediating structures and education.* Cambridge, MA: Ballinger.

Sizer, T. (1984). *Horace's compromise.* Boston: Houghton Mifflin.

Slavin, R. E. (1980). Effects of individual learning expectations on student achievement. *Journal of Educational Psychology, 72,* 520–524.

Slavin, R. E. (1983). *Cooperative learning.* New York: Longman.

Slavin, R. E. (1984). Component building: A strategy for research based instructional improvement. *Elementary School Journal, 84,* 255–269.

Slavin, R. E., Madden, N. A., & Leavey, M. B. (in press). Effects of Team Assisted Individualization on the mathematics achievement of academically handicapped and non-handicapped students. *Journal of Educational Psychology.*

Spady, W. G. (1974). The authority system of the school and student unrest: A theoretical exploration. In G. W. Gordon (Ed.), *Uses of the sociology of education.* Chicago: National Society for the Study of Education.

Stallings, J. (1980). Allocated academic learning time revisited, or beyond time-on-task. *Educational Researcher, 9,* 11–16.

Stallings, J. (1985). Effective elementary classroom practices. In R. M. Kyle (Ed.), *Reaching for excellence: An effective schools sourcebook.* Washington, DC: U.S. Government Printing Office.

Stipek, D. J. (1984). The development of achievement motivation. In R. Ames & C. Ames (Eds.) *Research on motivation in education* (Vol. 1). Orlando, FL: Academic Press.

Summers, A. A., & Wolfe, B. L. (1977). Do schools make a difference? *American Economic Review, 67,* 639–652.

Tammivaara, J. S. (1982). The effects of task structure on beliefs about competence and participation in small groups. *Sociology of Education, 55,* 212–222.

Tjosvold, D. (1978). Alternative organization for school and classrooms. In D. Bar–Tal & L. Saxe (Eds.), *The social psychology of education: Theory and research.* Washington, DC: Hemisphere Press.

Twentieth Century Fund Task Force on Federal Elementary and Secondary Education Policy. (1983). *Making the grade.* New York: Twentieth Century Fund.

Wang M. & Stiles, B. (1976). An investigation of children's concept of self responsibility for school learning. *American Educational Research Journal, 13,* 159–179.

Weber, G. (1971). *Inner-city children can be taught to read: Four successful schools.* Washington, DC: Council for Basic Education.

Weiner, B. (1979). A theory of motivation for some classroom experiences. *Journal of Educational Psychology, 71,* 3–25.

SIX

DIVERSITY AND EQUITY IN PUBLIC EDUCATION: COMMUNITY FORCES AND MINORITY SCHOOL ADJUSTMENT AND PERFORMANCE

JOHN U. OGBU

INTRODUCTION

In this chapter, I focus on the education of Black Americans and similar minorities but also compare them with other types of minorities. In the first part, I review past policies and strategies designed to improve the academic performance of Black American children, as well as review the theories that generated those policies and strategies. I then use data from California to show that past policies and strategies have not been particularly successful in eliminating the problem of low academic performance, although they have helped reduce it. The first part concludes with an assessment of the potential of the current reform movement to improve the academic performance of Black children and similar minorities. In the second part, I suggest how community factors contribute to the problem of low academic performance and thus must be taken into account in formulating policies to deal with the problem. The third part concludes the chapter with specific suggestions for intervention, focusing on community factors.

SOME CONVENTIONAL EXPLANATIONS, INTERVENTION POLICIES, AND STRATEGIES

Past policies and intervention strategies to improve the academic performance of Black children were based at least in part on prevailing explanations of children's academic performance. There are basically three types of conventional explanations that have guided, and to some extent still influence, intervention policies and strategies. One is institutional deficiency theory, which attributes the problem to faulty organization and functioning of the education system. The second is developmental deficiency theory or theory of cultural deprivation, which holds that Black children are unprepared for academic success in the public school because their parents are not capable of teaching the competencies a child needs to succeed. The third explanation is cultural discontinuities theory, which contends that the poor academic performance of the minority child is caused by conflicts between the child's cultural and language competencies and expectations on the one hand and the cultural and language competencies and expectations of the public schools on the other. These three strands of explanation have produced three different policy and intervention orientations: namely, school reform, rehabilitation of the Black child and family, and cultural compatibility education. That the "solutions" have not been particularly effective is evident in the persistence of low academic achievement. And this raises the important question: Will the present reform movement prove more effective in raising minority children's school performance? Before addressing this question, I briefly review past explanations, intervention policies, and strategies.

Institutional Deficiency Theory and School Reform

The institutional deficiency explanation began as a folk explanation, predating efforts of social scientists to study and explain the gap in academic performance of Black and white children. From the beginning of the public schools in the 19th century, Blacks have protested against their exclusion, segregation, and inferior education and have demanded equal education with whites. In the 1930s they increasingly pointed to "legal" dual school systems and segregated education along with "illegal" unequal distribution of educational resources in the South as the main reasons for the educational problems of Black children. In the 1960s Blacks and similar minorities added other factors, including overcentralization of school administration, lack of community control and participation, and insensitivity or prejudice of school personnel. Some even began to question the very existence of the schools as organized in the United States (Gittell, 1976).

Before World War II, social science explanations attributed lower school performance by Blacks to either heredity or home and community environments. Social scientists did not actually investigate the effects of school segregation and unequal distribution of educational resources on their school performance. They began to do so, however, after the United States Supreme Court declared in 1954 that school segregation by law was unconstitutional.

School reform through court actions thus began because of pressures from Blacks whose folk explanation blamed the system. Starting in the 1930s, Blacks and civil rights organizations sought to increase Blacks' access to more and better education through legal maneuvers. They filed lawsuits against the dual school systems of the Southern states, one of which resulted in the Brown v. Board of Education decision by the Supreme Court in 1954. The major concerns of the reformers before the 1960s were: (a) to end legal dual school systems, and (b) to give Blacks and whites equal access to educational resources (Ashmore, 1954; Clement et al., 1976; Ogbu, 1979a). It does not seem that the reformers were particularly concerned about what went on inside the schools or how what went on inside the schools affected the school performance of Black children.

The results of school desegregation and related reforms are mixed. School segregation by law no longer exists, but most Black students still attend public schools that are predominantly Black. School resources are no longer deliberately diverted from Black schools; however, school resources remain unequally distributed for other reasons. There is no national assessment of the impact of school desegregation and school integration on the academic performance of Black children; but available data indicate that the positive effect is limited (Berkeley Unified School District, 1985; Ogbu, 1979a; Schofield, 1982). Unfortunately, the reformers ignored two important issues. One issue is that schools are an agent of society at large and for that reason are rarely able to abandon their discriminatory policies and practices while society continues to subordinate and discriminate against minorities. Therefore, effective minority education reform can be accomplished only when it is accompanied or preceded by reforms in the status of minorities. The second issue is that the public schools are organized to prepare children for the labor market and that people go to school to get credentials for good jobs that pay well. Minorities go to school for the same reason and they are not likely to respond well to school reform if they are still forced to live in ghettos and are given little or no opportunity to benefit from their education in terms of good jobs that pay well.

Cultural Deprivation, Developmental Deficiencies and Rehabilitation of Minority Children and Families

Cultural deprivation emerged as a forceful theory in the 1960s. The central argument of the theory is that Black children come from families and a community environment that do not provide them with adequately organized "stimulation" for normal development. The theory often describes the culture of poor Black children as consisting of a list of indicators of poverty: parents lack education, parents are unemployed, families live in poor housing and in areas of the city with a high incidence of single-parent families and female-headed households, family members do not eat together, children are given too much responsibility at an early age, and parents do not read to children (Ogbu, 1978, p. 46). About 75% of Black children were said to be culturally deprived in the mid-1960s. It was said that because they were culturally deprived they were retarded in linguistic, cognitive, motivational, and social development and as a result failed in school (Ausubel, 1964; Bloom et al., 1965; Deutsch, 1967; Gottfried, 1973; Hunt, 1964, 1969).

The theory of cultural deprivation has been influential in educational intervention on behalf of minority and poor children since the second half of the 1960s. However, the term "cultural deprivation" is rarely used nowadays because of criticisms by minorities and others who regard it as inappropriate. Instead, substitute terms, such as cultural disadvantage, cultural differences, and at risk, which make the same assumptions, are used.

There are three types of intervention strategies generated by the theory of cultural deprivation, all of which emphasize the rehabilitation of minority children and their families. These are briefly described below.

Early Education. One specific hypothesis from cultural deprivation theory pertaining to academic achievement of minority children is that of failure of socialization. The central point of this hypothesis is that Black children do not perform well in school because their parents are not effective in teaching them appropriate language, cognitive, and learning skills required for the white, middle-class type of school success. Proponents of this hypothesis believe that Black children can, however, succeed academically if they are stimulated enough in infancy and early childhood to develop like white, middle-class children. This explanation has influenced policies and programs designed to improve minority school performance since the 1960s. It has led to preschool programs such as Head Start, which was designed to resocialize Black children. It has also led to programs for training low-income, Black parents on how to teach their children to develop appropriate competencies for school learning and adjustment (Rees, 1968; Stanley, 1973).

Although the early education strategy is widely accepted as a good rehabilitation remedy, the results have not always been satisfactory. Black children who participated in early education programs tended to score higher on IQ tests than other children who did not participate, but the IQ gains tended to wash out after a few years of public schooling. To prevent the washout phenomenon, Head Start and other early education services were subsequently extended into regular schooling, initially to the first grade and then to later grades. A recent study suggests, however, that one possible lasting effect of preschool programs for poor children is not the gains in IQ but rather the fact that the children learn "how to go to school" (Darlington, 1986; Lazar et al., 1982).

In one project, the Perry Preschool Project, some participants have been followed and periodically evaluated up to the age of 19. The evaluation at age 15 showed that children who went through the preschool programs had, on average, higher academic achievement test scores than their peers who did not attend preschool. They also were less involved in delinquent activities (Schweinhart & Weikart, 1980). At the age of 19, preschool program graduates "were less apt to be enrolled in special education classes, drop out of school, or be arrested." They were also more likely to be attending college or job-training programs or to be employed and self-supporting than their peers who had not gone through the preschool program (Berrueta–Clement et al., 1984).

Head Start and other preschool programs are good for poor, Black children and similar minorities, but they are based on an inadequate understanding of human development pertaining to cognitive, linguistic, motivational, and social-emotional skills (Ogbu, 1979b, 1981a,b, 1982a, 1985). In any given society or segment of society, children develop cognitive, linguistic, motivational, and social-emotional skills that are present and adaptive among members of their society or segment—and not simply because they are "stimulated." Thus, I have argued elsewhere that racial stratification caused Black Americans to occupy a particular cultural-ecological niche for many generations. As a result, they developed attitudes, self-concepts, learning habits, and linguistic, cognitive, motivational, and social-emotional skills required and fostered by that niche. Black parents and other socialization agents do quite well in transmitting these adaptive attributes to Black children and Black children successfully acquire the attributes as they grow up (Ogbu, 1978, 1979b, 1981a, 1985).

Compensatory Education. Preschool programs are designed to prevent poor, Black children from becoming "retarded" in terms of cognitive, linguistic, motivational, and social-emotional development and to help them develop middle-class competencies. Compensatory education programs, on the other hand, are designed to help older children make up for the middle-class competencies they did not develop in early childhood. Some programs are, of course, designed to change the ways schools operate in order to accommodate the children's deficiencies; and the school changes include curriculum modification, modification of teaching techniques, use of specialists, reduction of class size, and the like. Still other programs are designed to improve the relationship between school personnel and minority children and their families.

By and large, however, compensatory education programs are designed to rehabilitate or redeem older children from the influence of their home and neighborhood environments by resocializing them to develop competencies that are regarded as important for school success: language and communication skills, reasoning skills, perceptual skills, long attention span, motivation, pride in academic achievement, and feelings of self-worth (Ogbu, 1974, p. 209; 1978, p. 84).

Like preschool programs, the results of compensatory education programs for older children are mixed. In general they have not succeeded in reducing substantially the gap in academic achievement between Black and white children (Durham, 1972; Farber & Lewis, 1972; Goldberg, 1971; Ogbu, 1978; Passow, 1971).

School Integration, 1960s and Later. As already pointed out, before the mid-1960s the major argument for school desegregation/integration was that it would give Black and white students equal access to school resources. What went on inside the desegregated schools was not considered to have a significant effect on quality of educational opportunity (Ashmore, 1954; Clement et al., 1976; Ogbu, 1979a). The reason for not considering what went on inside the schools was probably that policymakers and members of Congress believed unequal access to school resources caused unequal academic achievement by Black children.

Coleman's survey (1966) appeared to cast doubts on the resource access theory by suggesting that Black and white schools in every part of the country had about equal resources in the mid-1960s *and* that where differences in school resources existed they did not appear to account for differences between Black and white students in academic achievement. His alternative explanation was that the differences in academic performance were due to "peer learning." According to the peer-learning hypothesis, low-income children benefitted academically from being in the same school with middle- and upper-income children. Coleman, therefore, suggested that school desegregation should be along class lines to help low-income students, Blacks and whites, because lower-class children gained by attending schools with middle-income students. And since most Black children fall into the low-income category, desegregation along class lines would also become desegregation along the race line (Clement et al., 1976, p. 26). Coleman's hypothesis thus introduced a new goal of school desegregation; namely, to improve the academic achievement of Black children by mixing them with white middle- and upper-middle-class children.

The peer-learning hypothesis shares the major assumption of cultural deprivation theory—that the families and communities of low-income Black children do not teach children appropriate academic attitudes and behaviors. The hypothesis suggests, too, that children can overcome these disadvantages if they interact in a mutually accepting manner with white, middle-class peers who serve as role models for success in school and later life (U. S. Commission on Civil Rights, 1967). Coleman said that the environment of an integrated school would offer children "substantial support for higher achievement and aspirations" because:

> The majority of children in such schools do not have problems of self-confidence due to race, for the school often reflects the mainstream of American society. The environment in such schools is well endowed with models of occupational success. (U. S. Commission on Civil Rights, 1967, p. 105; see also Ogbu, 1978; U. S. Senate Select Committee, 1972)

As in the case of compensatory education, the results of school integration are mixed. In general, while school integration is a desirable goal for social, political, moral and other reasons, it has had only a limited positive impact on the academic performance of Black children (Berkeley Unified School District, 1985; Ogbu, 1978; Weinberg, 1970).

In summary, the rehabilitation strategies—early education, parent education, compensatory education, school integration for peer learning—have not been particularly effective in raising the academic achievement of Black children partly because they are based on misconceptions. One misconception, already discussed, is that the causes of Black children's low academic performance lie in the biographies of individual children; the proponents of the rehabilitation strategies fail to explore how individual biographies might have been shaped by the collective historical and structural experiences of Black people. The other misconception is about development of adaptive human competencies. As indicated earlier, children develop their competencies as enduring attributes not merely because their parents or anyone else "stimulated" them sufficiently, but because the competencies are functional in their particular cultural-ecological niche.

Cultural Discontinuities and Cultural Compatibility Education

In the late 1960s both minority groups and some social scientists rejected the theory of cultural deprivation and, instead, proposed an alternative cultural explanation of the lower academic performance of minority children. Minorities argued that their cultures are different from white, middle-class culture which also serves as the culture of the public schools, and that their children have difficulties in school because schools ignore their cultures and force their children to learn in white, middle-class culture. This not only causes them to fail academically but also deprives them of their ethnic identity. To stop school failure and loss of identity, minorities proposed multicultural education, bicultural education, bilingual education, and the like (Boykin, 1980; Gibson, 1976; Ramirez & Castenada, 1974; Wright, 1970).

Social scientists who questioned the cultural deprivation theory included anthropologists, historical dialectologists, linguists, and some psychologists. Anthropologists, for example, pointed out that cultural deprivation and allied theories misunderstood and misrepresented the concept of culture. In their view there are no people in the world—poor people, ethnic minorities, tribal people, or peasants—who are "culturally deprived." Rather, they said, different populations have different cultures. As for school performance, anthropologists argued that minority children do not do well in school because of the cultural conflict caused by cultural and language differences. Philips (1976, p. 30) summarized this point of view: "Because they come from a different cultural environment, minority children do not acquire the content and style of learning which is presumed by the curriculum and teaching methods of the (public) schools."

Ethnographic studies show that some minorities such as American Indian groups have their own distinct cultures. For others, such as Black Americans, proponents of the cultural difference explanation have had to make concerted efforts to show they have separate cultures (Hannerz, 1969; Keil, 1977; Levine, 1977; Lewis, 1976; Valentine, 1979; Williams, 1981; Young, 1970, 1974). Some scholars have even pointed out distinct features of minority cultures that are in conflict with the mainstream culture minority children encounter in school (see Boykin, 1986; Kochman, 1981; Young, 1974).

By the late 1960s, the cultural difference explanation had gained legitimacy and formed the basis for policies and remedial strategies to improve the academic performance of minority children. Cultural differences were even given statutory recognition in two pieces of federal legislation; namely, the Bilingual Education Act of 1968 and the Ethnic Heritage Studies Act of 1972. These two acts also provided federal moneys for development and implementation of new programs stressing the role of cultural and language differences in education.

The strategy for improving the academic performance of Black children arising from the cultural difference explanation is that of cultural compatibility education. That is, curriculum, instructional technique, teacher–student relationships, and communication styles are more or less redesigned to be compatible with "the reality" of the children's cultural background. New approaches to teaching reading to inner-city, Black students will serve as an example of cultural compatibility education. Having established that a Black English dialect existed as a separate language system, proponents of the cultural/language explanation argued that the disproportionate number of Black children did not learn to read at the same pace and with the same ease as their white, middle-class peers because of language conflict. They suggested that there might be a kind of structural interference of Black dialect when Black children tried to read in standard English. Baratz (1970) describes the conflict as follows:

> When the middle-class child starts the process of learning to read, his problem is primarily one of decoding the graphic representations of a language he already speaks. The disadvantaged black child must also "translate" them into his own language. This presents him with an almost insurmountable obstacle since the written words frequently do not go together in any pattern that is familiar or meaningful to him. (p. 20)

It was therefore recommended that Black English dialect should be allowed in the classroom and that textbooks and curriculum materials should be written in Black dialect. It was also recommended that where instructional materials and textbooks are in standard English Black children should be allowed to use Black dialects. These remedies were tried but did not significantly improve the students' success in learning to read (Ogbu, 1982b; Simons, 1979).

Proponents of the cultural/language difference explanation are correct that Black students and other minorities may have their own culture and that their academic performance might be adversely affected by cultural conflicts. However, they have not gone far enough in their analysis to answer an important question; namely, why do other minorities (e.g., Punjabi of Yuba City, California, and Chinese Americans) do relatively well in school, and avoid the learning problems that are found among Black Americans, even though they have their own different cultures and languages (see Gibson, 1983; Ogbu, 1983)? Thus, the cultural difference explanation does not address the issue of variability in minority school performance; it fails to address the variability issue because the proponents study only those minorities who are not successful in school.

Persisting Academic Gap

The strategies of school reform, rehabilitation of minority children and their families, and culturally compatible education discussed above have had *some* positive impact on the school performance of Black and similar minority children. The weaknesses we noted do not mean that these programs are not needed; they are. However, available evidence indicates that these strategies have at best provided only a partial solution. Evidence of the persistence of lower academic achievement by Black children and similar minorities can be found both in local school districts, and in state and national statistics. We will use Berkeley and the state of California to illustrate the persistence of the academic achievement gap between Blacks and whites.

The evidence from Berkeley is taken from a 1985 report of a task force on academic achievement in the Berkeley schools. It is instructive to note, as the report points out, that the Berkeley schools have long been committed to providing quality education for their minority students. This commitment began in the 1960s when Berkeley became "one of the first communities in the nation to desegregate its schools voluntarily. Since then, successive school boards and administrations have renewed that early commitment to ensuring that Berkeley students are fully integrated academically and socially" (Berkeley Unified School District, 1985). This commitment and the attendant efforts have brought some improvements in the academic performance of Black students. However, a large gap still persists in the school performance of minority and white students. Thus, the task force report notes that "*on the average,* black students continue to perform substantially below white students—far below what school and community leaders could have imagined two decades ago, and far below what is acceptable to us today" (Berkeley Unified School District, 1985).

What is the evidence of lower school performance of Black and similar minority students in the Berkeley schools? On the California Test of Basic Skills (CTBS), Berkeley students as a whole score substantially higher, but Black and Mexican-American students substantially below the national average. The initial gap in reading and math scores is wide in the first grade and widens "consistently and progressively" each year throughout the children's public school career. This widening gap can be illustrated with the case of children who were in the first grade in 1977 when they were first tested and were in the eighth grade in 1984 when their latest test data were available. In 1977 white first graders scored at the 70th percentile on the CTBS, while Black first graders scored at the 51st percentile. Then in 1984, the whites as eighth graders scored at the 90th percentile, while the Black eighth graders scored at the 39th percentile. In math, white first graders in 1977 scored at the 82nd percentile and in 1984 scored at the 94th percentile. Among Blacks, however, the first graders in 1977 scored at the 64th percentile and in 1984 scored at the 43rd percentile. Similar initial gaps in reading test scores exist for 1977 and 1984. And the gap continues for later cohorts of Black and white students. Similarly, there are four times as many white students as Black students taking the Scholastic Aptitude Test (SAT), even though the proportion of Black and white students in the school system is about the same. No figures exist for differences in the SAT scores of white and Black students from Berkeley. Nationally, however, Black high school students score, on the average, 100 points below whites on the SAT (Berkeley Unified School District, 1985, p. 6).

In addition to these differences in achievement test and SAT performance, Black and Mexican-American students demonstrate lower performance on a wide variety of other academic measures. They are underrepresented in classes for the gifted and talented but overrepresented in special education and compensatory education classes. They are also overrepresented in lower and underrepresented in upper curriculum tracks in several subjects. And perhaps of greatest importance, they are more likely to be retained in grade and to drop out of school than white students.

Nor are these differences between minority students and white students confined to Berkeley. The situation for the entire state of california has been summarized in a recent report entitled *Excellence For Whom?* (Brown & Haycock, 1984). According to the report, Black and Hispanic students consistently score at the bottom of the achievement distribution at the elementary school throughout the state. The report says, for example, that:

> The average percentile rank for elementary schools with enrollment of over 50% black or 70% Hispanic is below 20 for all but one of the 1983 CAP survey/tests for grades 3 and 6. Schools with a combined majority of black and Hispanic students (but not with a majority of either) perform somewhat higher/better but still average in the bottom third for California elementary schools. (p. 14)

As in Berkeley, the achievement gap widens in the state as a whole as the children progress through the elementary school; this occurs even in school districts such as Pasadena and San Diego "where (as in Berkeley) serious efforts are being made to improve minority education."

The persisting problem of lower school performance of Black students and similar minorities is nationwide; it is not limited to particular school districts such as Berkeley, nor to particular states such as California. Nor is the problem limited to inner-city and barrio schools. Berkeley schools can hardly be called inner-city schools. It is not limited to segregated schools; Berkeley and San Diego schools can hardly be called segregated schools. There is substantial evidence that the problem of lower academic achievement is found in the inner-city schools and barrio schools of Chicago (Hess, 1985), New York (Clark, 1965; Hispanic Policy, 1984), San Francisco (Suarez–Orozco, 1986), San Diego (personal communication, 1986), Dallas (Hanna, 1985), and in relatively affluent suburbs such as Montgomery County, Ma., (Montgomery County Public Schools, 1984) and Fairfax County, Va. (Fairfax County Public Schools, 1985).

The Education for Excellence Movement: Back to Institutional Deficiency Theory

Institutional deficiency theory underlies the current education reform movement in the United States. Various reports (see Chapter 1) claim that students in the United States are not doing as well as they should in school. However, the reports disagree about precisely what is wrong with the schools. While minority education is not the primary focus of the reports, some nonetheless refer to the educational needs of minority and poor students (e.g., Boyer, 1983, p. 56; Goodlad, 1983, p. 147). Furthermore, a common theme is "the need for attaining the twin goals of equity and excellence" (Passow, 1984, p. 1). In spite of this common theme, close reading of the reports gives the impression that their overall emphasis is on attaining excellence. As McNett (1984) points out, the "most significant single theme [of the reports] is the idea that higher standards and improved academic performance should be expected of all children. There is no sense that some will not achieve. Education should raise its sights, set higher standards for both educators and students" (p. 1).

In proclaiming higher standards as a reformist goal, the reports seem to assume that both majority and minority students' academic performance depends on what goes on inside the schools and that what needs to be done to "fix" the schools and thereby improve students' academic performance is to manipulate or change those within-school factors (Weis, 1985a, p. 218). Among the needed changes in the schools are more instructional time, more course requirements, stiffer standards for promotion and graduation, and better pay for teachers (McNett, 1984). Some reports imply that by merely demanding higher standards, schools will motivate students to perform (Doyle, cited in Passow, 1984). It is doubtful, however, that this strategy will work for inner-city Blacks and other "marginal students," for, as Passow rightly notes:

> Those who have been involved in compensatory education and dropout prevention programs question this assertion, and with good reason. After all, their efforts have not always been effective and they might have done

better by forgetting all about various intervention strategies and programs and simply *announced* higher academic standards and expectations. (pp. 14–15)

What goes on inside the schools affects minority students' social adjustment and academic performance (Edmonds, 1986; Ogbu, 1974). But much more is involved. Recall the case of the Berkeley schools. The Berkeley School Board and school administrators have manipulated many of the within-school factors with dismal results. The reason is that community factors, and especially the folk system/cultural models and strategies that minority students and their families employ in their quest for education, are every bit as important as within-school factors in determining academic achievement. Yet, the reports and the current reform movement do not address these community factors. It is therefore doubtful that the reform movement will do better than past efforts in eliminating or reducing the academic performance gap between minority and white students.

On the whole, past and present explanations of the lower academic performance of Black students have certain weaknesses in common which render the policies and intervention strategies they generate less effective than desired. One weakness is that they are ahistorical, thereby failing to consider how collective historical experience of Black Americans in school and society might have shaped their perceptions of and responses to schooling. Second, the explanations tend to view schooling in the abstract, thereby failing to pay sufficient attention to the role of schooling as a cultural formula for preparing young people to participate in the job market and how job market opportunities have affected the minorities' perceptions of and responses to schooling. Third, the explanations have generally ignored the participants' point of view or their folk system. Finally, the explanations are noncomparative; that is, they do not seriously explore why some minorities in the United States and elsewhere succeed in school even though they possess cultural and other characteristics that researchers tend to associate with school failure.

COMMUNITY FACTORS AND MINORITY SCHOOL ADJUSTMENT AND PERFORMANCE

The difficulties faced by the proponents of the various explanations of school failure reviewed earlier can be avoided by comparing Blacks and similar minorities with the more academically successful minorities. When we compare the less academically successful with the more academically successful minorities we find that the two types differ not only in academic performance but also in their origins as minority groups, in the nature of their minority status, and in their cultural and language differences vis-à-vis white culture and the standard English language. They also differ in their identity, attitude toward school, and folk theory of getting ahead, all of which appear to affect how the minorities perceive and respond to schooling. I therefore suggest that the first prerequisite for understanding the community factors that contribute to low academic achievement is to recognize that there are different types of minority groups with different patterns of educational performance. A related prerequisite is to delineate the distinctive features of the minority types and how they enter into the process of schooling.

Kinds of Minorities

Through a comparative study of the histories and adaptations of various minorities in the United States and elsewhere, I have classified minority groups into three types (Ogbu, 1978). One type, *autonomous minorities,* are minorities primarily a minority in a numerical sense. They may possess a distinct ethnic, religious, linguistic, or cultural identity. However, even though they are not entirely free from prejudice and discrimination, autonomous minorities are not usually socially, economically, or politically subordinated. They also do not experience disproportionate and persistent problems in school adjustment and academic achievement partly because they tend to have a cultural frame of reference which demonstrates and encourages school success. Jews and Mormons represent this type of minority in the United States.

Immigrant minorities, the second type, are people who have moved *voluntarily* to the United States because they believed that emigrating to the U. S. would improve their economic status, social conditions, or political status. These expectations continue to influence the way immigrant minorites perceive and respond to societal barriers and other problems confronting them in America. Immigrant minorities do not usually experience persistent disproportionate problems in social adjustment and academic achievement in school. The Chinese in Stockton, Calif., and the Punjabi Indians in Yuba City, Calif., as well as Hispanics from Central and South America in San Francisco, are representative examples (Gibson, 1983; Ogbu, 1974; Suarez–Orozco, 1986).

Castelike or *involuntary minorities* are the third type. They are people who were originally brought into the United States society *involuntarily* through slavery, conquest, or colonization. Thereafter these minorities were relegated to menial positions and denied true assimilation into the mainstream of American society. American Indians, Black Americans,

Mexican–Americans, and native Hawaiians are examples in the United States. The Burakumin in Japan and the Maori in New Zealand are examples outside the United States. Involuntary minorities are seen to experience difficulties with social adjustment and academic achievement in school.

Discussions of minority education in the United States usually group Jews and Mormons with the majority whites who are successful in school. I also exclude them from further comparison in this chapter and focus instead on the immigrant and nonimmigrant minorities. These two types of minorities are compared with the dominant white group in their folk theory of getting ahead, in their degree of trusting relationships with the dominant group and societal institutions, and in their identity and cultural/language differences.

Distinguishing Features of Immigrant and Nonimmigrant Minorities

Opportunity Structure, Survival Strategies, and Folk Theories of Getting Ahead. Immigrant and involuntary minorities differ in their "theories" of how one gets ahead in the United States. But before we discuss these theories, we will clarify the role of schooling in getting ahead in the contemporary United States and other urban industrial societies. The clarification is necessary because those who are making educational policies or implementing intervention programs for minorities tend to ignore the fact that people go to school and work hard to succeed in school not out of love of learning but because they perceive and experience significant economic and other benefits of education.

Contemporary societies like the United States structure their schools to prepare citizens to support existing economic systems as workers/producers and consumers, and to teach them to believe in the systems. They also structure the schools to train citizens to support other institutions. American public schools, like schools in other societies, try to accomplish their task of recruiting people into the labor force by teaching young people the beliefs, values, and attitudes that support the economic system; by teaching them some practical skills such as reading, writing, and computation that make the system work; by enhancing the development of those personal attributes that are compatible with habits required at the workplace; and by credentialing people to enter the workforce. But if the public schools are to succeed in educating children from a particular segment of society, school credentials must play a positive role in people's folk theory of getting ahead. An example of such a positive role is to be found in the case of the white middle class. The latter's folk theory asserts that one gets a good job that pays well by getting a good education. Consequently, the middle class organizes schooling to prepare children in marketable skills and to offer credentials for labor force entry, remuneration, and advancement on the job. And because white, middle-class people have historically obtained jobs and earned wages commensurate with their school credentials, they have developed perceptions and responses that enhance academic success.

We will use the concept of status mobility system to clarify the connection between people's folk theory of getting ahead and their school perceptions and strivings. A status mobility system is the strategy of getting ahead in culturally approved ways in a society or a segment of society. Every society or segment has its own folk theory of getting ahead, even though different people may mean different things by the term "getting ahead." Each folk theory of getting ahead tends to generate its own ideal behaviors and ideal successful persons or role models—the kinds of persons widely perceived as people who are successful and get ahead because of their personal qualities and behaviors (LeVine, 1967). The personal qualities of the role models tend to influence the childrearing values and practices of parents and other agents of socialization. They also influence the attitudes and behaviors of children themselves as they get older and begin to understand the status mobility system of their people. Thus, in a population where academic success and school credentials enable people to get ahead, say, to obtain good jobs that pay well, people who have good jobs with good pay will usually be the ones who are well educated and who possess the qualities or competencies that are generally known to enhance academic success. In such a population parents' childrearing values and practices and other socialization forces will emphasize the qualities and strategies promoting academic success; young people will value these and strive to do well in school.

Frequently, however, minority groups encounter barriers that prevent them from obtaining jobs and wages commensurate with their education, contrary to the folk theory of getting ahead proclaimed by the dominant white, middle-class Americans. Immigrants and involuntary minorities have tended to perceive this barrier in the opportunity structure differently, and to respond to it differently because of their divergent histories and circumstances. Immigrants, due to their dual frame of reference (see below), may think that even if they are allowed only marginal jobs they are better off in the United States than they would be in their homelands; or they may think of their menial jobs and discriminatory treatment as temporary. Further, they may interpret their exclusion from better jobs as a result of their status as "foreigners," or because they do not speak the language well, or because they were not educated in the United States. Consequently, immigrants tend to share the folk theory of getting ahead characteristic of the white middle class and tend to behave accordingly, sometimes even in the face of barriers to opportunity. They do not necessarily bring such a theory from their homeland; they often accept the white, middle-class theory when they arrive in the United States (Suarez–Orozco, 1986).

Nonimmigrant minorites, however, perceive and respond differently. Since the nonimmigrants do not have a "homeland situation" to compare with the situation in the United States, they do not interpret their menial jobs and low wages as "better." Neither do they see their situation as temporary. On the contrary, they tend to interpret the discrimination against them as more or less permanent and institutionalized. Although they "wish" they could get ahead through education and ability like white Americans, they know they "can't." Consequently, they tend to develop a folk theory of getting ahead which differs from that of whites.

The situation is, however, paradoxical for minorities such as Blacks. When questioned directly, Blacks and similar minorities may declare like whites that in order to get ahead one needs a good education or good school credentials. By contrast, their actual strategies or behaviors for getting ahead do not support the white, middle-class folk theory like the immigrants' do. Indeed, intensive ethnographic interviews and observations reveal that Blacks do not really believe that they have the same chance of getting ahead as whites with similar school credentials. Further, Blacks try to change the rules by attacking the criteria for school credentials and employment, and then employ several alternative strategies for getting ahead. Among the survival strategies developed by Blacks are "collective struggle," "uncle tomming," "hustling," and the like (Ogbu, 1981c).

Degree of Trusting Relations with Whites and White-controlled Institutions. As noted above, immigrant minorities encounter and resent discrimination in the larger society and in school, but they do not perceive such treatment as institutionalized or permanent. Their responses can be described as "accommodation." The reason for the accommodation response is that many immigrants came to the United States to give their children the opportunity to get American education. For example, Suarez–Orozco (1986) reports from his recent study of Hispanic migrants in San Francisco that many parents "explicitly stated that they made great sacrifices to come to the United States so that their children could get an education and 'become somebody'. One mother went so far as to say that the only inheritance she could give her three children is 'this opportunity to study in this country. I have no money to leave them', she said, 'all I can leave them is an education' " (pp. 146–149). Immigrants frequently find their relationship with the public schools in the United States "better" than their relationship with the schools in their home countries. They speak favorably of the fact that in the United States their children are given free textbooks and other supplies.

In contrast, a deep distrust runs through the relationship between the public schools and the nonimmigrant minorities. In the case of Black Americans, one finds many historical episodes that have left them with the feeling that white people and the institutions they control cannot be trusted (Ogbu, in press). Public schools, particularly in the inner city, are generally not trusted to provide Black children with the "right education." This distrust arises partly from perceptions of past and current discrimination which, in the view of Blacks, is more or less institutionalized and permanent. This discriminatory treatment has, of course, been documented throughout the United States and throughout the history of Black people and Black education (Bond, 1966, 1969; Kluger, 1977; Ogbu, 1978; Weinberg, 1977).

Blacks reject segregated schools because they are judged inferior and distrust desegregated schools because they suspect that these schools perpetuate inferior education through many subtle devices such as "biased testing," misclassification, tracking, biased textbooks, biased and inadequate counseling, and so on. Furthermore, Blacks doubt that the public schools understand their children's educational needs. There is a strong feeling that the public schools do not understand the Black, male student, in particular. Thus, Blacks tend to attribute the low school performance of Black males to schools' inability to relate to Black males in ways that will help them learn.

Cultural/Language Differences. Based on comparative studies of cultural and language differences that children bring to school and the difficulties they encounter as a result of such differences, I have suggested classifying cultural and language differences in the school context into three types (Ogbu, 1982b). One is a *universal cultural/language difference.* All children face a transition from home to school involving adjustment to new cultural and language requirements, new social relations, and new styles of language use or communication. The transition also requires adjusting to new styles of thinking (Cook–Gumperz & Gumperz, 1979; Scribner & Cole, 1973). This type of cultural difference is not necessarily by itself associated with minority school adjustment and academic problems.

Primary cultural/language differences constitute the second type. These are differences that existed before two groups came in contact, such as before immigrant minorities came to the United States. Thus, Punjabi immigrants in Yuba City, Calif., spoke Punjabi, practiced Sikh, Hindu, or Moslem religion, had arranged marriages, and males wore turbans before they came to the United States where they continue these beliefs and practices to some extent.

The Punjabis also brought with them a different way of raising children. For example, they brought a way of training children in decision making and managing money that differs markedly from the way of the whites. White parents begin early to train their children to make their own decisions and believe that this will make them independent. From an early age they give children options and help them consider each option; by adolescence, white children make most of their own decisions. "By the end of high school," according to Gibson (1983), "many parents see their role as reduced largely to that of loving concerned advisor" (p. 80). Among Punjabis, on the other hand, many parents feel they make better decisions and that it is a parental responsibility to make decisions for their children; children, they believe, will learn to make good decisions from examples set by parents.

In money management Punjabi parents assume control of the money earned by their children and even use it for family needs. When children want something they ask parents; the parents decide whether it is an appropriate expense. Punjabi parents believe that their control of children's earnings ensures that the money is wisely spent and they also say that it enables them to maintain authority over their children. In contrast, white teen-agers control the money they earn and they spend it as they like without contributing to the running of the family.

The nature of primary cultural differences is better appreciated when we examine the situation of non-Western children attending Western-type schools in their own countries. The Kpelle of Liberia in West Africa will serve as a good example. The Kpelle situation was studied by Gay and Cole (1967), who wanted to find out how Kpelle culture and language affected children's learning Western-type mathematics in school. Gay and Cole therefore examined the kinds of mathematical concepts and activities present in Kpelle culture: arithmetic concepts, knowledge of geometry, indigenous measurement systems, and logic or reasoning.

They found that in arithmetic the Kpelle had concepts that were in some respects similar and in others different from Western concepts used in their American-type schools. For example, the Kpelle, like Westerners, classify things; but they do not carry out such an activity explicitly or consciously like Westerners. They have a counting system but it does not include concepts like "zero" or "number." And they do not recognize abstract operations such as addition, subtraction, multiplication, and division, although in their actual mathematical behaviors the Kpelle add, subtract, multiply, and divide things. Kpelle culture does not have many geometrical concepts and the ones it has are used very imprecisely. For example, things which are described as a "circle" include the shapes of a pot, a pan, a frog, a sledgehammer, a tortoise, a water turtle, a rice fanner, and so on. A tortoise shell, an arrowhead, a monkey's elbow, a drum, and a bow are all said to represent the shape of a triangle. The Kpelle measure length, time, volume, and money, but imprecisely. Totally lacking in their culture are measurements of weight, area, speed, and temperature. These differences in mathematical concepts and use existed before the Kpelle began to attend American-type schools. As I shall argue below, it is easier for bearers of primary cultural/language differences, namely, immigrants, to cross cultural boundaries than it is to cross barriers of the next type.

Secondary Cultural/Language Differences. We have examined closely the types of cultural/language differences and difficulties experienced by nonimmigrant minorities in the public schools and the way these children respond to cultural/language differences and difficulties. From our analysis it seems evident that the cultural/language phenomena faced by these children are not the same as the primary cultural/language differences described above. For instance, descriptions of the cultural differences faced by nonimmigrants usually stress differences in style, not differences in content as in the case of immigrant minority children and non-Western children in Western-type schools. Differences in the style of nonimmigrants have been described with respect to cognition (Ramirez & Castenada, 1974; Shade, 1982), communication (Gumperz, 1981; Kochman, 1981; Philips, 1983), social interaction (Erickson & Mohatt, 1982), and learning (Au, 1981; Boykin, 1986; Philips, 1976).

I have classified cultural differences of this type, which is more evident in style and meaning than in content, as secondary cultural/language differences. I define secondary cultural differences as those differences which arise *after* two populations have come in contact with each other or *after* members of a given population have come to participate in an institution controlled by another population, such as the schools for minorities and colonial peoples. In other words, secondary cultural differences develop as a response to a contact situation, especially one involving the domination of one group by another. This type of cultural/language difference is characteristic of nonimmigrant minorities. Although at the beginning of contact the minorities and the dominant group may be characterized by primary cultural differences, a new type of cultural difference begins to emerge later because of the minorities' need to respond to domination and all that it implies. For example, during slavery, white Americans used legal and extralegal means to discourage Black Americans from becoming literate. After slavery, whites created barriers in employment and other areas of life which effectively denied Blacks adequate social and economic benefits. These barriers extended to place of residence, public accommodations, political and legal rights, and the like. Under this circumstance, Blacks, like other nonimmigrant minorities, developed new ways of coping, perceiving, and feeling and these included a reinterpretation of their precontact behaviors and ideas.

Apart from style, another important feature of secondary cultural differences is cultural inversion. Cultural inversion is defined as a tendency for members of a subordinate population to interpret certain behaviors, events, symbols, and meanings as not appropriate for them because the behaviors belong to members of another population. At the same time, the subordinate minorities claim other—often opposite—behaviors, events, symbols, and meanings as more appropriate for them because they are not characteristic of members of the dominant group. Thus, appropriate behavior for Blacks is defined as being in opposition to the practice and preference of the dominant white Americans.

Nonimmigrant minorities use cultural inversion to repudiate negative stereotypes or derogatory images attributed to them by white Americans. Sometimes they use it as a strategy to manipulate whites or to get even with whites, or, as Holt (1972) puts it in the case of Black Americans, "to turn the table against the whites" (p. 194).

Cultural inversion may take several forms. These include hidden meanings of words and statements (Bontemps, 1969); different notions of time and its use (Weis, 1985b); different emphasis on language or dialects and communication styles (Baugh, 1984; Holt, 1972); or investiture of positive values on negative images and the like (Holt, 1972). It may also simply be an outright rejection of the dominant group's definition of appropriate behavior in a given setting like the school or workplace (Petroni, 1970). Cultural inversion is practiced selectively; that is, it occurs in some areas but not in other areas. And it seems to occur in those areas that minorities and whites have traditionally regarded as prerogatives of white people, such as academic work, high-status jobs, and related positions.

What bears emphasis is that cultural inversion results in the coexistence of two opposing cultural frames of reference or cultural ideals—one considered appropriate for minorities and the other for white people. Because of its close connection with their sense of collective identity, the cultural frame of reference of minorities is strongly associated with emotional attachment. Therefore, minority-group members who try to behave like white people or who try to cross cultural/language boundaries in areas defined as "white" may encounter opposition from their peers. Peer-group members oppose "acting white" or crossing cultural/language boundaries, partly because of collective animosity against whites and partly because it threatens their cohesiveness as a group (DeVos, 1984). Individual minority members themselves who try to "act white" or cross-cultural boundaries also experience inner conflicts from a shared sense of social identity and from uncertainty that they would be accepted by whites if rejected by their peers.

Thus, secondary cultural differences that characterize nonimmigrant minorities differ from primary cultural differences of the immigrants not only because the former emerged as coping mechanisms under subordination but also because of what they mean to the minorities and because they serve as boundary-maintaining mechanisms.

Collective or Social Identity. A final feature which differentiates immigrant from nonimmigrant minorities is the type of social identity minorities feel they have vis-à-vis white Americans. At least during the first generation, immigrants seem to retain the sense of peoplehood which they brought with them from their homeland to the United States. And it appears that the immigrants perceive this social identity primarily as different from the social identity of white Americans.

The nonimmigrant or involuntary minorities, on the other hand, have developed a new sense of social identity in opposition to the social identity of white Americans. This new identity was created after the nonimmigrant minorities had become subordinated and incorporated into American society and in reaction to the way white people treated nonimmigrant minorities in economic, political, social, and psychological domains. The treatment by whites included deliberate exclusion from true assimilation or the reverse, namely, forced assimilation (Castile & Kushner, 1981; DeVos, 1967, 1984; Spicer, 1966, 1971). Nonimmigrant minorities also developed oppositional identity because they perceived and experienced their treatment by whites as collective and enduring. They tended to believe they could not expect to be treated like members of the dominant group, regardless of their individual differences in ability, training, or education, because of differences in place of origin or residence, or because of differences in economic status or physical appearance. Furthermore, these minorities knew they could not easily escape from their birth-ascribed membership in a subordinate and disparaged group by "passing" or by returning to "a homeland" (Green, 1981). The oppositional social identity combines with new cultural coping mechanisms or secondary cultural differences and cultural inversion to make cross-cultural learning or "crossing cultural boundaries" more difficult than among immigrant minorities.

Whether we consider the case of the American Indians, or Black Americans, or Mexican-Americans, there have been numerous incidents in the history of each group which left the minorities with no doubt that their undesirable or unjust treatment was solely because they were not white Americans. An episode in the history of Black Americans will serve as an example of the experiences that caused nonimmigrant minorities to develop oppositional identity, vis-à-vis white Americans.

The incident took place in January 1923, long after blacks were emancipated from slavery. As reported by the CBS (1984) television program "60 Minutes," it began with an allegation that a Black man in Rosewood, Fla., raped a white woman. The accused man was not brought to a court trial as would be expected under the constitution of the United States. Instead, some 1,500 white men from the surrounding towns marched to Rosewood the night of the incident and the following day and killed 40 Black men, women, and children. Here all Black people were made responsible for the alleged offense of one Black person. Black Americans perceived and experienced countless incidents of this kind as both collective and enduring. As a result, they developed the belief that they were not treated like whites—regardless of their individual differences, regardless of their place of origin in Africa or residence in the United States, and regardless of differences in economic status or physical appearance.

Why Community Factors have More Adverse Effects on School Adjustment and Academic Performance of Nonimmigrant/Involuntary Minorities

Nonimmigrant minorities experience greater academic problems than immigrants, partly because the educational problems caused by community factors—opportunity structure, degree of trust/distrust, cultural/language differences, and identity—are different for the two types of minorities and partly because the minorities perceive, interpret, and respond differently to the educational problems they encounter in school. We will now consider how each of these community factors differentially affects the schooling of minorities.

Opportunity Structure, Survival Strategies, Folk Theories of Success and Schooling. Immigrant minorities, as we have seen, encounter discrimination in employment and other areas of life which, theoretically, should discourage them from pursuing education. However, this is not the case. Ethnographic studies show that immigrants not only possess folk theories of getting ahead emphasizing school success through hard work, but also that they match their aspirations with the necessary effort. The immigrants who believe and act this way do not necessarily come from societies where social and economic success depends on schooling and ability. Rather, they may develop their beliefs and behaviors *after* arriving in the United States. This is the case with Central and South American immigrants in San Francisco. Suarez–Orozco found that they have constructed a new folk theory of getting ahead with education playing a central role—despite the fact that success through education was not the folk theory operative in the immigrants' homelands.

The immigrants' folk theory and academic efforts are closely related to two other instrumental factors which enhance school success; namely, their favorable assessment of their chances to succeed in the United States, and their dual cultural frame of reference regarding upward mobility. The immigrants compare their accomplishments in the United States with the standards of their homelands, especially with the accomplishments of their peers "back home." And when they make this comparison they usually find plenty of evidence that they have made significant improvements in their lives and that there are good prospects for their children because of "better opportunity" in the United States. Immigrant parents take pains to let their children know that they have a better chance "to become somebody" in the United States than in their homelands; they also take pains to let them know that, as parents, they have made great sacrifices in order to provide the children with the opportunity to get American education and "to become somebody."

Finally, partly because parents sensitize children to sacrifices made on their behalf, children of immigrants feel a strong sense of obligation toward their parents. Interviews with both Asian and South American children indicate that they are keenly aware of sacrifices made by their parents in order to provide them with education and better opportunities "to become somebody" in the United States. And they are keenly aware, too, that such opportunities are more limited in their homelands (Suarez–Orozco, 1986). The children, therefore, listen to their parents who urge them to work hard in school.

Nonimmigrant minorities respond to barriers in opportunity structure differently partly because they have no dual frame of reference that enables them to assess their current status favorably. The only comparison they make is to the status of white Americans and that comparison makes the minorities resentful. Furthermore, the minorities have difficulty perceiving better future opportunities without struggle because of their belief that discrimination is institutionalized. Therefore, while their folk theory of getting ahead points to the importance of schooling, they simultaneously regard the theory as wishful thinking. In fact, ethnographic studies suggest that nonimmigrant minorities do not really believe they will get ahead like white Americans, even if they do have the same education. Analysis of their academic attitudes and efforts suggests that their folk theory of getting ahead does not particularly encourage individual perseverance in academic pursuit (see Fordham, 1985; Fordham & Ogbu, 1986; Matute–Bianchi, 1986; Ogbu, 1974, 1977). Moreover, as already noted, nonimmigrant minorities develop alternative or survival strategies that appear to be in competition with schooling.

When we examine what nonimmigrant minority parents teach their children about getting ahead through education, we find that without knowing it many parents appear to give their children contradictory messages. Thus, on the one hand they tell their children to get a good education and encourage them verbally to do well in school. But on the other hand, the actual texture of the lives of the parents in terms of low-level jobs, underemployment, and unemployment, also comes through strongly, reproducing a second kind of message powerful enough to undo their exhortations. Unavoidably, nonimmigrant minority parents discuss their problems with the system as well as those of relatives, friends, and neighbors in the presence of their children. The result is that nonimmigrant minority children increasingly become disillusioned about their ability to succeed in adult life through the mainstream strategy of schooling.

Turning to the children themselves, ethnographic studies suggest that they verbally express high interest in doing well in school and in obtaining good credentials for future employment in the mainstream economy. But they do not necessarily match their wishes and aspirations with effort, even though they know that to do well in school they have to work harder. Black and Mexican–American students in Stockton, Calif., for example, quite correctly explained that Chinese, Japanese, and white students in their school were more academically successful than they were because the former expended more time and effort in their schoolwork both at school and at home. The lack of serious academic attitudes and efforts appears to increase as nonimmigrant minority students get older and apparently become more aware of the reality that as members of a subordinate minority group they have limited future opportunities for getting good jobs even with good education. Simultaneously, they increasingly divert their time and efforts away from schoolwork into nonacademic activities.

Degree of Trust/Distrust and Schooling. The relationship between the schools and minority communities may raise similar educational problems for immigrants and nonimmigrants. However, the two types of minorities tend to interpret and respond to these problems differently. Three factors appear partly to account for the ability of immigrants to overcome barriers in school–community relations and thereby do well in school. One is that many immigrants see the public schools as offering an education that is far superior to the education available to them in their own homeland; therefore even when the immigrants are attending an inferior school in the United States they may believe the school to be of high quality. Their frame of reference for assessing the public schools is the quality of education in their homeland, not the quality of education in the white suburbs.

Second, some immigrants believe they are treated better by the public schools than they would be treated by the schools in their homeland. In ethnographic studies, immigrant students and parents often express both surprise and appreciation for the fact that they do not have to pay school fees and that they receive free textbooks and other supplies. The following excerpt from an interview with a Hispanic high school student in San Francisco illustrates this favorable evaluation of their treatment:

> In El Salvador life is very hard. To get an education there . . . even high school . . . it gets to be very expensive. You have to pay for your books, notebooks . . . everything, just like in college here. It is much harder to enter the university there. There is no help at all . . . the government gives you no help, that's the advantage here; there's help. There it is very hard to get any financial aid. (Suarez–Orozco, 1985, p. 16).

Even when the immigrants recognize, experience, and resent prejudice and discrimination in school, as in the case of Punjabi Indians in Yuba City, they appear to respond in ways that do not discourage them from doing well in school. They rationalize the prejudice and discrimination against them by saying that as "guests in a foreign land—they have no choice but to tolerate prejudice and discrimination" (Gibson, 1983, p. 66). Punjabi parents impress this attitude on their children and place the responsibility of doing well in school on the children themselves. Gibson describes the Punjabi strategy as follows:

> Punjabis rarely blame the educational system, or the teachers for a child's difficulties. Responsibility for learning rests, in the Punjabi view, with the individual. Punjabis are *not naive* about institutional and social barriers to success. They simply persevere, seeking ways to overcome obstacles in their path. Punjabi children are taught to do their best and to hold themselves accountable for their failures. If children fool around, squandering educational opportunities, they bear the consequence. (p. 149)

The overall impression one gains from analyzing ethnographic studies of immigrant minorities is that they teach their children to accept, internalize, and follow school rules of behavior and academic enterprise. Immigrant parents and communities seem to emphasize for their children the importance of acquiring job-related skills, proficiency in the English language, and basic skills in reading, writing, and math. They also emphasize that to succeed in these things children must follow the advice of teachers, school counselors, and other school personnel about rules of behavior and standard practices for academic success.

The perceptions and responses of nonimmigrant minorities to educational problems are strikingly different. These minorities do not have the immigrants' dual frame of reference that leads to favorable evaluation of the segregated and inferior education they *think* they are receiving. They compare their education with the education of white children in the suburbs, a comparison in which they always find the latter to be "better" for no justifiable reason—except discrimination. Furthermore, nonimmigrants interpret their treatment by the public schools within the context of the overall enduring conflicts between them and white Americans and the institutions controlled by whites. Thus, Blacks interpret their initial exclusion from the public schools and subsequent segregated and inferior education as designed to prevent them from qualifying for desirable jobs. Consequently, Black Americans have devoted a considerable part of their "collective struggle" toward compelling whites and the schools they control to provide them with "equal" and "quality" education.

One result of the enduring conflicts is that Blacks appear to have developed a deep sense of distrust of the public schools. Blacks more or less believe that they cannot trust the public schools to educate Black children in the same way as they educate white children. We find a similar sense of distrust among American Indians and Mexican–Americans.

In the case of Black Americans the situation becomes more complicated because the public schools themselves appear to approach the education of Black children defensively—through control, paternalism, or "contest," all of which are strategies that seem to divert attention and effort from the task of educating children.

Still another consequence of the conflicts and distrust is that Blacks and other nonimmigrant minorities have more or less come to interpret school rules and practices differently than whites and immigrant minorities. The immigrants, as will be shown in the next section, tend to endorse school rules and practices, much in the same way that middle-class whites do, as necessary, desirable, and compatible with their educational goals. However, inner-city Blacks and other nonimmigrant minorities interpret these same rules and practices as impositions of white culture that do not necessarily meet their real educational needs. Furthermore, as we shall see, nonimmigrant minority children define school rules and practices as "white" and therefore not particularly acceptable to them.

Because of the conflicts and distrust that exist in the nonimmigrant minorities' relationship with the schools and school personnel, and because of skepticism over school rules and practices, it is probably more difficult for nonimmigrant minority parents and communities to teach their children to accept, internalize, and follow school rules and practices that lead to academic success and social adjustment in school. Furthermore, it is probably more difficult for the children, especially as they get older, to accept, internalize, and follow the rules than it is for immigrant minority children (Ogbu, 1984).

Cultural Frame of Reference and Schooling. Primary cultural/language differences cause educational problems for immigrants both in interpersonal and intergroup relations as well as in academic work. The problem in interpersonal and intergroup relations may be due to the fact that children from some cultural backgrounds begin school with cultural assumptions about how to relate to other children or how to relate to adults that are different from the assumptions of their fellow students from other cultures. They are also different from the assumptions of the school and teachers. For example, in Punjabi culture children are brought up to defer to adult authority, but when the Punjabi child goes to the public school he is expected and encouraged to defend his ideas if they are in conflict with those of the teacher. Another problem faced by the Punjabi child has to do with the relationship with members of the opposite sex. Punjabi children are brought up to avoid eye contact with members of the opposite sex. But in the public schools, Punjabi girls are expected to look directly at male teachers and male students and Punjabi boys to look directly at female teachers and female students when speaking in order to be considered polite. Children who come from cultures lacking adequate mathematical and other concepts, such as the Kpelle of Liberia, must learn the necessary concepts before they can learn how to do mathematics. These are only a few of the problems caused by primary cultural differences for immigrant minority children and for nonWestern children attending Western-type schools.

However, there are significant features of the primary cultural differences which help the immigrants to overcome their initial problems eventually, adjust socially, learn more or less successfully, and perform well academically. One factor is that since the cultural differences existed *before* the immigrants came to United States, they do not serve as boundary-maintaining mechanisms that are more or less oppositional to similar features in white American culture and in the culture of the schools controlled by whites.

Second, because the primary cultural differences are not oppositional, immigrants are able to form a cultural model of schooling which
helps them participate both in their own culture and in the cultures of
white Americans and the public schools selectively without fear of losing their culture, language, and identity. Basically, the immigrants develop a cultural model of schooling that may be called an "alternation
model" (Ogbu, 1984) or "accommodation without assimilation model"
(Gibson, 1983). The essential ingredient of this model is that the immigrants do not equate school and classroom rules of behavior and standard practices with the rules of behavior and standard practices of white
American culture. Nor do they interpret academic success as a symbol of
being white. Immigrants do not necessarily want to give up their own
culture, language, and identity or assimilate into the white culture. So
they make a clear distinction between adoption of attitudes, knowledge,
and behaviors that enhance academic success for future employment on
the one hand and adoption of attitudes, knowledge, and behaviors that
lead to loss of cultural identity and to assimilation into white American
culture on the other hand.

We can illustrate the immigrants' model of accommodation without assimilation by describing the situation of an American who wants
to go to Paris for vacation but does not yet speak French. He thinks that
in order to have a successful vacation in Paris one has to learn to speak
French. Therefore, the American starts to learn to speak French. In so
doing, the American knows that he or she is not giving up the native
language; does not want to give up the native language; and, most
importantly, does not think that he or she is giving up the native language. Instead, the American *thinks* that he or she is learning French as
an additional language because it is needed to accomplish a particular
objective; namely, to have a successful vacation in Paris. The process of
learning here is perceived, experienced, and interpreted as additive.

So it is with immigrant minorities learning English and other aspects of the school curriculum and social life. Because the immigrants
separate attitudes and behaviors that enhance school success from attitudes and behaviors that make people "white," they do not think or
feel that their social identity, culture, or language is threatened when
they conform to school rules. Consequently, there is almost no evidence
of immigrants experiencing social pressures against adoption or ex-
pression of attitudes and behaviors conducive to social adjustment and
academic success. Nor do individuals adopting such appropriate attitudes and behaviors experience "affective dissonance" due to the fear
of losing peer and community support while uncertain of being accepted
by white Americans. Rather, immigrant minority students are encouraged by their communities, parents, and peers to conform to formal

demands of the school and classrooms—or, as Gibson (1985) puts it for the Punjabis, to "do what you have to do to get a high school education" but not to adopt other aspects of white American culture that immigrants consider undesirable. This is the model of schooling that "works" for the immigrants.

A related factor is that immigrant minorities often perceive the cultural and language differences they encounter as barriers to be overcome in order to achieve their long-range goal of obtaining good school credentials for future employment. They do not, therefore, go to school expecting the schools to teach them in their own cultures and languages. Rather, they go to school expecting and willing to learn the new culture and language.

Finally, because primary cultural differences are often differences in content, the problems they cause for immigrants tend to be specific and thus can easily be identified through careful ethnographic research. This specificity and identifiability make it easier to develop appropriate educational policies, programs, and practices to eliminate or reduce the negative impact of cultural differences.

What kinds of problems do secondary cultural differences cause for the nonimmigrant minorities in school? Some of the problems appear to resemble those we have noted for immigrant minority children; others appear to be different. One example of a similar problem is the eye contact described earlier for the Punjabi children in Yuba City. A similar problem has been reported for Puerto Rican children in New York City. According to Byers and Byers (1972, p. 20), white American children are taught to look directly at an adult when they are being reprimanded; and it is considered both disrespectful and an admission of guilt to look away in such a situation. By contrast, Puerto Rican children are brought up to look down respectfully when being chastised. Because teachers are not familiar with Puerto Rican culture, they often see the behavior of Puerto Rican children as disrespectful or an admission of guilt. In this case a problem arises because what is considered polite behavior by Puerto Rican minority culture is considered rude by the dominant white culture.

The second example of problems caused by cultural miscommunication is found in the education of Indian children. Dumont (1972, p. 365) reports that Oglala Sioux children who are usually "noisy, bold, daring, and insatiably curious" outside the classrooms tend to remain almost totally unresponsive to teachers' questions. He says that the children do not respond to the teachers' questions because they come from a culture where communication is not organized and controlled by adults.

Still another example of problems caused by cultural differences in expectation is described for Indian children in an Indian reservation school in Oregon. According to Philips, there were differences in rules which guide the use of speech in the Indian community and those in use in the public schools. In school, where white teachers require Indian students to behave according to white ways, the children do poorly in their academic work. But in classrooms where Indian teachers allow the students to behave as Indians do in the community, the Indian children do better in their academic work.

A fourth example is taken from the study of native Hawaiians who did not perform well when they were in classrooms organized in a conventional manner. However, when the classroom activities were re-organized to fit the Hawaiian pattern, school performance improved. For example, native Hawaiian children had difficulty learning to read. But after anthropologists studied the culture of their community, the knowledge was used to reorganize reading activities, so that the social and communicative interactions would reflect those of the children's home and community. The reading lessons were reorganized to resemble "a talk story," which is a major speech event in Hawaiian culture. A talk story is a local term for a "rambling personal experience narrative mixed with folk materials" involving adults and children (Au, 1981). This change resulted in improvements in the children's reading.

In general, those who have studied the problems caused by cultural differences for nonimmigrants point to differences in assumptions about relationships, communication, and behaviors. And they generally stress differences in style of interaction, communication, thought, and so on. Secondary cultural differences do not merely cause initial problems in social adjustment and academic performance for nonimmigrant minority children; the problems caused by secondary cultural differences tend to persist. It is thus not easy for bearers of secondary cultural differences to cross cultural boundaries.

One reason is that secondary cultural differences developed initially as a part of boundary-maintaining and coping mechanisms for the minorities under domination and exploitation by white Americans. Therefore, secondary cultural differences are more or less oppositional to equivalent features in white culture.

Second, because secondary cultural differences are oppositional and are closely associated with the sense of social identity and security among minorities, they tend to develop a cultural model of schooling which makes it difficult for them to participate in some aspects of the culture of white Americans and the culture of the public schools. Essentially, the nonimmigrants' model of schooling may be called a linear acculturation model, an assimilation model, or a displacement/replacement model. Minorities who have this model tend to equate school rules and practices that enhance academic achievement with the norms and cultural practices of white American culture; i.e., with the culture of their "oppressors" or "enemy." They define school knowledge as "white" knowledge, not that of the minorities; and they tend to interpret academic success as a symbol of being "white" or having successfully "acted white."

Because nonimmigrant minorities who subscribe to the displacement/replacement model of schooling do not make a clear distinction between the rules and practices that enhance academic success and the rules of behavior and practices of the white culture, they think and fear that adopting school norms will "displace" their own minority cultural norms and behavior practices, language and identity, and replace these with white norms, white behaviors, and white language and identity. Public school learning in the context of this model is thus a displacement/subtractive and replacement process: Adoption of school norms and standard behavior practices is to "act white."

There are, of course, social pressures against "acting white" both at school and in minority communities. Individuals who adopt attitudes and behaviors that enhance academic success or who are actually doing well in school are ridiculed and criticized by their peers as "acting white" or as "thinking they are white." Their peers apply discouraging pressures on them by calling them names like "Uncle Toms" (Petroni, 1970), "brainiacs" (Fordham, 1985; Fordham & Ogbu, 1986), or "gringos" (Matute–Bianchi, 1986), and by excluding them from peer activities. Family and community members also participate unknowingly in the social pressures against adopting the attitudes and behaviors that enhance academic success. For example, family and community people tend to make uncomplimentary comments about "talking proper" when a minority child is speaking standard English at home and in the community rather than using ethnic dialect. There is a psychological pressure in the form of "affective dissonance" against adoption of appropriate academic attitudes and behaviors. The individual student may be unwilling to adopt attitudes and behaviors that promote school success or to excel academically for fear of peer criticism and loss of peer support, and from a genuine belief that her actions may actually constitute "acting white." The nonimmigrant minorities' model of schooling creates a choice dilemma for minority students: If students accept the assimilation model of "acting white," they may indeed succeed academically but suffer peer criticism or ostracism as well as suffer from affective dissonance. If, on the other hand, students reject the assimilation model by refusing to act white, they will likely not do well in school because they will reject the attitudes and behaviors that enhance academic success. *The dilemma is that nonimmigrant minority students have to choose between academic success and maintaining their minority identity and cultural frame of reference.*

There is some evidence that reluctance and opposition to act white in the school context begins in elementary school and becomes more prevalent and stronger as children approach adolescence. This finding was reported in ethnographic studies of Indian students (Dumont, 1972; Philips, 1972, 1983), Black students (Fordham, 1985; Fordham & Ogbu, 1986; Petroni, 1970), and Mexican–American students (Matute–Bianchi, 1986). These studies suggest that the students come to school "resisting" the rules and standard practices of the classroom.

Under this circumstance, nonimmigrant students who want to succeed academically tend to adopt strategies that shield them from peer criticisms and ostracism. One strategy is to engage also in other activities that minorities define as appropriate for minority students. In the case of Black students, these include athletic and other team-oriented activities defined as "Black." Engaging in athletic and team-oriented activities is particularly important for Black male students who want to succeed academically (Fordham, 1985; Petroni, 1970). Another strategy that works for Black students is to camouflage success by assuming the role of a comedian or jester (Fordham, 1984, 1985; Ogbu, 1981b). By acting foolishly, the jester is able to cope with the pressures of school achievement and peers who do not endorse his striving for academic success. Still another strategy is for the student who wants to succeed to engage the services or protection of a "bully" in exchange for helping the latter with homework. In general, academically successful Black students should avoid bragging about their academic achievement (Fordham & Ogbu, 1986).

Another reason the problem of low academic achievement persists is that the nonimmigrants do not appear to interpret the cultural and language differences they encounter in school as barriers to be overcome but rather as markers or symbols of group identity to be maintained. They thus may "resist" adoption of school ways and insist on maintaining their ethnic or community attitudes, beliefs, and cultural practices. This is evident in the several examples of "problems" caused by secondary cultural differences described earlier. For example, a lack of fluency in standard English may be interpreted by nonimmigrant minorities as a sign of not being "white," rather than as a barrier to be overcome in order to learn to read well.

Finally, secondary cultural differences appear to be more diffuse and less specific when compared with primary cultural differences and so are the problems they cause in school. As noted before, secondary cultural differences tend to be manifested more in terms of "style" and "meaning" than content. These include differences in cognitive style (Ramirez & Castenada, 1974; Shade, 1982), communication style (Gumperz, 1981; Kochman, 1981), interaction style (Erickson & Mohatt, 1982), and learning style (Boykin, 1986; Philips, 1983). Because the differences are largely stylistic, and because the elements of opposition and ambivalence to white American culture are so prominent, it is more difficult to eliminate the problems created by secondary cultural differences through conventional programs that focus on content differences.

Summary

The barriers that arise from cultural and language differences, identity, inadequate opportunity structure, and community–school relations are an important cause of the difficulties experienced by minority children in social adjustment and academic performance in the public schools. But they do not explain why immigrant minorities do relatively well while nonimmigrant minorities perform poorly. The explanation of poor performance we have explored in this section lies in the differences in the way that immigrant and nonimmigrant minorities perceive, interpret, and respond to educational barriers because of their different histories and because of their different interpretations of and responses to their treatment by white Americans and white-controlled institutions.

Some immigrants brought with them certain cultural resources that encourage school success in America, such as the traditional respect for and value of education as a means for social mobility among the Chinese. But the immigrants may also bring other cultural resources that can discourage school success, such as the learning style of the Chinese that emphasizes external forms and rote memorization rather than observation, analysis, and comprehension expected in the public school; a language, such as Chinese language, that is very different from English; and an authority structure of the family, such as that found among the Chinese and Punjabi immigrants, which discourages socialization of children for independence and autonomy. But whatever positive or negative resources the immigrants bring to the United States, ethnographic studies suggest that situational factors associated with their immigrant status appear largely to generate perceptions and responses that enhance school success (Ogbu, 1983, p. 190).

For the nonimmigrant minorities, however, things are different. The fact that nonimmigrant minorities did not voluntarily become a part of U.S. society in order to achieve wealth, opportunity, and political freedom produces a different set of situational factors that generate perceptions and responses incompatible with school success. Figure 1 depicts the initial involuntary incorporation and subsequent treatment of nonimmigrant minorities which caused them to develop a pattern of responses that eventually formed their overall social reality; i.e., their cultural model or folk system. The nonimmigrant minorities developed survival strategies to cope with economic, political, and social exploita-

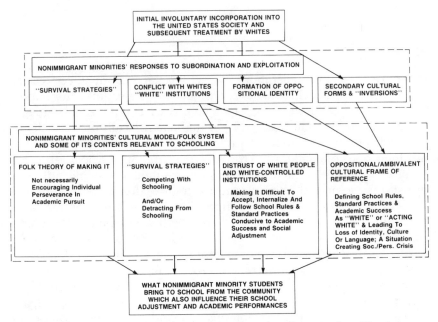

FIGURE 1: Involuntary incorporation of nonimmigrant minorities into American society.

tion. This development in turn shaped their theory of how to get ahead in American society, a theory that does not encourage academic learning and perseverance. The survival strategies also appear to be in competition with schooling. The persisting conflict between nonimmigrant minorities and white people, as well as white-controlled institutions, resulted in deep distrust of white people and the public schools, a development that makes it difficult for the minorities to accept and follow school rules and standard practices. Finally, the coping mechanisms or secondary cultural features developed by nonimmigrant minorities, together with their collective oppositional identity, led them to develop a cultural frame of reference that is in opposition to the white cultural frame of reference. In the minorities' cultural frame of reference, school rules, standard practices, and even academic success are defined as "white" or "acting white." And because they are so defined, they are not socially acceptable—at least not without some social and personal costs. These factors exist in nonimmigrant minority communities and are learned in varying degrees by minority children. They form an important part of the cultural knowledge and competence that the children bring to school and that in turn influence their school adjustment, learning, and performance—adversely.

POLICY IMPLICATIONS

Prerequisites

Three preliminary considerations will set the stage for my policy recommendations. First, principals and teachers must recognize the importance of what children bring to school: Their culture and language, which may be different from those of the majority culture; their identities, their perceptions and interpretations of the opportunity structure; and their perceptions and interpretations of minority-school relations. All of these factors influence the minority student's academic attitudes and efforts. Second, the schools must recognize that there are different kinds of minorities who are not affected in the same way by the same community and school factors. Third, both immigrant and nonimmigrant minorities face real external barriers that cause educational problems. Real improvements in the educational efforts and achievement of these minorities will come from continued and sustained efforts in school and society to undo the barriers that face all minorities or particular minorities. Effective educational reform for low-achieving minorities, in short, will require more than patching up assumed children's past and present "deficiencies."

Recommendations for Nonimmigrant Minorities

A comparative study leads to two related conclusions about the low school performance of nonimmigrant minority children. One is that a major reason for their low academic success is that they do not maintain serious academic attitudes and do not work hard or persevere in their schoolwork. In fact, nonimmigrant minority students could be characterized by what may be termed a "low-effort syndrome." The second conclusion is that this low-effort syndrome is due, in part, to several "community forces," including folk theories of "making it," interpretations of and responses to the job ceiling and related barriers to opportunity, conflict with and distrust of the public schools, and oppositional identities and cultural frame of reference (see Figure 1).

To improve the school performance of nonimmigrant minority students requires changing the students' inadequate and inappropriate academic attitudes and efforts—their low-effort syndrome—by addressing the community factors that generate them. Dealing effectively with community factors will require serious and sustained efforts to eliminate the broader societal forces which, in turn, generate and sustain the community factors.

Reduction of Societal Barriers, Sources of Conflict, and Other Community Factors

Since Brown v. Board of Education in 1954, public schools have been given a major role in America's attempt to break its historical pattern of discrimination against minorities and move toward a society of equal opportunity. The schools have played this role well, and there have in fact been major changes in both school and society over the past three decades. Blacks in particular have made impressive gains in politics, business, and education. There is now a substantial middle class within most ethnically distinct minorities, the wage gap has been closed somewhat, and test scores of minority children have improved relative to those of whites. Even so, even a cursory examination of special education enrollments, unemployment rates, poverty rates, out-of-wedlock birthrates, housing patterns, and similar social and economic indicators reveals that American society has eliminated neither its historical tendency to discriminate against minorities nor the effects of that discrimination.

In the face of this improving but still serious problem of American society, both the society at large and the schools must continue on the course set in motion more than three decades ago. American society must continue tough enforcement action to eliminate job, housing, and other discrimination. It is not common for dominant-group members of a society to give up discriminating against minorities voluntarily; therefore, it is important to continue vigorous civil rights activities to achieve these objectives.

The schools, for their part, must stand against even a hint of discrimination in hiring, firing, and promotions; they must do everything possible to promote understanding among ethnically diverse groups of students; and they must continue to address the problem of low achievement among minorities, even when the evidence of success is minimal. The values and practices of society will continue to change, albeit slowly, when those of its major public institution for children are clear.

Teaching Nonimmigrant Minority Students How to go to School

Ethnographic studies show that many nonimmigrant minority students do not know how to go to school and do not understand how the process of schooling is connected with the job market. Thus, the schools should ensure that beginning during the elementary grades students are taught to understand and practice the skills and strategies that have helped nonminority students succeed.

Two programs whose descriptions come closest to the approach envisioned in this recommendation are Marva Collins's school program in Chicago (CBS News, 1979) and Jesse Jackson's Program EXCEL (Cole, 1977). Marva Collins's approach has, according to reports, been successful in helping inner-city Black students understand that if they want to "go out into the world and command a job" after finishing school—which nearly all say they want to do—they must be capable and qualified. Collins' approach is explicit in defining capable and qualified to include proficiency in spoken and written English, spelling, math skills, and so forth. The children are made to understand, furthermore, that they need credentials to get good jobs and to get credentials they must learn to work hard, especially by doing their homework every night. With unambiguous goals and standards, and with parents' support, Marva Collins is said to teach inner-city children successfully how to learn and how to cross cultural and language boundaries successfully. Others can do the same.

Devise and Implement Programs to Increase Trusting Relations with Schools and School Personnel

Periodic conferences should be held in local school districts between the minority community and the schools. At the conference each side—the public school system and the minority community—should discuss its understanding of the educational problems or needs of minority children, its ideas of how to meet those needs, its responsibility in meeting the needs, and how the two sides can work together. Trusting relations will increase through open discussion of differences in the understanding of the educational needs and processes, areas of common interest and agreement, the responsibilities of each side, and how the two sides can work together. The school system should communicate the results of the conference to teachers and other school personnel and encourage their implementation, while minority participants should be responsible for letting community people know the outcomes of the conference and for encouraging their acceptance and implementation. Increased understanding and trusting relations growing out of such conferences will eventually affect what minority families and communities communicate to their children about the public schools and school personnel and how the children perceive and respond to the schools and school personnel.

Teach Nonimmigrant Minorities to Adopt a Cultural Model of Schooling Similar to the Model that "Works" for Immigrants

The first step toward helping nonimmigrant minority students adopt a more pragmatic view of schooling and increase their academic efforts without experiencing negative social pressure from peers is to make them aware of the nature and consequences of the low-effort syndrome. Current awareness programs for minority students tend to emphasize discovering racial and ethnic identities and pride. This is fine but not enough. It is not enough for nonimmigrant minority children to discover who they are or that they have their own racial or ethnic culture, language, and identity if the discovery reinforces the tendency to equate school learning with assimilation into white culture.

The next thing that should be done to help nonimmigrant minority students avoid the choice between cultures in the school context is to help them understand and adopt the immigrant minorities' model of *accommodation without assimilation, i.e., alternation model.*

The Role of the Community in Improving Academic Attitudes and Efforts

The communities of nonimmigrant minority children can play an important part in helping children improve their academic attitudes and efforts. The most important contribution communities can make is to help children differentiate the attitudes and behaviors that enhance academic success from the attitudes and behaviors that result in loss of ethnic identity and culture or that lead to linear acculturation. From our comparative study of minority cultures it appears that nonimmigrant communities themselves are implicated in defining certain attitudes and behaviors that lead to success as "white," not "Black," "Indian," or "Mexican–American." Minority communities must recognize that this attitude is part of the problem; they must then change the explicit and implicit messages they send to their children.

Minority communities can also help children channel their time and efforts from nonacademic activities into academic activities. One suggestion might be for the communities to sanction, rather than merely verbalize their wishes for, appropriate academic attitudes and persevering efforts as culturally rewarded phenomena. For example, the communities should provide their young people with concrete evidence that they approve, appreciate, and reward academic success in the same manner and to the same degree that they approve, appreciate, and reward success in fields such as athletics, sports, and entertainment.

REFERENCES

Ashmore, H. S. (1954). *The Negro and the schools.* Chapel Hill: University of North Carolina Press.

Au, K. H. (1981). Participant structure in a reading lesson with Hawaiian children: Analysis of a culturally appropriate instructional event. *Anthropology & Education Quarterly, 11,* 91–115.

Ausubel, D. (1964). How reversible are cognitive and motivational effects of cultural deprivation? Implications for teaching the culturally deprived. *Urban Education, 1,* 16–39.

Baratz, J. (1970). Teaching reading in an urban Negro school system. In F. Williams (Ed.), *Language and poverty: Perspectives on a theme* (pp. 11–24). Chicago: Markham.

Baugh, J. (1983). *Black street speech: Its history, structure, and survival.* Austin: University of Texas Press.

Berkeley Unified School District. (1985). *An equal education for all: The challenge ahead.* A report to the Berkeley Board of Education by the Task Force on School Achievement. Berkeley, CA: Department of Research and Evaluation.

Berrueta–Clement, J., Schweinhart, L. J., Barnett, W. S., Epstein, A. S., & Weikart, D. P. (1984). *Changed lives: The effects of the Perry Preschool Program on youths through age 19.* Ypsilanti, MI: High/Scope.

Bloom, B. S., Davis, A., & Hess, R. D. (Eds.). (1965). *Compensatory education for cultural deprivation.* New York: Holt, Rinehart, & Winston.

Bond, H. M. (1966). *The education of the Negro in the American social order.* New York: Octagon.

Bond, H. M. (1969). *Negro education in Albama: A study in cotton and steel.* New York: Atheneum.

Bontemps, A. (1969). *Personal communication.* Summer Workshop on Afro-American History and Culture, University of California, Los Angeles.

Boyer, E. L. (1983). *High School: A report on secondary education in America.* New York: Harper & Row.

Boykin, A. W. (1980, November). *Reading achievement and the social/cultural frame of reference of Afro-American children.* Paper presented at the National Institute of Education Roundtable Discussion on Issues in Urban Reading, Washington, DC.

Boykin, A. W. (1986). The triple quandary and the schooling of Afro-American children. In U. Neisser (Ed.), *The school achievement of minority children: New perspectives* (pp. 57–92). Hillsdale, NJ: Erlbaum.

Brown, P. R., & Haycock, K. (1984). *Excellence for whom? A report from the planning committee for the Achievement Council.* Oakland, CA: Achievement Council.

Byers, P., & Byers, H. (1972). Non-verbal communication and the education of children. In C. B. Cazden et al. (Eds.), *Functions of language in the classroom* (pp. 3–31). New York: Teachers College Press.

Castile, G. P., & Kushner, G. (1981). *Persistent peoples: Cultural enclaves in perspective.* Tucson: University of Arizona Press.

CBS News, Inc. (1979). "Marva." November 11, 1979.

CBS News, Inc. (1984). The Rosewood Massacre. *60 Minutes, 16*(47), pp. 16–22.

Clark, K. B. (1965). *Dark ghetto: Dilemma of social power.* New York: Harper.

Clement, D. C., Eisenhart, M., & Wood, J. W. (1976). School desegregation and educational inequality: Trends in the literature, 1960–1975. In National Institute of Education (Ed.), *The desegregation literature: A critical appraisal* (pp. 1–77). Washington, DC: U.S. Government Printing Office.

Cole, R. W. (1977). Black Moses: Jesse Jackson's push for excellence. *Phi Delta Kappan, 58*(5), 378–388.

Coleman, J. S., et al. (1966). *Equality of educational opportunity.* Washington, DC: U.S. Government Printing Office.

Cook–Gumperz, J., & Gumperz, J. J. (1979). From oral to written culture: The transition to literacy. In M. F. Whiteman (Ed.), *Variation in writing.* Hillsdale, NJ: Erlbaum.

Darlington, R. B. (1986). Long-term effects of preschool programs. In U. Neisser (Ed.), *The school achievement of minority children: New perspectives* (pp. 159–167). Hillsdale, NJ: Erlbaum.

Deutsch, M. (1967). *The disadvantaged child.* New York: Basic Books.

DeVos, G. A. (1967). Essential elements of caste: Psychological determinants in structural theory. In G. A. DeVos & H. Wagatsuma (Eds.), *Japan's invisible race: Caste in culture and personality* (pp. 332–384). Berkeley: University of California Press.

DeVos, G. A. (1984, April). *Ethnic persistence and role degradation: An illustration from Japan.* Paper presented at the American–Soviet Symposium on Contemporary Ethnic Processes in the USA and the USSR, New Orleans.

Dumont, R. V., Jr. (1972). Learning English and how to be silent: Studies in Sioux and Cherokee classrooms. In C. B. Cazden (Ed.), *Functions of language in the classroom* (pp. 344–369). New York: Teachers College Press.

Durham, J. T. (1972). Who needs it? Compensatory education. In R. R. Heidenreich (Ed.), *Urban Education* (rev. ed., pp. 5–10). Arlington, VA: College Readings.

Edmonds, R. (1986). Characteristics of effective schools. In U. Neisser (Ed.), *The school achievement of minority children: New perspectives* (pp. 93–104). Hillsdale, NJ: Erlbaum.

Erickson, F., & Mohatt, J. (1982). Cultural organization of participant structure in two classrooms of Indian students. In G. D. Spindler (Ed.), *Doing the ethnography of schooling: Educational anthropology in action* (pp. 132–174). New York: Holt.

Fairfax County Public Schools. (1985). *Annual report on the achievement and aspirations of minority students in the Fairfax County Public Schools, 1984–85.* Fairfax, VA: Author, Office of Research.

Farber, B., & Lewis, M. (1972). Compensatory education and social justice. In R. R. Heidenreich (Ed.), *Urban Education* (rev. ed., pp. 47–57). Arlington, VA: College Reading.

Fordham, S. (1984, November). *Ethnography in a black high school: Learning not to be a native.* Paper presented at the 83rd annual meeting of the American Anthropological Association, Denver.

Fordham, S. (1985). *Black student school success as related to fictive kinship* (Final Report). Washington, DC: National Institute of Education.

Fordham, S., & Ogbu, J. U. (1986). Black students' school success: Coping with the "burden of 'acting white'." *Urban Review, 18*(3), 1–31.

Gay, J., & Cole, M. (1967). *The new mathematics and an old culture: A study of learning among the Kpelle of Liberia.* New York: Holt.

Gibson, M. A. (1976). Approaches to multicultural education in the United States: Some concepts and assumptions. *Anthropology & Education Quarterly, 7,* 7–18.

Gibson, M. A. (1983). *Home–school–community linkages: A study of educational equity for Punjabi youths* (Final Report). Washington, DC: National Institute of Education.

Gibson, M. A. (1985). *Playing by the rules*. Paper presented at the 84th annual meeting of the American Anthropological Association, Washington, DC.

Gittell, M. (1976). School desegregation and the courts. *Social Policy, 6*(4), 36–41.

Goldberg, M. L. (1971). Socio-psychological issues in the education of the disadvantaged. In A. H. Passow (Ed.), *Urban education in the 1970s* (pp. 61–93). New York: Teachers College Press.

Goodlad, J. I. (1983). *A place called school: Prospects for the future*. New York: McGraw–Hill.

Gottfried, N. W. (1973). Effects of early intervention programs. In K. S. Miller & R. M. Dreger (Eds.), *Comparative studies of blacks and whites* (pp. 273–293). New York: Seminar Press.

Green, V. (1981). Blacks in the United States: The creation of an enduring people? In G. P. Castile & G. Kushner (Eds.), *Persistent peoples: Cultural enclaves in perspective* (pp. 69–77). Tucson: University of Arizona Press.

Gumperz, J. J. (1981). Conversational inferences and classroom learning. In J. Green & C. Wallat (Eds.), *Ethnographic approaches to face-to-face interaction* (pp. 3–23). Norwood, NJ: Ablex.

Hanna, J. L. (1985). *Understanding and coping with disruptive behavior in America: Like me, meddle me in a desegregated school*. College Park, MD: University of Maryland, unpublished manuscript.

Hannerz, U. (1969). *Soulside*. New York: Columbia University Press.

Hess, G. A. (1985, December). *Educational triangle: Elite schools, holding pens, and dropouts*. Paper presented at the meeting of the American Anthropological Association, Washington, DC.

Hispanic Policy Development Project. (1984). *Make something happen: Hispanics and urban high school reform* (12 vols.). New York: Author.

Holt, G. S. (1972). "Inversion" in black communication. In T. Kochman (Ed.), *Rappin' and stylin' out: Communication in urban black America* (pp. 189–204). Chicago: University of Illinois Press.

Hunt, J. McV. (1964). The psychological basis for using preschool enrichment as an antidote for cultural deprivation. *Merrill–Palmer Quarterly, 1*, 209–249.

Hunt, J. McV. (1969). *The challenge of incompetence and poverty: Papers on the role of early education*. Urbana: University of Illinois Press.

Keil, C. (1977). The expressive black male role: The bluesman. In D. Wilkinson & R. L. Taylor (Eds.), *The black male in America today: Perspectives on his status in contemporary society* (pp. 60–84). Chicago: Nelson–Hall.

Kluger, R. (1977). *Simple justice*. New York: Vintage Books.

Kochman, T. (1981). *Black and white styles in conflict*. Chicago: University of Chicago Press.

Lazar, I., Darlington, R., Murray, H., Royce, J., & Snipper, A. (1982). Lasting effects of early education. *Monographs of the Society for Research in Child Development, 47*, (1–2, Serial No. 194).

Levine, L. W. (1977). *Black culture and black consciousness: Afro-American folk thought from slavery to freedom*. New York: Oxford University Press.

LeVine, R. A. (1967). *Dreams and deeds: Achievement motivation in Nigeria*. Chicago: University of Chicago Press.

Lewis, D. K. (1976). The black family: Socialization and sex roles. *Phylon, 36*, 221–237.

Matute–Bianchi, M. E. (1986). *Ethnic identities and patterns of school success and failure among Mexican-descent and Japanese American students in a California high school: An ethnographic analysis*. Oak College, University of California at Santa Cruz, unpublished manuscript.

McNett, I. (1984). *Charting a course: A guide to the excellence movement in education.* Washington, DC: Council for Basic Education.

Montgomery County Public Schools. (1983). *A study of children at-risk: A report by the citizen's minority relations monitoring committee.* Montgomery County, MD: Board of Education.

Ogbu, J. U. (1974). *The next generation: An ethnography of education in an urban neighborhood.* New York: Academic Press.

Ogbu, J. U. (1977). Racial stratification and education: The case of Stockton, California. *ICRD Bulletin, 12*(3), 1–26.

Ogbu, J. U. (1978). *Minority education and caste: The American system in cross-cultural perspective.* New York: Academic Press.

Ogbu, J. U. (1979a). Desegregation, integration and interaction theory: An appraisal. In M. L. Wax (Ed.), *Desegregated schools: An intimate portrait based on five ethnographic studies* (pp. 84–103). Washington, DC: National Institute of Education.

Ogbu, J. U. (1979b). Social stratification and socialization of competence. *Anthropology & Education Quarterly, 10*(1), 3–20.

Ogbu, J. U. (1981a). Origins of human competence: A cultural-ecological perspective. *Child Development, 52,* 413–429.

Ogbu, J. U. (1981b). Societal forces as a context of ghetto children's school failure. In L. Feagans & D. C. Farran (Eds.), *The language of children reared in poverty: Implications for evaluation and intervention* (pp. 117–138). New York: Academic Press.

Ogbu, J. U. (1981c). *Schooling in the ghetto: A cultural-ecological perspective on community and home influences.* Washington, D.C.: National Institute of Education.

Ogbu, J. U. (1982a). Socialization:A cultural-ecological approach. In K. M. Borman (Ed.), *The social life of children in a changing society* (pp. 253–267). Hillsdale, NJ: Erlbaum.

Ogbu, J. U. (1982b). Cultural discontinuities and schooling. *Anthropology & Education Quarterly, 13*(4), 290–307.

Ogbu, J. U. (1983). Minority status and schooling in plural societies. *Comparative Education Review, 27*(2), 169–190.

Ogbu, J. U. (1984). *Understanding community forces affecting minority students' academic effort.* Oakland, CA: Achievement Council, unpublished manuscript.

Ogbu, J. U. (1985). A cultural ecology of competence among inner-city blacks. In M. B. Spencer, G. K. Brookins, & W. R. Allen (Eds.), *Beginnings: The Social and affective development of black children* (pp. 45–66). Hillsdale, NJ: Erlbaum.

Ogbu, J. U. (in press). Variability in minority responses to schooling: Nonimmigrants vs. immigrants. In G. D. Spindler (Ed.), *Education and cultural process.* Hillsdale, NJ: Erlbaum.

Passow, A. H. (Ed.). (1971). *Urban education in the 1970's.* New York: Teachers College Press.

Passow, A. H. (1984, December). *Equity and excellence: Confronting the dilemma.* Paper presented at the First International Conference on Education in the 1990's, Tel Aviv, Israel.

Petroni, F. A. (1970). "Uncle Toms": White stereotypes in the black movement. *Human Organization, 29*(4), 260–266.

Philips, S. U. (1972). Participant structure and communicative competence: Warm Springs children in community and classrooms. In C. B. Cazden, V. P. John, & D. Hymes (Eds.), *Functions of language in the classroom* (pp. 370–394). New York: Teachers College Press.

Philips, S. U. (1976). Commentary: Access to power and maintenance of ethnic identity as goals of multicultural education. *Anthropology & Education Quarterly, 7*(4), 30–32.

Philips, S. U. (1983). *The invisible culture: Communication in classrooms and community on the Warm Springs Indian Reservation.* New York: Longmans.

Ramirez, M., & Castenada, A. (1974). *Cultural democracy, bicognitive development and education.* New York: Academic Press.

Rees, H. E. (1968). *Deprivation and compensatory education: A consideration.* Boston: Houghton Mifflin.

Schofield, J. W. (1982). *Black and white in school: Trust, tension, or tolerance?* New York: Praeger.

Schweinhart, L. J., & Weikart, D. P. (1980). *Young children grow up: The effects of the Perry Preschool Programs on youths through age 15.* Ypsilanti, MI: High/Scope.

Scribner, S., & Cole, M. (1973). Cognitive consequences of formal and informal education. *Science, 182,* 553–559.

Shade, B. J. (1982). *Afro-American patterns of cognition.* Madison, WI: Center for Educational Research, unpublished manuscript.

Simons, H. (1979). Black dialect, reading interference, and classroom interaction. In L. B. Resnick & P. A. Weaver (Eds.), *Theory and practice of early reading* (Vol. 3, pp. 111–129). Hillsdale, NJ: Erlbaum.

Spicer, E. H. (1966). The process of cultural enclavement in middle America. *36th Congress of Internacional de Americanistas, Seville, 3,* 267–279.

———. (1971). Persistent cultural systems: A comparative study of identity systems that can adapt to contrasting environments. *Science, 174,* 795–800.

Stanley, J. C. (Ed.). (1973). *Compensatory education for children, ages 2 to 8: Recent studies of educational intervention.* Baltimore, MD: Johns Hopkins University Press.

Suarez–Orozco, M. (1985, May). *Opportunity, family dynamics and achievement: The socio-cultural context of motivation among recent immigrants from Central America.* Paper presented at the University of California Symposium on Linguistic Minorities and Education, Tahoe City, CA.

Suarez–Orozco, M. (1986). *In pursuit of a dream: New Hispanic immigrants in American schools.* Unpublished doctoral dissertation, Department of Anthropology, University of California, Berkeley.

U.S. Commission on Civil Rights. (1967). *Racial isolation in the public schools: A report* (Vol. 1). Washington, DC: U.S. Government Printing Office.

U.S. Senate, Select Committee. (1972). *Report: Toward equal educational opportunity.* Washington, DC: U.S. Government Printing Office.

Seven

An Issue of Survival: Education of Gifted Children

JAMES J. GALLAGHER

The education of gifted students (those who develop more rapidly their ability to *reason, comprehend, evaluate,* and *remember* than their age peers) has been a topic of periodic concern in American education. That concern seems to be expressed most urgently when the nation is worried about its strength or influence in the world.

American public education has long been struggling with two important goals: to create an environment in which excellence of teaching and learning can take place, and to create a learning environment in which every student has a right to maximize his or her own capabilities. Almost three decades ago, Gardner (1961) asked the question, "Can we be equal and excellent, too?" We are still struggling to find ways to answer "yes" to that question since both goals are important to us. The extensive development of professional schools and postgraduate education indicate our concern for *excellence,* while our commitments to universal education and school desegregation show our interest in *equity.*

How does *universal education* provide a special problem for gifted students? It creates a situation in many classrooms where the range of ability and performance can be very great, particularly in a diverse culture such as the United States. In a typical sixth grade, performance can range from a second-grade level to high school level of performance (Gallagher, 1985). To ask a teacher to provide a maximum education for the most advanced student, and for the most delayed student, and all those in between, is an educational task that we would not think of imposing on other instructors concerned with excellence. For example:

1. Would we expect the most gifted of violin students to attain the best development of his or her talents when the teacher has to teach a

group of fellow students how to bow so as to not sound like an alley full of cats?

2. Would we expect the most talented of golfing students to mature and improve his or her skills to a championship level when the golf instructor has to teach some beginning golfers how to avoid poison ivy in the woods?

3. Would we expect the most brilliant mathematics student to get the maximum education from a teacher who has to teach a group of fellow students how to add and subtract?

The intuitive answer to all of these questions has to be "no." Conscientious teachers have to cope with those students who are not achieving well, or even up to standard. While they may look wistfully at the brilliant student sitting patiently, waiting for something stimulating to happen, they are not often in a position to devote their full attention to them. The students labeled as gifted have often expressed themselves on this situation quite eloquently (Delisle, 1984):

- Well, some kids may disagree, but I think we should have more work and harder work, because what is the use of being gifted if there's nothing to be gifted about? (p. 65)
- School is boring when we review things I know by heart. (p. 78)
- I read a book or try to look interested. (I want to be an actress when I grow up, so this is good practice.) (p. 82)
- I like making things, not watching things be made. (p. 59)

Most observers would agree that issues dealing with gifted children are staging a minor revival on the local, state, and federal scene. Once again, as in the 1960s, we hear plaintive cries about our problems in teaching mathematics and science (Coleman & Selby, 1983). The cry for excellence is once more heard throughout the land, and excellence, by its very nature, throws a spotlight on gifted children. The fundamental question for policymakers and special educators is whether they can take advantage of that interest and establish solid programs before the public's interest is distracted again.

IN THE NATIONAL INTEREST

The profusion of reports on the current sorry state of American education (see Chapter 1, this volume) usually refers to the competitive status of the United States on the world scene. *A Nation at Risk*, published by the National Commission on Excellence in Education (1983), states:

If an unfriendly foreign power had attempted to impose on America the mediocre educational performance that exists today, we might well have viewed it as an act of war. We have even squandered the gains in student achievement made in the wake of the Sputnik challenge. Moreover, we have dismantled essential support systems which helped make those gains possible. We have, in effect, been committing an act of unthinking unilateral educational disarmament. (p. 5)

It should not be surprising that other cultures would experience a similar conflict. Gallagher (1984) drew a distinction between two political philosophies that are represented in most modern societies and which have an impact on educational programs for gifted students. The conflict is whether the greater emphasis in a society should be placed on *production and accomplishment*, or whether the emphasis should be on the *equitable distribution* of the society's resources. If the focus is on *production*, then gifted students and their full development become an important aspect of the educational and cultural program of that society. Taiwan (Wu, 1983), China (Butler, 1983), and the Soviet Union (Brickman, 1979) all represent societies that place an emphasis on production and accomplishment, despite a theoretical commitment to equal distribution of resources. This allows such cultures to emphasize special programs and special schools for gifted and talented students as a means of developing the intellectual talent desired in those societies.

Similar programs are identified in Israel, a nation facing manifest crisis and threat, and therefore committed to the full development of its intellectual resources (Bitan, 1976; Butler–Por, 1983; Landau, 1979; Smilansky & Nevo, 1975). On the other hand, cultures that do not find themselves under serious or direct threat often stress equity and consequently emphasize the support of programs helping those students who are less favored or who have fewer opportunities. These are illustrated by Australia (Larsson, 1981), France (Terrassier, 1981), and Sweden (Husén, 1974).

The wide diversity of cultural values and views in the United States suggests that both production and equity are brought into play in various communities under sometimes conflicting educational objectives. As we view world problems in the near future—international conflicts, hunger, population explosion, pollution—our society should be vitally interested in the conservation of intellectual resources.

The rationale for special resource allocations for programs for the gifted rests upon a different foundation from that for other areas of exceptional children. In the case of children who are deaf, mentally retarded, learning disabled, or with a variety of other special problems, the concept of *vertical equity* describes the underlying social value that provides the rationale for special programming. *Vertical equity* means the *unequal treatment of unequals in order to make them more equal.* Through the acceptance and support of state and federal programs for handicapped children, the society has shown its willingness to endorse that value.

Support for programs for gifted children rests upon societal self-interest as well as personal fairness. In the 1960s a major spurt of interest was clearly tied to fear of Russian space domination (Goodlad, 1964). The current surge of concern centers on the economic challenge being presented to the United States from a variety of countries. The argument is presented as follows:

1. Other countries have proven their ability to compete successfully with the United States in technological areas where we have previously been superior.
2. Our limited labor power and high standard of living puts us at a potential disadvantage in future competition.
3. We need to develop the most advanced of our creative skills so that we can, through design and invention, continue to be leaders in economic development.
4. We can accomplish this end only by providing an excellent education to the best of our students; current evidence would lead us to believe that we are falling far short of these goals.

One such indication is the average mathematics scores for eighth-grade students across 14 different countries (Figure 1). This and similar international comparisons usually show the United States near the bottom. Coleman (1984) reports that U.S. inferiority continues even when one compares only the top 1% of students in several cultures.

Although there is an urgency in the country for improving general standards of educational excellence, there is a special need for providing the most capable of our students the best educational experience we can, since it is this group that will originate many of the major innovations and creative advances that will spur America's resurgence.

We can all agree that a nation aspiring to be a major factor in world technology will not be successful if it provides a rich education for only a thin minority of its citizens—a well-educated, elite, leadership group—while the majority of the society is composed of semiskilled or unskilled workers. The modern technological engine is driven by scientists, economists, engineers, teachers, bankers, businessmen, artists, professors, doctors, etc. Without these persons to provide the needed support systems, no leader, no matter how brilliant, will be able to bring society forward.

In this chapter we will be concerned with the answer to the questions:

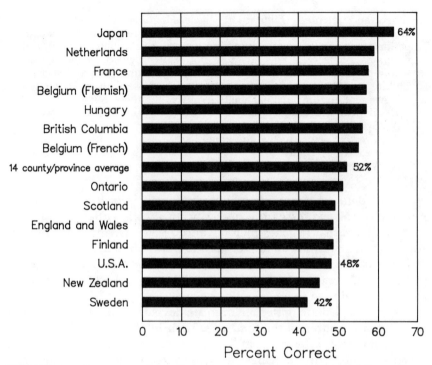

FIGURE 1:   Average mathematics scores for students in the eighth grade:
1981–82. (Source: U.S. Department of Education, 1985.)

- Who are gifted children?
- What problems do they create in education?
- What are the desired procedures for special education of these students?, and
- What public policies should we promote to expand education of the gifted?

THE DISTINCTIVENESS OF GIFTED STUDENTS: WHO ARE THEY?

We should first determine who we are discussing and how these students are different from average children so that we can see how the schools need to adapt to meet their needs.

Definition

The most commonly used definition of the gifted was developed by a national commission and embedded in a report by Sidney Marland, then U.S. Commissioner of Education (Marland, 1972):

Gifted and talented children are those identified by professionally qualified persons who by virtue of outstanding abilities are capable of high performance. These are children who require differentiated educational programs and service beyond those normally provided by the regular school program in order to realize their contribution to self and society. Children capable of high performance include those with demonstrated achievement and/or potential ability in any of the following areas:

1. General intellectual ability
2. Specific academic ability
3. Creative or productive thinking
4. Leadership ability
5. Visual and performing arts. (p. 10)

This definition commits educators to look for *potential* as well as *performance* and expresses the necessity for a differential program for these students that matches their advanced potential and performance. Although there have been numerous attempts to broaden the definition of gifted children beyond the *academic* and *intellectual*, most programs still use identifying instruments such as IQ tests and achievement tests that rely heavily on these two dimensions.

Strictly speaking, gifted children are developing intellectually more rapidly than children of the same age. Their intellectual performance is not qualitatively different from that of other youngsters, but they are capable of intellectual activities 3 to 4 years in advance of their own age by the time they reach school (Robinson, 1977). There is not much remarkable about a student playing chess, but playing competitively with adults at age 6! That *is* remarkable because of the age at which these skills matured.

Another key characteristic of gifted children is that they show a wide range of *intraindividual* differences. Namely, their cognitive development may be proceeding much faster than their social development, and this uneven pattern of development causes problems for gifted children themselves, their families, and the schools.

Characteristics

Much of what we know about the differential characteristics of gifted children comes from the monumental, longitudinal study of Lewis Terman and his associates, who followed about 1,500 gifted children (top 1% on IQ tests) for a period of 50 years (Oden, 1968; Sears & Barbee, 1977; Terman, 1954). The results of their studies have been largely confirmed by smaller efforts addressed to the same questions (Gallagher, 1985).

Basically, the Terman study shed the gifted student of many myths that have grown up around the topic, especially that they were "sickly" or "emotionally disturbed." The gifted students in this longitudinal study turned out on the average to be superior in most other domains as well as their intellect. In areas of physical health, mental health, sociability, and attainment in later life, among others, these students performed in a highly superior fashion to normative groups on the average, although there were always dramatic individual exceptions to the general rule of developmental superiority.

While the Terman sample no doubt ignored many minority gifted individuals through its methods of selection (IQ test scores), and may have shortchanged creativity as a key identifying characteristic, there is little reason to doubt the essential soundness of the finding that these children are generally above average in most areas of development.

The role that families play in the full development of such children is another frequently asked question. In the Terman studies the predominant characteristic of the parents was that they were highly educated and generally well-to-do economically, although there were interesting exceptions to that general finding.

Another approach to this question of the family's influence was carried out by Bloom (1982). He has investigated the factors that seemed to influence the development of world class performers in the sciences, arts, and athletics by retrospectively interviewing 25 world class performers in each field, plus some of the significant others around these performers. His goal was to determine the nature of the productive environment that brought forth these successful individuals. The factor that he found most impressive was that of parental encouragement, urging the child to high levels of performance, and creating opportunities for further learning. Consider the different reaction of two sets of parents when a young child picks up the violin or attempts to play it in imitation of some adults he or she has seen. One parent may say, "Put that violin down. It's very valuable and you might break it." Another parent might say, "Look, Max, our son is showing musical talent. We must see to it that he gets music lessons." These differential parental reactions played out over time seem to make a difference.

Since Bloom did his study retrospectively, that is, starting with the world class performers as adults and looking back to their childhood, we have no knowledge of how many parents have said to a child that he or she must have music lessons and nothing much came of it. There seems to be little doubt that parental encouragement is one factor that can add to intellectual productivity and will perhaps even interact with the factor of increased opportunities for schooling. Such parents with high ambitions for their child will make sure that the child receives the highest quality and level of schooling possible.

PROGRAM ADAPTATIONS FOR GIFTED STUDENTS

There are three general ways to modify the school program for gifted students in order to provide them with a more appropriate program. You can change where the instruction takes place, the *learning environment;* what is taught, *content;* and the skills to be mastered, *skills* (Gallagher, 1985).

Learning Environment

In terms of learning environment, the goal for gifted students is to group them together for some type of special instruction so that they can learn more complex ideas at an accelerated rate. Figure 2 summarizes various ways to achieve such grouping. Grouping is done to: (1) reduce the variability of achievement and ability in the instructional group, (2) allow gifted students to interact with one another, and (3) allow them access to a highly qualified teacher.

Figure 2 indicates the rankings of 1,200 teachers, administrators, and parents interested in gifted education on types of learning environment modifications. At the elementary school level, the resource room was clearly the most popular choice. At the secondary school level, the most popular choice was special classes, particularly advanced placement classes that earn college credit while the student is still in high school. The strategy of independent study was also popular with secondary school respondents.

Special schools for gifted students were not favored, primarily because they separate gifted students so thoroughly from their age-mates. Even so, there are a few examples of special schools for gifted students in science and mathematics, such as the Bronx High School of Science (Kopelman, Galasso, & Strom, 1977) and the North Carolina School of Science and Mathematics (Eilber, 1981). However, these schools are for senior high school students. The later in the school career the gifted student is, the more likely that educators and parents will accept substantial ability grouping as a part of the solution to more effective education. Of course, there is almost complete ability grouping when the student gets to professional school or advanced graduate work.

Content

What should gifted students be taught? One of the fundamental problems facing the education of the gifted is what to teach. What is the differentiated curriculum that we should provide to gifted students?

The rapid expansion of knowledge in recent years has led to an

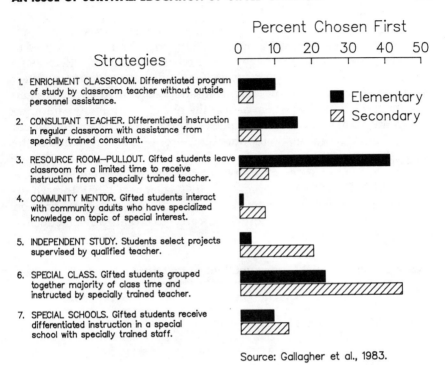

FIGURE 2.   Ranking of administrative strategies by teachers,
             administrators, and parents ($N = 1200$).

avalanche of new information in practically all content fields. The available time to teach this relevant information, however, has not changed very much. There are still 12 grades before college. Despite the gradual lengthening of graduate and professional programs, instructional time in the public schools has not increased. The school year in the United States is limited to 180–200 school days of about 5 hours each day. We can calculate a maximum of 1,000 hours of instruction a year, or if the gifted child is in a resource room program that provides 1 hour a day of special instruction, there is a maximum of 200 hours a year of special instruction.

The situation is complicated when, with so many ideas to learn, the gifted student is forced to do assignments on knowledge he or she already has mastered. The serious question for the educator, then, is how to make a decision between the competing sets of information that might be taught. The chase after total mastery of all available knowledge is clearly doomed, so the goal is to learn significant ideas, models, and theories with multiple applications.

High-ability students need differential content presented, since they already will know much, but not all, of what would be presented to the average student at their age level. Renzulli, Smith, and Reis (1982) suggest a process of *curriculum compacting*, finding out through a pretest what students already know, then planning a sequence of activities and lessons designed to help them master the rest of the unknown information in the regular curriculum as quickly as possible. The gifted student would then be free to go on to something else. What is the nature of the "something else?"

Table 1 summarizes four types of content differentiation: *acceleration, enrichment, sophistication,* and *novelty* (Gallagher, 1985). In each instance, substantial content knowledge and skills mastery is required on the part of the teacher in order to carry the units to an effective conclusion.

TABLE 1:   Differential Curriculum Content for Gifted

Type	Description	Example
Acceleration	Content is designed to match the gifted student's attainment and consists of curriculum usually reserved for older students.	A program of algebra or geometry provided in elementary school for gifted students.
Enrichment	Materials are designed as extensions to regular grade objectives but elaborate and extend those objectives to give the gifted student a broader understanding.	If the regular grade objective is the mastery of the westward movement in the U.S., the gifted students can read histories, short stories, biographies, diaries of settlers, etc., so as to deepen and personalize their understanding of that movement.
Sophistication	Materials are designed to allow the gifted student to master larger systems of ideas and concepts beyond those expected of the average student.	While the average students are learning about the American Revolution, gifted students are trying to grasp the essence of revolutions, and their commonalities across geographical boundaries and historical eras.
Novelty	This content represents material and ideas not covered in the regular curriculum but deemed interesting and profitable for the gifted student.	Gifted students pursue the question of how new technologies change human mores and patterns (i.e., TV or jet planes or nuclear energy), a synthesis across content disciplines.

Source. Gallagher, 1985.

The process of *curriculum acceleration* brings more advanced curriculum to younger children. Mathematics is often the area in which this curricular adaptation takes place because of its hierarchical organization, so the gifted students may take algebra and geometry well in advance of their age-mates. *Curriculum enrichment* merely extends the regular classroom objectives with additional material and experiences. This works best whenever the special program for gifted students is being integrated with the regular classroom program, as may be the case in the "resource room" organizational setting. *Curriculum sophistication* is used to take advantage of the ability of gifted students to master more complex systems of ideas and allows them to focus on major scientific laws, principles, or literary patterns across eras. These more complex ideas would be difficult for the average or below-average student of a similar age. *Curriculum novelty* introduces gifted students to material not covered in the standard curriculum but which might be useful for someone who will be in advanced science or in professional leadership positions. The role of technology in changing social values and mores is one example of curriculum novelty; the study of statistical probability as a base for thinking about scientific ideas would be another.

All of these methods attempt to extend the intellectual challenge faced by gifted students by providing additional content for their stimulation and intellectual development.

Skills Development for Productive Thinking

Another major area of differential educational objectives for gifted students is the intent to help them develop more fully their productive thinking skills and to encourage them to become more independent thinkers, "self-starters," who do not have to depend on teachers for their ideas or directions. An extensive literature has emerged from these attempts to encourage creative thinking, problem solving, and problem finding among gifted students (Feldhusen & Treffinger, 1980; Getzels, 1982; Meeker, 1982).

The underlying assumption of most of this work, whether it be brainstorming, synectics, future problem solving, or other special approaches, is to free up the capabilities of students for originality and the free flow of ideas, abilities that may have atrophied as a result of a routine classroom fact and memory diet. The story that if Thomas Edison had gone to school, instead of being removed from school by his mother, he might have ended up inventing a longer lasting candle instead of the light bulb, is an indication of the presumed ill effects of standard schooling on imagination and creative thought.

Treffinger (1980) sums up the educational purposes for stimulating creativity as follows:

1. Creative learning is important because it helps children be more effective when adults aren't around.
2. Creative learning is important because it creates possibilities for solving future problems that we can't even anticipate.
3. Creative learning is important because it may lead to powerful consequences in our lives.
4. Creative learning can produce great satisfaction and joy. (pp. 9–13)

Special teacher-training procedures are needed to execute such exercises and procedures effectively, and integrate the differentiated content with skills development in productive thinking. Yet only 10 states currently certify teachers in gifted education.

Jackson (1983), referring to science teachers and their inability to conceptualize the *problem-finding* and *problem-solving* processes that are at the heart of scientific inquiry, commented: "The notion of science as a process, a mode of inquiry, seems not to have caught on among those using the inquiry oriented materials. . . . For most teachers, science is still a noun, not a verb" (p. 151). This failure to present science or other content as a strategy for seeking an approximation to the truth is a serious one for the student who wishes to *problem find* and *problem solve* instead of regurgitating a long string of facts (Getzels, 1982). It seems clear that we cannot rely on teachers, without training, to stimulate these thinking abilities.

SPECIAL PROBLEM AREAS

The greater part of this chapter has been devoted to plans for the gifted child of high ability and high academic performance coupled with a strong desire to learn. There are a number of subgroups of gifted children who do not fit that general pattern and who deserve special attention.

Gifted Underachiever

Gifted underachievers seem to have high ability as measured by tests, teacher ratings, and self-report, but are performing at a mediocre or worse level in school. We have lost track of this issue in the United States with only a couple of meaningful published works in the last decade on this topic. It nevertheless remains a very significant issue because of the loss of intellectual potential for the individual and for the society.

The only two studies that have reported strong positive results from intervention programs with these students are one by Whitmore (1980) on a program in California and another by Butler–Por (1982) on a program in Israel. Whitmore described a program for underachieving children in the primary grades that focused on the goals of improving self-concept, remediation of specific learning problems, and developing achievement motivation in school. The heavy emphasis on personal support and guidance from the teacher over a 2-year period yielded strong achievement gains far beyond normal expectations, and these gains were maintained in a follow-up study.

Butler–Por reported significant gains from a program for pre-adolescent underachievers that stressed "reality therapy" and established a contract jointly arrived at by teacher and student which involved various tasks and rewards to be executed in a short time frame. Such expectations of personal responsibility caused improvement in grades as well as in behaviors such as tardiness and absences.

Both of these studies stressed emotional support of the students and an intensity of effort measured in months and years that has often been missing from other attempts to change the underachievement pattern. It appears that schools may often underestimate the amount and length of effort needed to make a difference in the achievement and development of these children.

Gifted Women

A second area that has not yet yielded to clear and definitive results is the dimension of gifted women. Although our measures of general intellectual ability unfailingly show an equality between the sexes, the same equality is not true when one gets into more specific content fields, such as mathematics or literature. A great deal of attention has been given recently to mathematics because most of our mathematics and science searches have yielded many more boys than girls at the upper end of the performance scale (Benbow & Stanley, 1983). This result has caused a great deal of reflection. Fox (1977), among others, has been instrumental in trying to devise special mathematics programs for girls. She even suggests that girls should be segregated by sex for instruction until they gain confidence in their own mathematical abilities. Under current conditions, they are often discouraged by more assertive males before they have a chance to establish their own capabilities.

Gifted Minorities

Another major issue still not adequately faced by the field of gifted education is the need for special programmatic adaptations for students from culturally different or culturally diverse groups. Such cultural differences often cause students with special intellectual gifts to go unrecognized when standard procedures are used. Consequently, one area of emphasis in recent years has been special procedures for more adequate talent identification (Mercer & Lewis, 1981; Renzulli, 1979).

In addition to better methods of identification, we face the issue of identifying program modifications that should be made for gifted minority students. Frasier (1979) pointed out that many minority youngsters have the added burden of "upward mobility" and need counseling to help them with the feelings of alienation that come from leaving one's own subculture and trying to become a member of mainstream society. Wolf (1981) and Exum (1979) both stress a differentiated curriculum that focuses on personal identification with cultural roots and self-identity. Exum suggested seminars on topics such as African art, slavery, Black reconstruction, racism as mental illness, and world emergence. Such topics would provide an analogous background to that received in the standard curriculum for children from European ethnic backgrounds.

Maker (1983) stresses programs of transition or trial placement for those culturally different gifted children of high potential, but who may be lacking in basic skills. There is a shortage of documented programs to provide special services to minority children with special talent. Many of the suggestions noted here remain untested, or in need of systematic evaluation.

PROGRAM EVALUATION

The growing concern about the effectiveness of educational programs in general has resulted in a rapidly growing industry of program evaluation. Programs for educating gifted students, since they involve additional costs, are clear targets for program evaluation efforts, often designed to establish accountability. Such evaluations pose major questions:

1. *Are the differentiated program elements in place?* There is not much purpose in conducting a sophisticated program analysis if the basic program has not been implemented. If the teachers are not developing more sophisticated content or teaching productive thinking skills as expected, then why go to the bother of measuring the impact on students?

2. *Did the program have the anticipated impact on the target students?* The basic issue here is whether the students are different in some measurable way from their status before the program began. Do they have more content knowledge? Do they show mastery of a different set of skills? Are their attitudes or interests different? Did the program do what it was supposed to do?

3. *Did some unanticipated consequences occur?* Program evaluations should be on the alert for findings that could not be anticipated in the original program design. Do the students show unusual tension or anxiety in the program? Have they shown an increase in enthusiasm for school as a result? Sometimes these unanticipated findings may be more important or interesting than the expected results.

There are a variety of technical difficulties faced by those who evaluate programs for gifted children. Among these difficulties is the fact that the *expected* academic gains for gifted students over any time period would be above average! So the mere presence of above-average academic growth is not necessarily a program endorsement. Conversely, the test instruments used in program evaluation may often not be appropriate for gifted students, since the tests may not measure the higher-level thinking processes that are at the heart of the differentiated curriculum. Such tests often do not have enough "ceiling" to allow gifted students to show their full range of knowledge or abilities.

A summary of recent evaluations of programs for the gifted was completed by Gallagher, Weiss, Oglesby, and Thomas (1983). Their review produced four primary conclusions:

1. *Skills training.* Programs that focus on skills development and are devoted to enhancing productive or creative thinking almost uniformly report positive results. Attempts to train *originality, fluency,* or *flexibility,* and other such characteristics are observed to be successful within the special training situation itself. In these training programs, the teacher is provided with special strategies designed to help develop creative thinking and problem solving (Delisle & Renzulli, 1982; Torrance, 1969). However, limited evidence is available on the transfer of productive thinking skills to other tasks or environments (Mansfield, Busse, & Krepelka, 1978).

2. *Content differentiation.* Another major educational objective is to provide a more complex curriculum experience to the gifted student than is possible to provide to the average student. The type of content acceleration exemplified by the Study of Mathematically Precocious Youth (SMPY), currently implemented in many parts of the country, seems to be effective, with few negative side-effects (Ben-

bow, 1982; George & Denham, 1976). Lack of carefully designed comparison or control groups limits the interpretation of many of the reports, but we are reassured that no major social or emotional damage to gifted students appears to accompany the presentation of advanced curriculum efforts such as the SMPY (Keating, 1976).

3. *Learning environment.* Much emphasis has been placed on *where* the gifted child receives either special skills training or content enrichment. The teacher always plays a critical role in the effectiveness of the program, regardless of where the child is placed. It is now considered likely that *where* the gifted child is placed in an educational setting is less important than *who* teaches the child and *what* the nature of the lessons is (Kulik & Kulik, 1982).

4. *Acceleration.* A gifted student may well be in the educational system for as many as 20–25 years. Increasing attention is being paid to techniques to reduce the total amount of time a student spends in education before beginning a career. The most popular acceleration strategy in current practice is the Advanced Placement Program, which allows high school students to gain college credit by taking special advanced courses in high school. Strong cost effectiveness data have been provided suggesting a major economic benefit from this program (Casserly, 1979). Other programs have demonstrated that it is possible to accelerate youngsters in specific subject areas such as mathematics without any tangible damage or concern for the youngster (Benbow & Stanley, 1983).

Overall, the message appears to be that the program changes generally seem to accomplish their goals and that the investment in these programs appears justified. Existing evidence, however, is sparse and evaluation studies flawed. A much stronger effort is needed to document effective special services for gifted children.

PUBLIC POLICY NEEDED FOR GIFTED EDUCATION

Every state currently has some form of programmatic effort designed to assist local schools in the education of gifted children, but this sometimes merely means the identification of someone on the administrative staff in the state Department of Education as their "coordinator of gifted education." A total of more than $200 million can now be identified as being provided to local school systems by the 50 states to aid in this effort. This amount can range from no provision in a few states to more than $30 million in Pennsylvania, the state with the highest allocation for gifted education (Mitchell, 1981).

What needs to be done from a public policy standpoint that is not now being done? One of the striking omissions is any direct aid for gifted education from the federal level. This contrasts rather strikingly to the more than $1 billion currently allocated for handicapped children (Kirk & Gallagher, 1986). Despite the fact that both groups are included in the category of exceptional children the public policy actions are very different to handicapped and gifted children.

Even more important than the level of funding, however, is the *type of activity* that would be supported through federal funds. Practically all local and state funds currently are spent on direct service delivery in the schools (i.e., teachers' salaries). Thus, federal funds should be used to support research, development, leadership training, demonstration, and dissemination. Without these activities no field can grow or prosper.

Gallagher (1982) proposed a five-point program for federal support that would cost no more than $50 million (a small amount in federal budget terms), but would nonetheless have a quality-raising, *catalytical* effect on the education of gifted children:

1. *Leadership training.* Past experience with the development of programs for handicapped children and for vocational education has shown the importance of preparing, through postgraduate education, key administrative leaders (Martin, 1976). This small cadre of trained leaders and administrators can be counted on to take important roles in state departments of education, teacher-training institutions, and research institutes. The development of their ideas and their leadership could influence the field for the next two decades.
2. *Continuous in-service training.* It is clearly not enough to identify outstanding teachers and assign them to special programs for the gifted. Further, there is no likelihood that universities, through pre-service training programs, can provide the specialized training necessary for teachers of the gifted. What is more likely is that existing elementary- and secondary-teacher training programs can provide the base upon which an intensive in-service training program, specially devoted to programmatic modifications for the gifted, can be built. Therefore, funds need to be made available to states and local communities to allow for these in-service training programs to develop and multiply.
3. *Research and development.* In the search for quality programs, there is perhaps no more needed element than careful research on various aspects of gifted education. The growing trend to designate already severely limited research funds for specific target groups, such as the handicapped or the economically disadvantaged, has reduced to

almost nothing the resources available for research on gifted education. As long as such designated funds exist, it seems important to
add a small amount of money specifically for gifted education, to
stimulate research dealing with the instructional process, curriculum innovation, thinking processes, and program evaluation. Such
knowledge is useful in all states, and research has been accepted as
one clear federal responsibility.

4. *Demonstration programs.* The expenditure of small sums of money to
publicize innovative and exemplary programs can place an educational spotlight on successful programs for gifted students in urban,
rural, and suburban areas. By judicious selection, programs can
focus on special issues, such as enhancing the education of minority-group gifted students, creating strong programs in mathematics
and science, and operating programs for gifted women and other
long-neglected groups, as well as show what can be done in more
traditional program areas.

5. *State leadership.* In other fields of education, one of the most productive investments that the federal government has made is to add to
the state leadership team someone who is specially interested in,
trained in, and committed to the program area needing development and expansion. It has been demonstrated in a number of instances that the presence of such a trained and committed individual has been the key to further development of programs within
a state. Therefore, providing small sums of seed money that allow
state departments of education to add to their staffs for the purpose
of program planning for the gifted could be a useful investment.

The issue of additional costs always occupies the attention of decision makers. How much additional money do these programs cost?
Gallagher, Weiss, Oglesby, and Thomas (1983) collected data from more
than 100 programs using either the *consultant teacher, resource room,* or
special class model and came to the conclusion that the additional cost of
educating gifted students ranges from an additional 15% to 40% of per
pupil cost. This cost makes gifted education one of the least expensive
programs for exceptional children; costs for other special education programs run 200% or higher than average per pupil cost. Examples of such
programs are those for the learning disabled, mentally retarded, blind,
deaf, and multiply handicapped children (Kakalik, Furry, Thomas, &
Carney, 1981). Figure 3 provides a comparison of costs for various types
of exceptional children.

A recent North Carolina state publication (Aubrecht, 1986) has
addressed the issue of "What is an Appropriate Education for Gifted

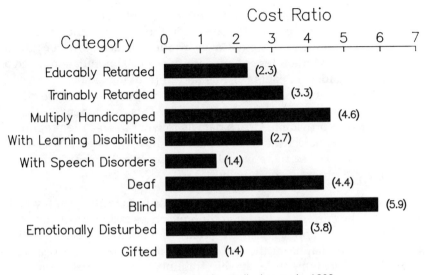

Source: After Gallagher et al., 1983.

FIGURE 3:   Cost index related to costs of educating exceptional relative to nonexceptional children.

Students?" The following points that match with the federal program described by Gallagher are highlighted in that report:

1. A differentiated program from preschool through secondary school with increased educational grouping as the student approaches the secondary level. This program would focus upon both differentiated curriculum content and thinking-skills mastery.
2. Acceleration of 1 to 2 years would be considered for all gifted students unless contraindicated by socioemotional adjustment factors. There is no reason why the brightest of our students must spend a quarter of a century in classrooms. When we save 2 years of their career through acceleration, we add enormously to their individual, and society's, productivity.
3. We need to increase dramatically the support services that come through *research, development, demonstration,* and *dissemination* to maintain and improve the quality of educational services that we are delivering to gifted students. In particular, we need more attention to curriculum development so there is a continuing supply of significant content available to teachers, particularly at the elementary school level.
4. A significant effort needs to be made in teacher training, probably

focusing at the in-service and summer school level. Regular classroom teachers need to be introduced to the methods and differentiated curriculum that seems to be needed. Teachers, often given minimal preparation for coping with this special population, need a firm foundation in content fields and in thinking skills.

5. There should be a requirement for all special programs for the gifted that they have an evaluation component. This component would be designed to provide feedback data as to what degree the program's instructional objectives were being met, how the students were responding, etc., so there would be an incentive to upgrade and improve the program continually.

The field of education for gifted students has clearly been revived, in part, by the current and future economic crises facing American society. Special education services for gifted students that appear effective are now applied haphazardly, and special dimensions such as research, curriculum development, leadership training, and demonstration need support to maximize human potential. The full delivery of quality services that provide a more effective education for gifted students will not automatically appear. However, it can be accomplished by a deliberate set of public policy decisions.

REFERENCES

Aubrecht, L. (1986). *What is an appropriate education for a gifted student?* Raleigh, NC: North Carolina Association for the Gifted and Talented.

Benbow, C. (1982). Consequences in high school and college of sex differences in mathematical reasoning ability: A longitudinal perspective. *American Educational Research Journal, 19,* 598–622.

Benbow, C., & Stanley, J. (Eds.). (1983). *Academic precocity.* Baltimore: Johns Hopkins.

Bitan, D. (1976). Israel. In J. Gibson & P. Chenells (Eds.), *Gifted children: Looking to their future* (pp. 322–327). Tiptree Essex, England: Anchor.

Bloom, B. (1982). The role of gifts and markers in the development of talent. *Exceptional Children, 48,* 510–522.

Brickman, W. (1979). Educational provisions for the gifted and talented in other countries. In A. Passow (Ed.), *The gifted and the talented* (78th Yearbook of the National Society for the Study of Education; pp. 308–330). Chicago: University of Chicago.

Butler, S. R. (1983). The talented child in the Peoples Republic of China. In B. M. Shore, F. Gagné, S. Larivée, R. Tali, & R. Tremblay (Eds.), *Face to face with giftedness* (pp. 271–289). New York: Trillium.

Butler–Por, N. (1982). *The phenomenon and treatment of academic achievement in children of superior and average ability.* Unpublished doctoral dissertation. University of Wales, Cardiff, Wales.

Butler–Por, N. (1983). Giftedness across cultures. In B. Shore, F. Gagné, S. Larivée, R. Tali, & R. Tremblay (Eds.), *Face to face with giftedness* (pp. 250–270). New York: Trillium.

Casserly, P. (1979). Helping able young women take math and science seriously in school. In N. Colangelo & R. Zaffrann (Eds.), *New voices in counseling the gifted*. Dubuque, IA: Kendall/Hunt.

Coleman, J. (1984, December). Excellence and equality in education. Address at Conference on Excellence vs. Equity in Education, Tel Aviv, Israel.

Coleman, W., Jr., & Selby, C. (1983). *Educating Americans for the 21st Century*. Washington, DC: National Science Board Commission on Precollege Education in Mathematics, Science, and Technology.

Delisle, J. (1984). *Gifted children speak out*. New York: Walker.

Delisle, J., & Renzulli, J. (1982). The revolving door identification and programming model. *Exceptional Children. 48*, 152–156.

Eilber, C. (1981, Fall). Report card: The first year at the School of Science and Math. *Popular Government, 23*–26.

Exum, H. (1979). Facilitating psychological and emotional development of gifted black students. In N. Colangelo & R. Zaffrann (Eds.), *New voices in counseling the gifted* (pp. 312–320). Dubuque, IA: Kendall/Hunt.

Feldhusen, J., & Treffinger, D. (1980). *Creative thinking and problem solving in gifted education* (2nd ed.). Dubuque, IA: Kendall/Hunt.

Fox, L. (1977). Sex differences: Implications for program planning for the academically gifted. In J. Stanley, W. George, & C. Solano (Eds.), *The gifted and the creative: A fifty year perspective* (pp. 113–140). Baltimore: Johns Hopkins.

Frasier, M. M. (1979). Counseling the culturally diverse gifted. In N. Colangelo & R. Zaffrann (Eds.), *New voices in counseling the gifted* (pp. 304–311). Dubuque, IA: Kendall/Hunt.

Gallagher, J. (1982). A plan for catalytic support for gifted education in the 1980's. *Elementary School Journal, 82*, 180–184.

––––––. (1984). Excellence and equity—A world-wide conflict. *Gifted International, 2*(2), 1–11.

––––––. (1985). *Teaching the gifted child* (3rd ed.). Boston: Allyn & Bacon.

Gallagher, J., Weiss, P., Oglesby, K., & Thomas, T. (1983). *The status of gifted/talented education: United States survey of needs, practices, and policies*. Los Angeles: National/State Leadership Training Institute.

Gardner, J. W. (1961). *Excellence: Can we be equal and excellent too?* New York: Harper & Row.

George, W., & Denham, S. (1976). Curriculum experimentation for the mathematically talented. In D. Keating (Ed.), *Intellectual talent: Research and development*. Baltimore: Johns Hopkins.

Getzels, J. (1982). The problem of the problem. In R. Hogarth (Ed.), *New directions for methodology of social and behavioral science: Question framing and response consistency*. San Francisco: Jossey–Bass.

Goodlad, J. (1964). *School curriculum reform in the United States*. New York: Fund for the Advancement of Education.

Husén, T. (1974). *Talent, equality and meritocracy: Availability and utilization of talent*. The Hague: Nijhoff.

Jackson, P. (1983). The reform of science education: A cautionary tale. *Daedalus, 112*(2), 143–166.

Kakalik, J., Furry, W., Thomas, M., & Carney, M. (1981). *The cost of special education.* Santa Monica, CA: Rand.

Keating, D. (Ed.). (1976). *Intellectual talent: Research and development.* Baltimore: Johns Hopkins.

Kirk, S. A., & Gallagher, J. J. (1986). *Educating exceptional children* (5th ed.). Boston: Houghton Mifflin.

Kopelman, M., Galasso, V., & Strom, P. (1977). A model program for the development of creativity in science. *Gifted Child Quarterly, 21,* 80–84.

Kulik, C., & Kulik, J. (1982). Effects of ability grouping on secondary school students: A meta-analysis of evaluation findings. *American Educational Research Journal, 19,* 415–428.

Landau, E. (1979). The young person's institute for the promotion of science. In J. Gallagher (Ed.), *Gifted children: Reaching their potential* (pp. 105–109). Jerusalem: Kollek.

Larsson, Y. (1981). *Provision for the education of gifted and talented children in Australia* (Occasional Paper, No. 13). Sydney, Australia: Department of Education, University of Sydney.

Maker, J. (1983). Quality education for gifted minority students. *Journal for the Education of the Gifted, 6,* 140–153.

Mansfield, R., Busse, T., & Krepelka, E. (1978). The effectiveness of creativity training. *Review of Educational Research, 48,* 517–536.

Marland, S. (1972). *Education of the gifted and talented* (Report to the Congress of the United States by the U.S. Commissioner of Education). Washington, DC: U.S. Government Printing Office.

Martin, E. W. (1976). A national commitment to the rights of the individual— 1776–1976. *Exceptional Children, 43*(3), 132–134.

Meeker, M. (1982). *Divergent production of semantic units.* El Segundo, CA: SOI.

Mercer, J., & Lewis, J. (1981). Using the system of multicultural pluralistic assessment to identify the gifted minority child. In I. Sato (Ed.), *Balancing the scale for the disadvantaged gifted* (pp. 59–66). Los Angeles: National/State Leadership Training Institute on the Gifted and Talented.

Mitchell, P. (Ed.). (1981). *A policymaker's guide to issues in gifted and talented education.* Washington, DC: National Association of State Boards of Education.

National Commission on Excellence in Education. (1983). *A nation at risk: The imperative for education reform* (A Report to the Nation and the Secretary of Education). Washington, DC: U.S. Government Printing Office.

Oden, M. (1968). The fulfillment of promise: Forty-year follow-up of the Terman gifted group. *Genetic Psychology Monographs, 77,* 3–93.

Renzulli, J. (1979). *What makes giftedness?* (Brief No. 6). Los Angeles: National/State Leadership Training Institute on the Gifted and Talented.

Renzulli, J., Smith, L., & Reis, S. (1982). Curriculum compacting: An essential strategy for working with gifted students. *Elementary School Journal, 82,* 185–194.

Robinson, H. (1977). Current myths concerning gifted children. In I. Sato (Ed.), *Gifts, talents, and the very young* (pp. 1–11). Los Angeles: National/State Leadership Training Institute on the Gifted and Talented.

Sears, P., & Barbee, A. (1977). Career and life satisfactions among Terman's gifted women. In J. Stanley, W. George, & C. Solano (Eds.), *The gifted and the creative: A fifty-year perspective.* Baltimore: Johns Hopkins.

Smilansky, M., & Nevo, D. (1975). A longitudinal study of the gifted disadvantaged. *Educational Forum, 39,* 273–294.

Terman, L. (1954). The discovery and encouragement of exceptional talent. *American Psychologist, 9,* 221–230.

Terrassier, J. (1981). The negative Pygmalion effect. In A. Kramer (Ed.), *Gifted children: Challenging their potential* (pp. 82–84). New York: Trillium.

Torrance, E. (1969). *Creativity.* Belmont: Dimensions.

Treffinger, D. (1980). *Encouraging creative learning for the gifted and talented.* Los Angeles: National/State Leadership Training Institute.

U.S. Department of Education. (1985). *Second International Mathematics Study.* National Center for Education Statistics.

Whitmore, J. (1980). *Giftedness, conflict and underachievement.* Boston: Allyn & Bacon.

Wolf, M. (1981). Talent search and development in the visual and performing arts. In I. Sato (Ed.), *Balancing the scale for the disadvantaged gifted* (pp. 103–116). Los Angeles: National/State Leadership Training Institute on the Gifted and Talented.

Wu, W. T. (1983, November). *Evaluation of educational programs for intellectually gifted students in junior high schools in the Republic of China.* Paper presented at the meeting of the National Association for Gifted Children, Philadelphia.

Part Three

Uses of Information and Educational Indicators

EIGHT

EDUCATIONAL INDICATORS WITHIN SCHOOL DISTRICTS[1]

WILLIAM W. COOLEY

Educational research that is conducted specifically for school districts would profit greatly if the emphasis were shifted from discrete studies of particular programs or policies, which generally fall under the rubric of program evaluation, to a continuous activity of data collection and analysis, which has been referred to as monitoring and tailoring (Cooley, 1983). Reform efforts in education have tended to assume that the best way to improve educational practice is to adopt a new program that seems to address a particular problem, implement that innovative program, and then evaluate the program to determine its effectiveness in dealing with the problem. Berman (1980) calls this the technological-experimental paradigm of educational change.

Formal, summative program evaluations that attempt to estimate the impact of a particular program or policy on student outcomes tend to produce results that often should not be used, because of their invalidity, or cannot be used because valid impact studies, if they can be done at all, take too long to be timely. Worse than that, such studies represent a substantial opportunity cost. That is, they require so much time and effort that other, potentially more useful approaches, are not employed.

An alternative to the experimental paradigm, one which has not been widely used in education but which has considerable promise, is the cybernetic paradigm. It involves developing and monitoring a variety of performance indicators. Then, whenever an indicator moves into an unacceptable range, an attempt is made to determine just where that condition is most severe. Focused corrective action is then taken which tailors practice. Although monitoring and tailoring resembles the cyber-

---

[1]Portions of this chapter were drawn from Cooley (1983).

netic model used in controlling physical systems (as in the thermostat), there are some very important differences when applying it in an educational system, as Sproull and Zubrow (1981) point out.

More specifically, compared with physical systems, available educational indicators are more fallible, it is usually less clear what an unacceptable range is, and it is not as obvious what the corrective action must be when an indicator moves into an unacceptable range. It certainly sounds hopeless. However, the monitoring and tailoring approach can be designed in ways that take these shortcomings into account and can serve a very useful function within an educational system.

A district-wide needs assessment conducted in Pittsburgh in 1980–81 (Cooley & Bickel, 1986, pp. 183–196) is useful to illustrate the main features of a monitoring and tailoring approach. One purpose of monitoring indicators is to help school districts establish priorities for improving the system. In that assessment, we worked up a variety of district-wide data that indicated the condition of the educational system in the district. The indicators included observed variables, such as student attendance, very simply derived variables, such as student–teacher ratio, or more complex, indirectly measured latent variables, such as socioeconomic status. The original unit of observation may have been students, classrooms or schools, and the level of aggregation used depended on the point to be made. What is common to indicators is that they are a function of a construct that describes some aspect of educational phenomena that people care about. More on constructs in a moment.

Extensive dialogue with the superintendent and board members regarding these indicators led to the establishment of the priority areas for improving the educational program in the district. The dialogue concerned the degree to which the indicators seemed to be in an unacceptable range, as well as which indicators were getting at more fundamental problems which in turn might be affecting the performance of other indicators.

So one function of indicators in a monitoring and tailoring system is to contribute to district-wide priority setting. Examining a variety of indicators (in the form of district-wide aggregates) makes such priority discussions more productive. Since the objective is to improve the performance of the system, district-level aggregates are important for a dialogue about what aspects are in greatest need of improvement and, over time, for indicating whether progress is being made.

The other useful way to examine a performance indicator is to look at how it is distributed. Noticing where unusually low performance is occurring on a priority indicator provides a basis for guiding the action system that is supposed to improve that performance. The unit of analysis for examining distributions, whether it is students, classrooms, or schools, must be consistent with the unit that is the focus of the action system. Let's examine this important point a little more carefully.

As part of the district-wide needs assessment, we analyzed all the achievement data from the district that we could find—in terms of 5-year trends, contrasts across grades, and differences among the various subject areas. The results of these analyses suggested that a major problem within achievement was reading in the primary grades. For example, district-level aggregates indicated (on a criterion-referenced basis) that approximately 25% of the students were leaving the third grade with inadequate reading comprehension to deal with the fourth-grade curriculum. If those skills were not learned in the primary grades, subsequent remedial efforts became more and more costly and seemed less and less effective.

Further looks at the data (this time at the classroom level) revealed some second- and third-grade classrooms in which little or no reading growth was occurring in the course of the year for students placed in those teachers' classrooms. Note that in this particular example the indicator is not end-of-year achievement level but achievement growth, the units being monitored are classrooms, not individual students or schools, low growth was a trend for a given teacher's students, not a one time event, and initial student abilities were also taken into account in comparing growth.

Now the question is, what is to be done when the growth in reading ability of students assigned to a particular teacher is discovered to be low, year after year? Tailoring requires a deployable resource, an action system, that can respond to such indications. In its response, the action system must recognize that the indicator is fallible. A procedure is needed for confirming the indication. In this particular case, the person who responds to the indicator might be an instructional supervisor, trained in clinical supervision and capable of visiting that classroom, initially to confirm (or disconfirm) the indication that reading instruction is not going well in that classroom. If a problem is then confirmed, diagnosis of the situation is needed, coupled with corrective action, generally employing intensive clinical supervision.

As another example, if district-level aggregates indicate that student absence has moved into an undesirable range, and if the action system available for correcting truancy consists of social workers treating individual students and their families, then the extreme cases in the distribution of student-level truancy rates would be the focus of that action system. If other levels of aggregation revealed a classroom or school with particularly low attendance, further investigation might reveal the need for another kind of action system that can work with particular teachers or schools to create a more attractive learning environment.

One assumption central to the monitoring and tailoring approach is that important significant improvements can be made in the educational system through fine-tuning the system. Some might call it a form of incrementalism (Lindblom, 1972). Recognizing that, it also must be emphasized that there indeed may be fundamental changes that must be made in the system in order to adjust to fundamental changes that occur in society. But it does seem rational to make sure that current programs and policies are working as well as possible before trying some dramatic departure from current practice. I am not saying that schools should not innovate. There comes a time when the sabertooth curriculum has to go. But when a problem is detected in a school district, the tendency is to launch a district-wide solution, generally involving a new program, rather than determine just where (i.e., in which schools or classrooms) things are not working well and tailor practice to improve performance. The district-wide innovation can frequently disrupt those schools or classrooms in which things had been working smoothly, and seldom corrects situations where they were not. Without focused assistance, some principals or teachers will not implement the new solution any better than the previous practice. Too little has been done to get the programs that are in place working well. What is impressive in the results of national evaluations of compensatory education, for example, is the vast variability in effectiveness among sites implementing the same instructional model, not differences between models. (See, for example, Cooley & Lohnes, 1976, for a discussion of this important point.) A monitoring and tailoring system can help a district decide how to focus its available energies for staff development and remedial attention.

Now let us take a little closer look at two of the major components of such a system, the indicators and the action systems.

MAJOR INGREDIENTS OF A MONITORING AND TAILORING SYSTEM

Indicators

It helps to think about possible indicators in terms of major constructs. One set of constructs relates to the efficacy of the system as it prepares students for adulthood. Here it is important to have indicators of such constructs as entering student abilities and interests, their educational programs and progress in them, and achievement and other personal outcomes that are indicative of their expected future. This set represents the familiar system constructs of inputs, processes, and outcomes. Cooley and Lohnes (1976) have suggested one way of organizing such data.

Another set of constructs is needed to describe the quality of the present experience. Schooling is a large part of everyone's life. It is important to seek indicators of the richness of the present experience as well as satisfy the clamor for indicators of how well the students are being prepared for adulthood. For example, Epstein's (1981) measure of the quality of school life is a useful indicator.

A third set of constructs is necessary to satisfy the need to consider whether the system is fair. Questions concerning the equality of educational opportunity dominate policy discussions, and indicators that can reflect such inequities in the system can make those debates more productive. Disaggregations of fairness indicators can also reveal where more resources may be needed to correct currently unjust distributions. Class size is an example of such an indicator.

Dialogue regarding inequities in an educational system is admittedly not a straightforward affair (e.g., Green, 1971). But arguments in terms of the appropriateness of different indicators makes those discussions less abstract. Also, concern soon shifts from noticing the inevitable differences in student outcomes and justifiable differences in resource allocations, to unjust inequities in opportunity to learn. Having indicators from all three domains (efficacy, quality, and equality) also facilitates discussions about "balancing" the different demands on the schools (e.g., quality of the present experience versus preparation for the future; demand for excellence versus the need for equity; liberal education versus training marketable skills). Data have a way of stimulating productive priority debates.

For all constructs, it is important to develop multiple indicators and to be able to display them at multiple levels (i.e., student, classroom, school, and district levels). Because this requires considerable information processing, an essential ingredient is to build a computer-based information system that allows the development and display of the necessary indicators. Today such computer systems are quite feasible.

One problem in using indicators is that it is frequently possible to corrupt them. That is, indicators are corruptible if it is possible to affect the indicator without affecting the underlying phenomenon that the indicator is attempting to measure. For example, if suspensions are being monitored as one indicator of school climate, and if having many of them reflects poorly on the principal, it's very easy to see how principals could modify their behavior with respect to issuing suspensions (or reporting them!) and still have the same level of chaos in that building. The corruptibility of indicators is one reason why it is important to have multiple indicators of the same construct and to refine them continuously. This is an important task of the evaluation researcher in such a system. It is important to point out that indicators will be corrupted more readily if rewards or punishments are associated with extreme values on that indicator than if the indicator is used for guiding corrective feedback.

A lot can be learned about the construction and use of indicators in education from the research on social indicators that emerged as an active area among social scientists in the mid-1960s. That work was stimulated by two secretaries of health, education, and welfare, John Gardner and Wilbur Cohen, who felt that social indicators could provide a better basis for federal social policy (Land & Spilerman, 1975). Krathwohl (1975) organized an Educational Testing Service Invitational Conference on this theme in 1975. There now are entire books and journals devoted to social indicators research. MacRae (1985) provides an excellent summary of the use of policy indicators, including their contribution to the public debate on such complex issues as equity and social integration. In education, the book by Johnstone (1981) is particularly relevant.

It must be noted, however, that there has been considerable debate about the utility of the social indicators movement. There seem to be two major problems with the use of educational indicators. One is the widespread emphasis on federal-level aggregates. Noticing that a national indicator has moved into an alarming range encourages the launching of federal solutions to an isolated problem. That can easily produce programs that end up being counterproductive because of the counterintuitive ways in which large, complex systems react to change (Meyers, 1981, p. 20). Everyone has their favorite example of an unintended negative side-effect from a well-intentioned innovation.

The other weakness in the educational indicators movement, and this is a weakness shared with all types of social indicators, is the tendency to justify indicators as a way of estimating the impact of educational programs and policies. To do that, of course, requites rather well-specified causal models. Economists have been at this for a long time, and it seems clear that their causal models are usually inaccurate. It is important to work on developing models that can describe, even predict, how indicators change over time, how they interrelate, and how they seem to be influencing one another. But adequately specified causal models may be a long way off, even at the district level. Meanwhile, indicators can play an important role in monitoring and tailoring systems within school districts. Now a few more words about action systems.

Action Systems

If system improvement is to follow from monitoring, the information system must be "connected" to an action system. It is very important how this is done because it is usually not clear why a student, or classroom, or school, is in an undesirable range on some valued indicator. Indicators are a function of many factors in the system. Indicators can only tell you where to look for possible problems. For that reason, the action system that is called into play must be first and foremost a diagnostic system. Corrective action is generally not clear from the indicators because our causal models for explaining their rise and fall are still not adequately specified.

The monitoring and tailoring approach requires the availability of services that can be deployed to correct the most serious cases that are found within a district. At the student level, those who deal with extreme cases on such indicators as attendance, suspensions, and achievement growth would be social workers, counselors, and remedial tutors. Specialists trained in clinical supervision would work with principals and teachers who are low on classroom level growth indicators, and a school improvement team would work in schools that are extreme on building level indicators.

Notice that I am not calling for new staff to perform these functions. What the information system does is show how existing personnel might focus their energies. It also helps to justify that focusing. Guided by an unexamined sense of equality, those capable of this type of corrective action tend to be spread so thin they cannot possibly be effective.

So the necessary action systems are financially feasible because they represent a way of focusing the efforts of existing personnel. Of course it is one thing to be feasible, and quite another to be effective. But even here there is reason to be optimistic. One basis for the optimism is the documentation of a school improvement effort (Cooley & Bickel, 1986). Focusing upon seven elementary schools that had a history of low student achievement, the director of that program and his school improvement team have demonstrated how monitored student progress data, accompanied by focused, team supervision are capable of improving the quality of instruction.

Another basis for optimism is the growing literature on effective teaching and effective schooling. For example, by carefully examining the behavior of unusually competent teachers, Leinhardt (1983) has found that these teachers gain considerable amounts of instructional time through the use of well-rehearsed, easily operationalized classroom management routines. The effective schools research has been summarized in a special issue of *Educational Researcher* (Bickel, 1983). This literature is beginning to describe ways in which schools and classrooms can be organized to improve educational outcomes. Such results contribute to the knowledge base needed for guiding the type of focused, clinical action required in monitoring and tailoring. But our Pittsburgh experience is also making it clear that Purkey and Smith (1983) are correct when they point out that school improvement, though certainly possible, is never easy. What monitoring and tailoring can do is indicate potentially fruitful ways in which corrective energy can be focused, and provide a basis for new hope as indicators begin to improve.

There is a question that quite properly arises as one begins to build a computer-based monitoring system: Is it humane? Part of the answer to that question is a series of other questions. For example:

- Is it humane to expose children year after year to a teacher who is apparently unable to improve the reading performance of children in his or her charge?
- Is it humane to have a child absent 160 days in a school year without so much as a home visit because the social worker's energies are being diverted by a principal to the task of preparing the justification for long-term suspensions?
- Is it humane for a school district to solve the problem of an unsatisfactory principal's performance by an annual game of musical chairs among principals in the hopes that eventually a principal will end up in a school in which the parents don't complain?

The other part of the answer is to note that the monitoring and tailoring system must be designed in a way that recognizes the fallibility of the indicators and the inadequacies of our causal models in determining why an indicator has moved into an undesirable range. It is not designed, for example, to issue pink slips to teachers whose students turn in an unsatisfactory standardized achievement performance.

It seems to me that the most effective way to establish monitoring systems is within schools. There are many reasons why I believe this, but the most compelling is the need to keep the monitoring system "connected" to the action system. If improved student performance is the main desired outcome, then that action must be within schools. The rest of this chapter considers what such a system might look like.

SCHOOL-BASED MONITORING SYSTEMS (SMS)

People began discussing the potential use of computers to assist in the management of educational systems as soon as computers began to be available in the late 1950s and early 1960s (see, e.g., Goodlad, O'Toole,

& Tyler, 1966). Since that time, all large school systems and even many of the smaller districts have developed computer support for central administrative functions. Sometimes these central systems include data on individual students, but these tend to be restricted to data that are needed for central administrative tasks, such as computing average daily membership for state subsidies or home socioeconomic status for federal compensatory education distributions.

Central systems tend to serve central functions, and they almost never get to the part about how to help principals and teachers improve the effectiveness, pleasantness, and fairness of their educational environments. The demands of the central environment tend to overwhelm both the hardware and software resources of the central computer system. In the 1960s, when school-based systems were first tried, the costs were just too prohibitive to justify the effort, both in terms of the costs of the hardware and the costs of developing and maintaining such systems. Baker (1978) provides an excellent summary of these earlier efforts.

Several things have happened in recent years that are encouraging a reconsideration of school-based monitoring systems. The most obvious, of course, is the emergence of the powerful, relatively inexpensive microcomputer. Being able to purchase for less than $5,000 the computer power that would have cost hundreds of thousands of dollars in the 1960s is clearly a major factor in the renewed enthusiasm for developing school-based information systems.

Another important development is the availability of software for establishing data base management systems. The new applications software such as Knowledge Manager (Micro Data Base Systems, 1984) make it quite easy to develop automated information systems for schools and do it in ways that make modification relatively easy, and ad hoc inquiries possible (that is, not all possible retrieval requests need to be anticipated by the developers of the system). Another development that makes school-based computer systems feasible today is the desktop scanner, which facilitates a variety of data-entry tasks, including automatic scoring of student tests and reading attendance forms. The relatively inexpensive, accurate, programmable scanner eliminates the big expense of hand-entering data. Finally, the development of the inexpensive modem and the associated telecommunications software makes it possible to export summaries of school data to the central computer as well as import to the school computer, data that are centrally available for students in that school. Similarly, as students transfer from school to school, so can their computer-based records. This concept of distributed processing, which has been emerging in the 1980s, is contributing greatly to the reconceptualization of how school district information systems might be designed.

The Goals of a School-based Monitoring System

As is usually the case, the consideration of the functions and characteristics of information systems should be preceded by a consideration of the goals for such a system. In general, the goals of a School-based Monitoring System (SMS) are much the same as the goals for the educational system in the first place. A possible difference is that when one takes on the task of defining an automated information system, it is much more important to be precise and explicit regarding goals, if those goals are to guide the development and implementation of relevant indicators.

The general goals that have tended to guide our work are: (1) improving student achievement, (2) enhancing the quality of school life, and (3) providing equal opportunity to learn. To be useful in systems design, these very general goals need to be defined more explicitly. Then, data relevant to the goals need to be specified, collected, and organized into indicators that can both facilitate knowing how well the educational system is progressing toward realizing these goals and guide in their realization. It is also important to recognize that a given indicator may be relevant to more than one goal. Student absence is a good example. Absence is an indicator of achievement because an absent student is engaged in less school learning than a present student. In addition, attendance data aggregated at the classroom or school level can indicate rather unpleasant facts about the quality of school life by showing classrooms or schools that students are avoiding. Finally a student who is unable to attend classes because of difficulties in the home does not have the same opportunity to learn as a student whose home expectations are to be in school.

Improving the quality of the school experience includes reducing the rigidity with which schools tend to operate. A major problem in breaking up the built-in rigidity of the school and its traditional format of classroom organization is the increased amount of information demanded in more adaptive instructional systems. It is relatively uncomplicated for the traditional teacher to keep track of what happens each day with 25 students. Very little information is required when all children progress through the same instructional materials at about the same rate, varying only in how much they learn from the exposure. When all students are on page 38 in the arithmetic textbook, that single number defines where the class is. When this neat process is broken down and individual students are allowed to work at different levels and rates, the teacher has 25 times as much information to monitor for that same class. If students are also allowed to move toward different objectives or toward the same objective through different modes of in-

struction, the information-processing problem becomes even more severe. Back in 1967, McLuhan and Leonard were arguing:

> School computers can now help keep track of students as they move freely
> from one activity to another whenever moment by moment or year by year
> records of students' progress are needed. This will wipe out even the
> administrative justification for schedules and regular periods, with all
> their anti-educational effects, and will free teachers to get on with the real
> business of education. (p. 23)

So in creating a SMS, it is important not to just "automate" the
information requirements of the current system, but also to reconsider
the broad aims of the educational system and to seek ways of realizing
goals that have been more elusive, such as enhancing the quality of the
school experience.

Functions of School Monitoring Systems

There are many possible functions for an automated information system
within a school. The first and foremost is just plain record keeping.
There is a critical need in schools to keep records of who is there, what
students are doing, and how well they are doing. These records may be
required by federal law, state code, or local board policy, and they are
omnipresent. So, one function of an automated School-based Monitoring System is to satisfy those needs for record keeping, including modifying the files as students come and go.

A second major function of a SMS is generation of reports. A
serious problem in schools is having information easily distributed to all
who might need to know. For example, home information, including
emergency phone numbers, that teachers might find useful as they attempt to strengthen school–home relationships, can easily be distributed to all teachers from school-based computer files. Once a school
data base is up and running, it is amazing how many different applications can be identified in terms of supplying printouts of various kinds
to different professionals in the building who have a need to know. A
third function of the information system is record retrieval. This is not
the routine generation of reports but the function of searching for specific records, or sets of records with specific features, that might require
special attention. For example, pulling out all the data on a specific
student for a parent conference or scanning for students with combinations of failing grades and high absenteeism can easily be done in such
automated systems.

A fourth function is data analysis. One turns to the computer for
ease of record keeping, report generating, and record retrieval, but the

great strength of the computer is its ability to do complex analyses quickly and easily. One of the challenges in developing such information systems today is to build into these systems the expertise of a data analyst so that the benefits of such analyses are available to people in the schools. That is, you do not necessarily expect principals to know how to apply multiple contingency analyses to a set of data, but the types of questions which might benefit from such analyses can be anticipated by system developers and the results made available to users.

The final function of the SMS is to provide information for monitoring indicators and tailoring practices. Computer scientists call this the "process control application" of automated information systems; it is the application of cybernetic models to improve the educational system. The goal of this function of the monitoring system is to identify ways to tailor the school and its curriculum to the individual needs of the learner, rather than to make the individual learner adjust to the offerings of the typical classroom instruction.

CHARACTERISTICS OF EFFECTIVE INFORMATION SYSTEMS

Certainly one characteristic of an effective information system is that it contains data that are reasonably current and accurate. Central systems often fail to maintain data dependability. That is, if the focus is exclusively on centralized data bases for district-wide planning and accounting functions, and data flow is only from the school to the central computer, there is no reason to believe that the central files will be current and accurate if the people in the school are not using the data. Thus, it is essential to have the data become part of the operating system in the local school. If data that eventually are transmitted to the central system are used on a day-to-day basis within schools, it is much more likely that the centrally available data will be current and accurate.

One of the major problems that has plagued information systems is how to maintain current and accurate files. To overcome this problem, the SMS must include incentives for the local school to emphasize timeliness and accuracy in its file maintenance. For example, scoring the criterion-referenced tests in a school district can provide such incentives. When the Pittsburgh Public Schools launched its Monitoring Achievement in Pittsburgh (MAP) program, it was designed as a centrally scored achievement monitoring system. Even with the most heroic of efforts, that central system could only produce 2-week turnaround on the test scoring and reporting. Insofar as such tests are designed to guide the day-to-day instructional planning, the fortnightly turnaround is insufficient. However, with a scanner attached to the local school microcomputer, it is capable of scoring tests on the day they are given, of sending reports to students, teachers, and principals, and of automatically updating the school's information system with student performance and pacing data.

Local scoring of tests not only creates incentives for maintaining current files, it also helps improve the accuracy of files. For example, with scoring taking place and the results being viewed the same day, errors that can creep into a testing system can be easily found, corrected, and the results rescored. An example of such a clerical error might be a teacher indicating the wrong form of the facing sheet that controls test processing for that homeroom. If a central system scores several thousand such batches (one for each classroom), errors are usually not detectable and the inaccurate data become part of the centrally available file. Of course, when the printouts eventually reach the teacher, the teacher will notice the error and discard the results, but meanwhile, they are part of the central system and are unlikely to be purged or corrected.

Another important point here is that locally used data files reduce the likelihood of indicators becoming corrupted. That is, if data are collected and used within the local school to help in school planning and improvement, suspicious data (e.g., an overzealous teacher may have administered a test using nonstandard procedures) can be more easily detected and corrected. Data that are used exclusively for a centralized accountability system are far too easily corrupted and they will be corrupted if teachers and principals sense that they are being used in unfair ways in their own evaluation. So the shift in emphasis from data being used for local school improvement as opposed to central system accountability will result in a central data base that is sufficiently dependable for central planning and monitoring.

Another important feature of a SMS is to have built-in checks for noticing out-of-range data. For data that are being hand-entered, this feature should be part of the data-entry procedures. That is, as key strokes occur, any out-of-range character is immediately detected and brought to the attention of the keyboard operator through audio and visual cues. Similarly, data captured in other ways, such as through scanners or files imported from other computers, need to be screened for out-of-range data. Again, the advantages of distributive processing are obvious. Detecting out-of-range data centrally results in a more cumbersome set of procedures for correcting errors. If errors are detected within the school where the correct values can be more easily established, it is relatively easy.

One reason to adopt school-based monitoring systems is to make it possible to examine a broad range of data in an integrated fashion. For example, principals are often on the receiving end of a wide variety of computer printouts from different sources. They may get attendance reports from the central student accounting system, test results from the state assessment programs and/or the district's standardized test scoring service, listings of students eligible for compensatory education, report card grade summaries, or locally developed criterion-referenced test results. With a school-based student information system, such files can be imported into the school computer so that relationships among these various indicators of student progress can be examined and inconsistencies noted and followed up. Effective information systems make it possible to examine a wide variety of student data in a correlated manner.

In addition to facilitating the examination of trends across domains of data, effective information systems make it possible to examine data over time. For example, longitudinal data can help to spot a student whose achievement growth seems to have leveled off, or one whose truancy rate has suddenly increased, or one whose grades have begun to decline. This type of "early warning system" can be built into a SMS if longitudinal data are available.

Another powerful analytical tool is longitudinal data aggregated to the classroom level. For example, a principal who can study relationships between curriculum pacing and student achievement growth for all classrooms in the school has a better chance of exerting instructional leadership than one who does not have access to that kind of data. An effective information system makes it possible to examine data at the student, classroom and school levels. Longitudinal trends for the school as a whole are important in assessing how well the school is moving toward its goals.

One possible by-product of a school-based microcomputer system is an increase in the level of inquiry on the part of the professional staff. When data are easily available and data displays are arranged in provocative combinations, serious professionals will tend to "browse" through those displays. Then, when they encounter a surprising result, they will look to see if there are other instances of that phenomenon or look for factors that may have brought it about. Inquiry can be a guiding force in school change, but the tools for conducting inquiry must be available. An effective information system, which allows for ad hoc inquiries, is such a tool.

Specifications for a SMS

A SMS system must have built in incentives for school personnel to use the system. The local school SMS must offer the kinds of data that principals need in order to provide classroom level diagnostic information effectively to plan a program of staff development. It must provide test scoring services that teachers are willing and able to use, information to the social workers regarding chronic truancy and attendance patterns, and information directly to teachers on the available instructional materials that would be particularly helpful for the students in that classroom given recent test results.

The school-based SMS should have the following features:

1. It has an integrated software package that provides data management facilities and communication capabilities, making it easy to download files from the district's central computer which are relevant to the school and send summaries of school-level data back to the district files at the level of detail the district needs for system-wide purposes.

2. It includes a scanner that provides test-scoring services as well as updates the school-based student files with the latest achievement information.

3. It is menu-driven so that school personnel are able to begin to use it easily, and it can generate CRT displays as well as produce printouts that principals can easily share with other professional staff in the building.

4. It has an easily learned set of commands for making inquiries that were not anticipated in the menu options.

5. It has a secure password system so that unauthorized users cannot have access to confidential data that they have no right to see.

There are several commercial systems currently available that perform some of these functions, but none of them provide the flexibility required to meet the needs of every school system. Given the availability of sophisticated application packages, I think it is highly advantageous to develop and adapt these systems to local differences, such as the types of criterion-referenced tests being used, ways in which student tracking and attendance accounting is conducted, the types of special services available in the building for students, and so forth. Good applications packages also make it easier to be adaptive to the current central computer's file structures and methods of handling data.

REFERENCES

Baker, F. B. (1978). *Computer managed instruction: Theory and practice.* Englewood Cliffs, NJ: Educational Technology Publications.

Berman, P. (1980). *Toward an implementation paradigm of educational change.* Santa Monica, CA: Rand.

Bickel, W. E. (1983). Effective schools. *Educational Researcher, 12*(4), 3–31.

Cooley, W. W. (1983). Improving the performance of an educational system. *Educational Researcher, 12,* 4–12.

Cooley, W. W., & Bickel, W. E. (1986). *Decision-oriented educational research.* Boston: Kluwer–Nijhoff.

Cooley, W. W., & Lohnes, P. R. (1976). *Evaluation research in education.* New York: Irvington.

Epstein, J. L. (1981). *The quality of school life.* Lexington, MA: Heath.

Goodlad, J. I., O'Toole, J. F., Jr., & Tyler, L. L. (1966). *Computers and information systems in education.* New York: Harcourt, Brace.

Green, T. F. (1971). Equal educational opportunity: The durable injustice. *Philosophy of Education,* 121–156.

Johnstone, J. N. (1981). *Indicators of education systems.* London: Kogan Page.

Krathwohl, D. R. (chairman). (1975, November). *Educational indicators: Monitoring the state of education.* Proceedings of the 1975 ETS Invitational Conference, New York.

Land, K. C., & Spilerman, S. (Eds.). (1975). *Social indicator models.* New York: Sage.

Leinhardt, G. (1983). Overlap: Testing whether it is taught. In G. F. Madaus (Ed.), *The courts, validity, and minimum competency testing* (pp. 153–170). Boston: Kluwer–Nijhoff.

Lindblom, C. (1972). *Strategies for decision making.* Urbana: University of Illinois.

MacRae, D. Jr. (1985). *Policy indicators: Links between social science and public debate.* Chapel Hill: University of North Carolina Press.

McLuhan, M., & Leonard, G. B. (1967). The future of education. *Look, 31,* 23–25.

Meyers, W. R. (1981). *The evaluation enterprise.* San Francisco: Jossey–Bass.

Micro Data Base Systems. (1984). *Knowledge manager.* Lafayette, IN: MDBS.

Purkey, S. C., & Smith, M. (1983). Effective schools—A review. *Elementary School Journal, 83,* 427–452.

Sproull, L., & Zubrow, D. (1981). Performance information in school systems: Perspectives from organization theory. *Educational Administration Quarterly, 17*(3), 61–79.

NINE

THE USE OF STUDENT IMPROVEMENT SCORES IN STATE AND DISTRICT INCENTIVE SYSTEMS[1]

DUNCAN MacRAE, JR., and MARK W. LANIER

IMPROVING SCHOOLS BY MEASURING STUDENTS' IMPROVEMENT

Educational reform, like policy proposals in many other areas, risks being trapped in a cycle of new initiatives and disappointing results. Such cycles result not simply from fluctuation in our national goals for education, but also from the fact that our collective public enthusiasm often exceeds our knowledge about what will work. For this reason we need, as a nation, to give more steady public and private support to the incremental improvement of education. We need to spend more effort in trying out proposed reforms repeatedly in practice, preferably on a small scale; assessing each such trial carefully to see whether it improves education; and designing the next trial in view of the knowledge we have gained, rather than basing it simply on our hopes. We must learn to substitue smaller, better-informed, local cycles of school improvement for larger, national cycles of optimism and disillusionment. Even in those rare instances when a large-scale change is needed, we still need to refine it in detail by successive trials.

Our capacity to learn from experience requires not only careful design of our evaluations, but most importantly, measurement of what we have accomplished. The goal of a school or teacher is to produce

[1]Revised version of a chapter in Duncan MacRae, Jr. (Ed.), "Improving North Carolina's Public Schools," University of North Carolina at Chapel Hill, 1985, unpublished report. We are indebted to Patricia Dalton, Ron Haskins, James J. Gallagher, and Kinnard P. White for helpful suggestions, but they are not responsible for our errors.

learning,[2] so that, after an educational treatment, students have some knowledge or ability resulting from it that they did not have before. An apparently obvious way to measure this learning is by looking at students' *improvement* in the desired respect, i.e., comparing their knowledge or ability before and after the treatment. Yet measures of students' improvement have rarely been used in reviewing and evaluating educational policies; and even in recent years when they have been tried, few clear successes in their use have been observed. Our aim in this chapter is to examine the use of pupil improvement measures to advance the performance of teachers and schools, discuss their revealed and potential problems, and consider conditions under which they may be more useful.

Statistics on students' learning can potentially be used in several ways to improve that learning, including both formative and summative evaluation (Millman, 1981).[3] Their use in formative evaluation (Scriven, 1967), i.e., as part of an ongoing internal process within a school, is discussed by Cooley in this volume, and by Cooley and Bickel (1986). In contrast, Dill, in this volume, points out the potential formative value of national indicators of student achievement, even when they are not based on improvement, to define problems for the nation or states.

Our concern in this chapter is with incentive systems at an intermediate level—that of the state or district. Although improvement statistics at these levels could be used for formative purposes, we are concerned with comparisons among schools or among teachers, used as an ingredient in evaluations and in rewards for effectiveness. In general form, the policy that we wish to consider is a simple one: When state or district authorities wish to know which schools and teachers have done well, instead of using only the absolute levels of achievement of pupils in each school, they should use the corresponding levels of *improvement*. There are numerous variations on this procedure, however, as well as potential pitfalls; thus our eventual recommendation will be to study concrete incentive systems, varying their conditions in detail, through a carefully designed set of successive trials. If we can make these incentive

---

[2]We assume this to be the goal, although conceivably the teacher may be seen "solely as a classroom manager" (Millman, 1981, p. 146). We shall speak of learning of knowledge and ability, but our discussion applies to traits of character as well.

[3]To avoid misunderstanding, we must state that we do not favor the use of such statistics as the sole criterion in incentive systems, both because of problems of reliability and validity and because of the danger of biases resulting from such use (MacRae, 1985, Chapter 9). Moreover, we do not necessarily recommend that only existing standardized tests be used, since some of the critiques bearing on both validity and stability have specific reference to these tests.

systems workable, they will then contribute to the assessment and improvement of numerous other efforts to enhance learning. We are concerned here with a general approach to the use of indicators of pupil achievement, but not with specifying the subjects that the public schools should teach. The wave of reforms proposed in recent years has centered about pupils' learning of key subjects taught in the schools. Some observers wish to extend this list of subjects to include other qualities, such as character and citizenship, taught either explicitly or implicitly. In addition, our society has a continuing concern with the distribution of learning among groups of children who may differ in race, sex, social class, handicaps, or initial level of achievement. No matter which of these goals we seek, however, or what policy we propose for furthering them, we need to obtain and use the best possible evidence bearing on whether the chosen policy results in more learning. The measurement of these contributions is thus a central task for all our deliberations on educational policy and for policy review and evaluation.

MEASURES OF STUDENTS' IMPROVEMENT AND THEIR USES IN INCENTIVE SYSTEMS

Recent "movements" in education (e.g., accountability, minimum competency, basic skills, and effective schools) have stressed the importance of student achievement levels. Many school districts annually report the level of achievement scores in each school in the district, or the proportion of pupils who have attained a specified level. This information can be important if it validly indicates pupils' capacities, but it is less useful for telling what a school has contributed to them. These achievement scores depend on many factors over which schools have, at best, limited control because they reflect the effects of parental inputs before the school year began, pupils' initial ability or achievement, and other nonschool factors. The scores cannot, therefore, tell us what a specific public policy, or a particular school or teacher, has contributed to learning. Instead, the test scores reported tell us the present *status* of students (i.e., what their level of achievement is now).

We can come closer to measuring the contribution of a policy, or the effectiveness of a teacher, if we measure *improvement* in test scores, rather than simply considering the present level of test scores. Improvement scores, which can be calculated in several different ways, have the common feature that they compare current achievement with some measure of expected achievement, usually based on past test scores. These measures of improvement should be useful in incentive or feedback systems and can provide information relevant for educational policymakers, administrators, and teachers themselves when based on valid measures of the effects sought. In incentive systems, outsiders wish to assess and reward the performance of teachers or schools in producing students' learning. In internal feedback systems, teachers themselves examine their performance in order to teach better. In either case, measures of improvement can be used to give special attention to pupils who enter an educational experience at a disadvantage, because they set aside those pupils' starting achievement level. They can also be used, if we wish, to identify schools or teachers who are most effective in teaching pupils with lower starting levels. Multiple measures of improvement might also be used to provide feedback as to the subjects in which a given school or teacher was doing better or worse.

If we could measure student achievement before and after a learning experience by means of exactly equivalent tests, the comparison of before and after scores would yield a clear measure of student improvement over that period; and if all the change in that period was due to instruction, this comparison would measure the effectiveness of the teacher or school. Often, however, we use a noncomparable "before" measure—a test on the same subject matter not comparable with the "after" test, or a measure of ability or socioeconomic status. In this case (as in the preceding one), the comparison of "before" measures and "after" scores is typically made by regression or analysis of covariance (Hoffer, Greeley, & Coleman, 1985, p. 82; Millman, 1981, p. 161), in which the "before" measure is used as a covariate. The result is then a measure of *relative improvement*. Although it does not tell just how much a group of students learned, it permits a fairer comparison between schools or teachers by equating their students on the covariate(s).[4]

If we are able to compare the learning produced by various teachers or schools, we may be conducting a type of quasi-experiment, in which one teacher or school serves as a comparison for another; the result, at best, will be a measure of the differential effects of the teachers

---

[4]These procedures assume that the dependent variable and the covariate are related linearly to learning. This assumption would not hold, for example, for a single dichotomous question. It would be questionable if the "before" test or covariate measured only skills learned in the grade in question but not variations in earlier preparation; then those pupils who were inadequately prepared would still begin by scoring "zero," together with those adequately prepared. Similarly, an "after" test that measured only the minimum required skills to be learned in that grade would give the same score for those who learned more than that grade taught as for those who learned just what was required. Finally, the assumption of linearity would not be equally valid for various transformations of a test score, such as raw scores, standard scores, grade equivalents, or percentiles.

or schools compared. Thus, White (1975) refers to the variable being measured as "relative performance." There are, of course, standard experimental and quasi-experimental methods for assessing interventions (Cook & Campbell, 1979; Cronbach, 1982). These methods use improvement in student test scores when assessing the effects of specific educational programs and thus have applications in some types of incentive systems (e.g., in performance contracting for instructional programs).

In a number of policies recently adopted by states and school districts in the United States, statistics on improvement in student test scores have been used as indicators of the performance of teachers or schools and as a basis for providing rewards or incentives. We call this the *indicator-incentive system* approach, meaning that measures of improvement on an indicator are used (possibly among other criteria) as a basis for rewarding schools or teachers differentially. This approach is intended to improve education by setting a standard and inducing educators to strive toward that standard. This approach assumes, by analogy with the market, that educators with this motivation will be more likely to seek out examples of success and emulate them. This assumption is not universally true, however. An indicator system based on improvement was instituted in the Atlanta public schools in 1972–73, in cooperation with the Urban Institute. Without special incentives, without effort on the consultants' part to show schools or teachers how to do better, and with only a 1-year trial, the system produced no perceptible effect on administrative or teaching practices (White, 1975).

The question is sometimes raised as to whether the procedure of measuring improvement is applicable to criterion-referenced as well as to norm-referenced tests. The availability of national norms for a test is usually irrelevant for indicator-incentive systems, because all that matters in these systems is the comparison of average improvement among schools or teachers in a state or school district; this comparison can be made without reference to national norms, or indeed to any prior norms. Indicator-incentive systems can use norms based on improvement, however. Thus, last year's distribution of average improvement scores in a given school district might be used as a basis of comparison for this year's. For this reason, specially designed local tests could be as good as or better than nationally standardized tests for measuring improvement.

The question whether improvement can be measured with criterion-referenced tests has more meaning if it is interpreted in terms of the *domain* of subject matter covered by the tests, and the *transformations* performed on test scores. Gronlund (1985, p. 13), for example, defines a criterion-referenced test as dealing with "a clearly defined and delimited domain of learning tasks." With this definition, as long as achievement in this domain can be considered to vary linearly with the test score, all the procedures we discuss for measuring improvement on tests in general are applicable; if the domain is properly chosen, the test(s) used may also be especially valid. Gronlund defines an "objective-referenced" test as "interpretable in terms of a specific educational objective." If this objective is represented by a cutoff score, it transforms the initial range of scores into a dichotomy such as "mastery" versus "nonmastery." Dichotomous variables are difficult to use for individual improvement scores. For a class or a school, the proportion achieving mastery might be compared at the aggregate level with the average "before" score of those same students, or more sophisticated techniques, such as logit regression might be used. More important, however, is the fact that this dichotomization uses test information very inefficiently in comparison with the numerical test score. If we wish to find out how well a teacher brings students up to "mastery" level, we need only to use the numerical test score and omit from the analysis those students who reach a level considerably above mastery, or weight them less heavily. We *do* need to know how effective the teacher is in bringing educationally disadvantaged students up *toward* mastery, and a simple dichotomization will fail to reveal this. In short, we do not believe that objective-referenced or criterion-referenced tests require any distinct procedures of analysis for measuring improvement.

Measures of improvement can be used not only in indicator-incentive systems, but also to seek general causes of school or teacher effectiveness. First, experiments and quasi-experiments to reveal the effects of specific educational treatments on achievement can use improvement measures as dependent variables.[5] Second, research on school and teacher effects (e.g., Epstein, 1985; Good, 1983; Murnane, 1975; Rutter et al., 1979; Summers & Wolfe, 1977, 1984; Wellisch, MacQueen, Carriere, & Duck, 1978) is most appropriately conducted using measures of improvement or corresponding use of "before" measures as independent variables. Alexander, Pallas, and Cook (1981) have shown the superiority of prior test scores to measures of SES, when the former are available, by reanalyzing a given data set in both ways. Factors contributing to learning such as the leadership of the princial, the quality of the colleges attended by teachers, or teachers' skills in classroom management have been suggested by studies of this kind that seek general causes of improvement. Such studies seek to state *general models of causa-*

---

[5]More precisely, the "after" score can be used as a dependent variable and the "before" score or other control variable can be used as a covariate.

tion as bases for policy choice, and to extend these models to a larger population of schools.

A major statement of such models concerning effects of classroom management, proposed for use in North Carolina's schools, is incorporated in the Carolina Teaching Performance Assessment System (CTPAS) (Wyne, White, Stuck, & Coop, 1984). Teachers with high ratings on classroom performance, based on the CTPAS, are expected to be more effective than others in producing learning by similar pupils. Such an expected effect, however, although inferred from research, requires repeated testing to show that it actually occurs in practice (White, Wyne, Stuck, & Coop, 1983). Without this further measurement of outcomes, the assumption of uniform causal models in a specified population would remain untested, with regard to both the transition from nonexperimental research to practice and the diversity of teachers' and schools' paths to effectiveness.

These two approaches—indicator-incentive systems and policies based on general models of the causes of learning—are similar in some ways, yet have different advantages and disadvantages. If they are used to guide educational policy, each must involve some notion about how we can act to produce improvement; both, in other words, involve notions about what causes learning. When we use information about general causes of learning, however, we tend to deal with *general* characteristics of schools or teachers that are assumed to affect improvement similarly over a large number of schools. This approach cannot easily be adapted to particular local circumstances or detect unique but effective local programs. At the same time, it has an advantage: When we do research on such causes, we do not usually reward teachers or schools for the information they give or for their pupils' scores, and the data are not likely to be biased for this reason.

The indicator-incentive approach has just the opposite advantages and disadvantages. It is highly adaptable to local circumstances; if we find a school (or teacher) that regularly produces large improvements, we can study and reward this school even if it does not conform with any previously observed general pattern. Such an approach allows for local initiative and experimentation, so that schools and teachers can seek their own paths to excellence.

On the other hand, the attachment of specific rewards or penalties to test scores can result in practices that undermine the validity of test scores and statistics based on them. Although "teaching to the test" is not wholly undesirable when tests reflect what should be taught (i.e., when test content and a desired curriculum are well matched), the actual teaching of the test (e.g., when teachers acquire advance copies of tests and teach test items) is an undesirable consequence of the incentive approach. This problem was a serious concern in Dallas, for example, when rewards were associated with high improvement scores and teachers began requesting more copies of the test in advance. "Teaching to the test" can be especially problematical if tests and curricula are not well matched, if emphasis is placed on test-taking skills rather than skills that tests purport to measure, or if curricula and instructional content are narrowed to reflect only what is tested (Frederiksen, 1984). To the extent possible, these potentially adverse effects should be measured, by including tests to which incentives are not attached and by comparison of student performance on different tests, as part of testing programs using the indicator-incentive approach (LeMahieu, 1984).

Our task here is to review indicator-incentive systems, their problems, and conditions for their future success. The success of these systems depends on teachers' and administrators' knowledge of models of causation, because the changes made in response to incentives must be directed intelligently toward students' improvement. Some educators who seek to make changes to increase improvement may try to select these changes exclusively from their own experience. Others may be able to choose from a wider and better range of possible changes if they can examine successful schools and classrooms, seeking to follow their example; or study the research literature, especially studies of general models of causation. Elsewhere in this volume, House and Lapan suggest that intuitive trial and error is preferred by teachers over technically rational models of causation. However, several other contributors, especially Epstein, imply that new alternatives rather than those already widely used should receive greater attention. Regardless of the sources of change, indicator-incentive systems will be successful if they stimulate changes resulting in real improvement in student achievement. Our ultimate criterion for the success of an indicator-incentive system should be students' learning, in relation to the cost of having such a system. When we evaluate the effects of such a system, learning should be measured by indicators independent of those to which incentives are attached. Intermediate criteria, which ultimately affect learning, also include the acceptability and possible implementation of such a system, and include its intelligibility to all concerned.

RECENT EXAMPLES OF INCENTIVE SYSTEMS USING STUDENT TEST SCORES

A wide variety of incentive systems for teachers and schools have been proposed recently by states and districts across the nation. These vary on many dimensions, such as the criteria used for assessing excellence and the types of rewards given. Madaus (1985) dates the origins of incentives based on student test scores to "15th century Italy, where a master's salary depended on his student's performance," to "Adam Smith in the 18th century," and to "John Stuart Mill and Horace Mann in the 19th" (p. 614). Coltham (1972) reports an unsuccessful English experiment in "educational accountability" in the 19th century. However, these earlier incentive systems employed levels of test scores rather than improvement in test scores. Proposals to use students' *improvement* on test scores as a criterion for comparing schools and teachers have a history easily traceable to the early 1970s (Lieberman, 1970; McDonald & Forehand, 1973; White, 1975), though without producing clear success. Incentives based on students' improvement received renewed attention during the flood of educational reforms in the early 1980s, appearing in a variety of policies aimed at assessing and rewarding school or teacher effects. Some of these policies offer nonmonetary rewards (Wynne, 1984), which may lead to greater acceptance and less "teaching to the test," but perhaps less overall effect, than monetary ones. Most policies, however, either directly or indirectly link financial incentives to improvement in student test scores.

By limiting our focus to policies based on improvement in test scores, rather than the level of test scores,[6] we select for attention a small proportion of the teacher and school incentive plans recently advanced by states and districts. These plans, involving merit pay, career ladder, master teacher, and similar arrangements, vary tremendously in their details (see Calhoun & Protheroe, 1983; Cohen & Murnane, 1985; Education Commission of the States, 1984; Educational Research Service, 1979; U.S. Department of Education, 1984), but rarely rely on test scores as a component in evaluation. Administrators in most states and districts have strongly discouraged any linkage between student test scores and incentive systems.

Despite opposition, financial incentives have been or soon will be provided in several states and districts based on improvement in student test scores. The most common plan offers incentives to schools

---

[6]We omit discussion of compensatory programs for schools and districts with low average test scores. One problem with such programs is the negative incentive that penalizes schools and districts by lowering compensatory aid when their test scores rise. A second type of policy not considered in detail links either test scores or improvement in test scores to school accreditation. Recent reforms in Mississippi and Missouri have provided such linkage (Walton, 1984). The incentives in such programs can be financial and punitive, as in Mississippi (i.e., loss of state funding is the "stick"), or nonmonetary and positive, as in Missouri (i.e., higher accreditation ratings are the "carrot").

deemed meritorious with all teachers in those schools sharing equally in the awards. Descriptions of some of these plans, derived in part from unpublished sources, such as telephone interviews with administrators and reports of limited circulation, will show the types of indicator-incentive systems that have been created.

In 1983, California enacted its Education Improvement Incentive Program (Fetler, 1986). By 1985, California secondary schools were awarded a total of $14.4 million, based largely on comparisons of average annual test score improvement for 12th graders. Individual schools received a maximum of $400 per pupil, while district awards ranged from roughly $120,000 to $1.57 million. Problems with the program identified by administrators include reliance on school averages rather than improvement by individual pupils, validity of the test, the penalty for high average scores in previous years, and the proctoring procedures used. The last concern stemmed from suspected and confirmed manipulations of scores, resulting in implementation of a revised system employing lay proctors. Future plans outline expansion of the incentive program, if it is successful, to other grade levels (Fetler, 1986). Even so, the governor's line item veto could be the proverbial wrench that stops the wheel. Yet, in its chief state school officer, Bill Honig, California has a strong proponent of the indicator-incentive approach and of school award programs using many criteria in addition to test scores (Honig, 1984).

The South Carolina Education Improvement Act of 1984 called for development of both a Teacher Incentive Program and a School Incentive Program, as well as 58 other reforms (see McDonnell, 1984; Southern Regional Education Board, 1985, pp. 20–21). The School Incentive Program (SIP) distributed about $7 million to schools for pilot testing in the 1985–86 school year. Improvement in test scores from South Carolina's criterion-referenced Basic Skills Assessment Program (BSAP) and from the norm-referenced Comprehensive Test of Basic Skills (CTBS) is a necessary condition for receiving awards. Only if achievement gains exceed a minimum threshold are other criteria (e.g., attendance data or school climate variables) considered. The minimum acceptable level of BSAP improvement reflects an increase in the percentage of students above mastery, determined through examination of past data, and, from CTBS, an analysis of the top and bottom quartiles.

The South Carolina Teacher Incentive Program (TIP) was conducted as an experiment in 1985–86 with three variants in 11 districts, each variant incorporating student achievement data. The first, a "campus" approach (later modified to stress individual rewards), used the data from SIP, which are aggregated at the school level, and rewards all teachers in meritorious schools who have received at least satisfactory performance evaluations. This last provision is designed to overcome objections such as those raised in Dallas (discussed below) that some nonmeritorious teachers were rewarded simply because they taught in meritorious schools. Some of this criticism in Dallas came from teachers, which is ironic because one objective of reward systems at the school level is the fostering of collegiality among teachers (Bellin & Bellin, 1973, pp. 138–39).

The other two variants in TIP, bonus and career-ladder plans, use a portfolio format that draws together various types of information to evaluate individual teachers. Under the bonus model, annual stipends set by the local district (recommended at $2,000 to $3,000) are awarded to qualifying personnel. In the career-ladder model, the size of stipends depends on placement at one of three career levels (around $1,250 at Level I, $2,750 at Level III). In both plans, a district committee, working with teachers, will develop the evaluation portfolio, which by state mandate must include measures of students' improvement. In addition to BSAP and CTBS scores, where available, tests developed by teachers, tests from textbooks, classroom products, and other instruments and materials can be used as evidence of achievement growth. Beyond achievement growth, five other components enter into the evaluation process; two of them, for example, are (a) extended duties and (b) personal development through graduate study, workshops, travel, and research. Due to the experimental and flexible approach of the Teacher Incentive Program and the ambitiousness of both the teacher and school programs, it is surprising that each program is assigned to only one administrator and even more startling that the administrator of the teacher program is in a "sunset" position. Apparently, very little technical assistance (e.g., with test score transformations) will be available from the state level to guide districts in these new directions.

In Florida, the Omnibus Education Act of 1984 created the District Quality Instruction Incentives Program, in which districts were asked to submit plans for distributing a total of $20 million to meritorious schools and teachers. This program became a union issue, as those districts affiliated with the National Education Association (NEA) have refused to participate. As a result, only 33 of Florida's 67 districts (i.e., those affiliated with the American Federation of Teachers) are participating in the program. As in South Carolina, test score improvement is a requirement for any award to schools, after which other criteria can be considered. Several alternative methods for computing gains in achievement (e.g., several types of regression analyses; an increase in the percentage of students improving 10 or more percentile points) were suggested by state officials. All but 2 of the 33 participating districts adopted some form of regression analysis to assess predicted versus actual achievement.

In this decentralized plan, each district determines the shares of its allocation given to schools, teachers, support personnel, and other recipients. Such decentralized plans offer the advantages of enhanced political feasibility, adjustment to local conditions, and the accumulation of knowledge from various "trials." At the same time, such decentralization results in duplication of administrative planning and effort, problems in comparing programs across districts, and variations in the emphasis placed on student performance versus other criteria.

Moving from state plans to school district plans, the incentive system implemented in Houston has been cited as an example of "new style merit pay attempts" that reward teachers based on "output measures like student performance on standardized tests" (Bacharach, Lipsky, & Shedd, 1984, p. 28). Teachers who meet a number of prerequisites are eligible for awards if their school has made "outstanding educational progress," determined by ranking the average gain scores for schools within groupings based on the proportion of low-income families (Hatry & Greiner, 1985, p. 141). The merit school program in the Dallas Independent School District has also received national attention (e.g., Jordan & Borkow, 1983, p. 24) and will be the only district plan discussed in detail.

The Dallas school award program was built on a solid foundation of methodological expertise. Using a very extensive data base, Webster and Olson (1984) experimented with past data and many alternative statistical procedures in order to develop fair rankings for schools of any size and any grade configuration found in the Dallas system. Eight measures for ranking schools (all correlated at or above the .91 level) were presented to the program's oversight committee. The measure selected, a lower-bound estimate of the mean, individually standardized gain in achievement for a school, was designed to avoid rewarding unstable average gains.

Each type of school (i.e., K–3, K–6, etc.) was then ranked, using this statistic. Teachers in the top 25% of schools in each ranking were then awarded a merit bonus of $1,500, with support staff in selected schools receiving lesser amounts. This incentive system has the aforementioned potential benefit of fostering collegiality and is an improvement over systems built on insufficient data bases and dependent on questionable methodologies. At the same time, it is subject to the criticisms that it rewards both good and bad teachers and that it encourages unethical behavior. After the first year of awards, the Dallas program was abandoned for exactly these reasons. According to one administrator, the most common complaint about the plan was the assertion that "everyone [in a merit school] shouldn't benefit." Others feel that the negative publicity brought on by reports of teacher requests for advance copies of tests and by rumors of investigations into improper behavior by teachers contributed to the program's demise.

These examples of improvement-based incentive plans are indicative of the many forms that such programs can assume and suggest some of the problems that must be considered in designing and analyzing such policies. Generally, the major problems can be organized under the two topics of "valid measurement" and "effective use." We now turn our attention to a detailed discussion of these two problems.

PROBLEMS IN THE MEASUREMENT OF SCHOOL AND TEACHER EFFECTS

Information

The first requirement for an improvement-based incentive plan is that the content to be taught in the various subject-matter areas where incentives are to be provided must be measured validly. This requires a diversity of tests, the administration of which may be costly. Second, the relevant achievements or qualities must be tested at least annually. Third, the scores must be connected to serial numbers so that scores from one time of administration can be matched with scores from another by computer; scores identified by pupils' names are not only somewhat less secure, but also cause both errors and inconvenience in matching. Those school systems that have introduced indicator-incentive systems have usually had computer data bases of test scores recorded in comparable form so that a given pupil's scores from one year can be quickly compared with those from the next. However, some states have enacted provisions for incentives even when the data necessary to estimate pupils' gain scores were not available.

Tests and Transformations

There are differences of opinion as to the best transformation of raw test scores to use (i.e., grade equivalent scores, scale scores, percentile ranks, etc.). The measurement of improvement thus requires detailed decisions about the particular tests to use and the transformation of test scores. Developers of the California Achievement Tests (CAT) recommend that developmental scale scores be used for arithmetical computations (e.g., the subtraction of pretest score from posttest score in computing gain scores). These scale scores were used by Guth (1984) in his analysis of school effectiveness in North Carolina. Some researchers interested in measuring improvement in achievement have relied on grade equivalent scores (e.g., Heyns, 1980), a transformation that was used in the Dallas merit school program (Webster & Olson, 1984). Still others have employed national percentile rankings (e.g., Wellisch, Mac-Queen, Carriere, & Duck, 1978). These transformations need to be compared in terms of the stability of the school and teacher effects that they indicate.

Statistical Measures

There are also questions as to the best statistical procedure to use in measuring improvement over time (i.e., average difference scores, regression residuals, etc.). It is clear, however, that measures of improvement should be based only on data for those students who remain in the sample both before and after the educational experience in question. Laymen accustomed to using annual published statistics on average status of pupils may be inclined to compare these from year to year; but such judgments based on noncomparable populations in different years should be avoided if possible (this was the occasion of some debate in the Dallas system and is a source of informed criticism in the California program). We here face a question of balancing validity against intelligibility, perhaps involving education of the public.

The most easily understood measure of improvement, the simple "gain" or difference score, has been strongly criticized (e.g., Cronbach & Furby, 1970) because of its possible unreliability for measuring gains of individual students. Other scholars (e.g., Rogosa & Willett, 1983; Williams & Zimmerman, 1977; Zimmerman & Williams, 1982) have responded more recently that average gain scores can be useful under some conditions. Moreover, several authors (e.g., Guth, 1984; Marco, 1974; Webster & Olson, 1984) have suggested that, in many cases, alternative measures may be largely equivalent.

One alternative to the gain score is a regression residual (residualized gain score), in which a pupil's score is compared with an expected value based on prediction of pupils' current scores from earlier scores. In its simplest form this regression uses the score from only one previous testing. More complex methods use two or more previous tests for prediction (Webster & Olson, 1984). Rogosa, Brandt, and Zimowski (1982) have proposed that growth curves for individual pupils be estimated as a way of further reducing variance due to differences among pupils; a rate of growth characterizing the pupil, independently of treatments, should be closely associated with "ability" or "aptitude." This approach requires at least three observations over time per pupil.

An additional problem concerns pupils with extreme pretest scores partly due to error; such scores will tend to regress toward the mean on later tests, and this will bias estimates of teacher effects. McLean and Sanders (1983) deal with this problem by using an estimation model proposed by Henderson (1975; see below).

Furthermore, as we shall show below, even the best improvement measures can include learning that does not result from the policy, school, or teacher in question. As a result, additional controls for non-manipulable background variables, such as socioeconomic status, may need to be included in regressions. This sort of control can be especially important when we test achievement in subjects for which there is no easily measurable achievement base, such as a new foreign language or a distinct, new mathematical skill.

So far we have assumed that a particular transformation of scores and a particular measure of improvement can be chosen and used. Some who measure improvement may, however, be unwilling to assume that a transformation can be found that measures equal intervals of achievement. In this case, they will no longer have confidence that they can compare gains of pupils who begin at different levels. They may then have to make separate comparisons of groups of schools or teachers that teach different grades or different social groups, and that thus start at different levels of achievement (Fennessey & Salganik, 1983; Heyns, 1980, p. 17). This has been done in California's accountability program (Fetler, 1986) and in Houston (Hatry & Greiner, 1985, p. 141), for example. Such limited comparisons seem to treat teachers and schools more fairly; but they have been criticized as setting lower standards for disadvantaged groups.

Stability

Both the public and experienced educators believe that we should expect certain effective schools and teachers to stand out year after year. Efforts to show such stability have been disappointing, however, as a series of systematic studies show. More specifically, these studies show that the correlations between improvement scores across years are much lower than might have been expected. Reviewing three studies, Glass (1974, p. 13) reports 1–year stability coefficients (correlations over student groups in successive years) for residual gain scores of teacher effects in grades 1–3, of .00 to .78 with 35 of 45 coefficients, and all coefficients for subject matter averages, equal to .49 or less. Rosenshine (1970, pp. 648ff), citing four studies of elementary and secondary teaching that found stability coefficients generally "about .35 or much lower," claims that "evidence on the consistency of teacher effects is weak." Alexander, McPartland,

and Cook (1980, pp. 21ff) report coefficients for residual school effects ranging from .05 to .59 for Baltimore schools, grades 3–5. Forsyth (1973, pp. 10–11) found a correlation of .28 between school regression residuals for two consecutive cohorts of high school students. Finally, Rowan, Bossert, and Dwyer (1983, p. 26) report coefficients of .19 and .24 for school residuals from regressions including SES variables, for grades 3–6. Indeed, Rowan (personal communication, Sept. 10, 1984) concludes that "our . . . inability to stably measure instructional effectiveness represents a *substantive* finding—school and teacher effects are weak and unstable."

We know of only one statistical study of stability of school or teacher effects, regardless of the methods used, that shows associations uniformly as high even as .5. McLean and Sanders (1983), using a special estimation method to reduce the effect of error variation,[7] found three coefficients averaging .51 for the stability of a sum of mathematics, language, and reading scores for teachers in grades 3–5; the median of nine coefficients for individual subjects was .45.

These findings pose a serious problem for the use of improvement statistics in causal models, as public indicators, or as ingredients of incentive systems. In causal models, this property of the statistics may be partly responsible for the relatively low correlations that are typically observed between policy variables and students' improvement. In indicator-incentive systems, it raises the possibility that the list of schools singled out as "most effective" in one year will have little overlap with the list for the next—as the Montgomery County, Md., schools have found (Myerberg & Splaine, 1983, pp. 76–79). This problem of instability will hamper efforts to develop incentive systems based on school or teacher effects.

However, Dyer, Linn, and Patton (1969, p. 601) present evidence that improvements in different subject-matter areas correlate much more closely than do gains across cohorts, suggesting that greater stability might be attainable in the use of these measures. After randomly subdividing the classrooms in a large sample of school districts, these researchers correlated the residuals from prediction equations between pairs of subject-matter subtests and obtained values ranging from .62 to .84. Similarly, Guth (1984) found that the correlations between mean

---

[7]The possible superiority of this method needs to be examined by comparing it with other methods on the same data. McLean and Sanders' use of Henderson's (1975) "mixed model" resembles the "empirical Bayes" approach of Raudenbush and Bryk (1986, p. 5), which they report also reduces certain random errors in the analysis of school effects. The lower-bound estimate of the school mean used in Dallas (Webster & Olson, 1984) also has the same purpose.

school gain scores in reading, language arts, and mathematics ranged from .5 to .7 in his 122 schools. These results suggest that the differences between successive groups of pupils in the studies cited earlier did not involve as much random error as the low stability coefficients would suggest. Rather, there may have been systematic, nonrandom differences between student groups in succeeding years—such as differences in ability, motivation, or their social environment—not captured by achievement measures. A challenge to future research is to discover and measure the relevant systematic differences so as to control for them and increase the stability of the resulting measures.

Improvement versus Effects of Policies or Schools

Improvement scores go far toward removing the gross differences among student populations that are reflected in mere indicators of current achievement status. They nevertheless reflect any and all factors that may contribute to learning during the period studied. Some of this learning may occur in the home or elsewhere rather than in the school. The learning of what is measured by our incentive-related tests is desirable; but if policies, schools, or teachers are to be given credit for learning, it must be learning for which they are responsible or which they can influence.

Although improvement measured over a calendar year can reveal much about the effectiveness of schools or teachers, Heyns (1978) has shown that improvement on annual tests reflects not only the effect of the schools, but also that of summer learning. It is possible that summer learning is "differentially affected by the classroom behavior of the teacher of the previous year" (Rosenshine, 1970, p. 653) or other school factors, but the determinants of summer learning have more likely origins in the home. In the summer, students from higher-income and white homes gain relative to those from lower-income and Black homes (see also Murnane, 1975, pp. 86–89). The bias thus produced in annual improvement indexes is reduced when only the period from fall to spring is considered. Measures of improvement obtained in this way would further narrow the advantages enjoyed by schools from higher-income areas, putting all schools on a more nearly equal basis for the assessment of their effectiveness. Fall and spring testing might thus permit a more valid measure of improvement. In addition, it would reduce the possible propagation of bias due to one year's "after" measures constituting next year's "before."

We need also to reconsider the use of social and economic variables as statistical controls in the measurement of improvement. We have suggested that, in incentive systems, comparisons across schools may be appropriate only when they involve schools whose pupils come from similar social backgrounds. Our argument was based on the problems associated with the measurement of improvement, but comparisons among schools with similar student bodies might also be a crude and inexpensive way of controlling on "before" conditions. A related approach would be to use measures of improvement, but to control statistically for family background characteristics such as socioeconomic status and parental education (Hoffer, Greeley, & Coleman, 1985, p. 84). Such controls might be justified even if fall–spring testing were done, because the effect of the home parallels that of the school even during the school year. Before we go to extremes in controlling for extraschool conditions, however, we must recognize that some of these conditions may in fact be part of an educational program. Many school programs, for example, encourage parental participation, and some even train mothers to function as teachers of academic subject matter. Thus, we must control those contributory variables for which the school, or the policy in question, is not responsible, but not arbitrarily control extraschool effects that our teachers, schools, or policies help produce.

These and other problems associated with measuring students' improvement point to the need for research and experimentation that will aid decisions based on improvement scores. In planning this research, we must therefore look to the decision processes in which these statistics might be used and try to anticipate their possibilities and limitations in use. The following sections address these needs and present recommendations for the use of improvement measures.

PROBLEMS IN THE USE OF IMPROVEMENT MEASURES

Unintended Consequences

Even if we could measure improvement validly and stably, the use of these measures in incentive systems would still give rise to problems because the persons affected need to learn to accept and use such measures for policy purposes. This problem of understanding and use is a generic problem of policy indicators (MacRae, 1985, Chapter 9). When indicator-based incentives are provided in a limited number of curricular areas, effort and resources may well be transferred to these areas from others—for example, from music and art (if they are not part of the incentive system) to reading and mathematics. Such biases in curricular content may well have more lasting impact than simply teaching to the test. Moreover, while teaching to the test can be problematical, it is probably not as destructive to the educational process and to the ethics of participants as is teaching the test itself. This latter type of unintended consequence has apparently occurred in several recent programs, pointing to the need for multiple indicators and for limited incentives, as well as for test security.

Cohen and Murnane (1985) have studied a number of successful incentive plans and found that their success may be temporary, making further improvement more difficult after a certain degree of improvement is produced. If such plans contribute to the elimination of poorer teachers and the recruitment of better ones, the resulting homogenization may lead to universal rather than selective rewards. Thus, the plans may be more effective before this sort of routinization occurs, when there are greater contrasts among the teachers.

Opposition

Equally serious is the possibility that people affected by the incentive system will oppose the establishment of the system in the first place. Teachers may be concerned that the measurements would be invalid; administrators may be worried that the additional testing would be cumbersome to carry out. The continuing opposition of teachers to merit pay proposals extends to test-based incentive plans, as illustrated by the opposition of the NEA in Florida. The arguments underlying such opposition must be considered seriously; proposed incentive systems must be pilot tested carefully; evidence of their fairness and workability must be provided; and teachers and their organizations must be allowed to participate in the planning of incentive systems (Johnson, 1986).

Fairness to teachers may require equalization of school conditions that affect their effectiveness, such as their other responsibilities, materials, and facilities (Haertel, 1986, pp. 48–49); but incentives should be provided to improve these conditions if they are manipulable, even if teachers do not control them. For example, Campbell (1984, p. 38 and note) suggests that performance measurement can be used to compare alternative textbooks in a given subject. More generally, he suggests (p. 44) that distortion of measurements, and objections to incentive programs, could be reduced if we evaluated programs that present staffs could adopt, rather than evaluating persons or social units.

TOWARD BETTER IMPROVEMENT-BASED INDICATOR-INCENTIVE SYSTEMS

Our accounts of existing indicator-incentive systems and the general findings on instability of improvement scores suggest that working recipes for successful indicator-incentive systems are not yet available. Even where new programs have led to changes, these changes have not been successfully institutionalized. The general principle of measuring improvement still seems desirable, but further study and trials are necessary before it can be put into practice reliably. For this reason, we shall now recommend several courses of action that would increase our knowledge of improvement measures and their potential for use in educational policy. Our recommendations will center on the need for better information concerning improvement and incentive systems.

Research for Better Measurement of Improvement

Additional research should be conducted using available data from standardized tests. Various transformations of test scores and various methods for computing improvement measures should be compared to determine the effects on the stability of improvement measures.

In addition to exploring the stability of measures of students' improvement based on standardized tests, we need also to examine the validity of these measures. At first glance, improved achievement would seem to be our major criterion for policy choice. There are a number of reasons, however, why particular test scores may not be appropriate measures of policy goals. Tests, as we have noted, often do not measure just what a given school or teacher is expected to teach. A study of fourth-grade mathematics tests and texts by Freeman et al. (1983), for example, concluded that "the proportion of topics covered on a standardized test that received more than cursory treatment in a textbook was never more than 50%." For this reason, we must be sure that tests used in incentive systems are chosen with close attention to the specific goals of instruction in the grades and subjects considered.

Even with well-chosen tests, other factors may contribute to invalid measurement. Some teachers may "teach to the test," responding to the emphasis on standardized tests by spending time on particular types of questions. Similar but more gradual effects may also distort the curriculum (Haertel, 1986, pp. 51–52). In addition, students in one class may be more highly motivated than those in another on the day of the test. In at least one instance, students have collectively reduced their scores in protest, to deprive their school of an award. Alternatively, some incentives may lead students "not to do their best on the initial examination" (Haertel, 1986, p. 50). Thus, although objective statistics have a definite value, they also have risks. One way to reduce these risks is to supplement tests with qualitative or quantitative indicators of teacher and school quality, and to use multiple indicators, together with some discretionary judgment, when awards are made. If systematic judgments or ratings of teachers or schools by qualified observers are available, we should test whether these measures rank schools or teachers in the same way as do average improvement statistics. Also, data on attendance, discipline problems, and other aspects of educational processes and outcomes should be compared with improvement measures in the identification of trends and relationships. A set of steps to reduce many of these risks is also proposed by Haertel (1986, pp. 54–55).

Needed Data

We have noted earlier that the notion of student improvement is a very general one; it can refer not only to test scores in reading or mathematics but also to measures of achievement in music, German, vocational preparation, or other special courses taught by only a fraction of the schools in a given state. We ordinarily think of the required administrations of standardized achievement tests as the major basis for comparison of schools or teachers, but we must also recognize that they measure general aspects of achievement that may not match the particular subjects that should be taught in individual schools or classrooms. Such a mismatch is especially likely to occur in high schools, where pupils follow more diverse curricular paths than in elementary schools. If these diverse courses represent real differences in the needs of local communities or groups of students, then we must use diverse measures of achievement that fit them more closely.

An individual school, and even a school district, is limited in its capacity to give and use tests in a wide variety of subjects. If only one school in a district or one district in a state administers a special standardized test in a given subject, levels of achievement and improvement can be compared with national norms, but pupils' improvement cannot be compared with that of pupils in other schools or school systems in that area.

Comparability among schools, and provision of incentives among such schools, can be fostered by action at the state level. A central state educational agency may facilitate these comparisons of schools by encouraging schools to enter into competition in a variety of subject matter areas for which suitable tests are available. Such an agency, rather than simply allowing each school district to choose and obtain tests independently, might provide a "menu" of tests representing the main subjects in which instruction is offered and for which valid tests are available.

A school that wishes to determine its relative place in producing improvement in one subject—and perhaps to receive rewards for high performance in that subject—could then choose from this menu and administer the corresponding tests before and after that subject was taught. The results would then be reported to the state agency for computation of improvement scores (or this computation could be done locally), and comparison could be made with anonymous statistics on other schools that had chosen the same test. This arrangement should be tested on a trial basis to determine its feasibility.

Trial Uses of Measures of Improvement

States and localities that enact incentive systems based on measures of improvement may find that these systems do not work exactly as planned. In all likelihood, they will face problems, ranging from simple cheating to more subtle forms of "teaching to the test." Moreover, if incentive systems are implemented at the state level, states may fail to gain information on how to improve them because of a lack of well-chosen comparison groups; comparisons across states, although useful, are unlikely to provide adequate matching. Questions of fairness also affect the choice of comparison groups (Haertel, 1986). It is nevertheless possible to devise workable indicator-incentive systems, such as those used by Cooley (1983; this volume) in the Pittsburgh schools. Procedures employed by Cooley include using criterion-referenced tests at the school and district levels; coordinating carefully with district authorities; employing multiple measures of student learning and behavior that include measures of attendance, vandalism, achievement, and other personal outcomes;[8] combining this statistical information with administrators' and teachers' personal knowledge of conditions in the schools; and using all this information in guiding the actions not only of teachers and administrators, but also of social workers and others who can deal with the various problems of the schools. Cooley refers to this procedure as "monitoring and tailoring"—monitoring the situation of each school by statistical and other sources of information, and tailoring the administrative decisions of the school district so as to adjust them to the current needs of that district. A related approach, recommending the use of multiple indicators of a school's performance in administrative decisions, is advanced by Sproull and Zubrow (1981).

The use of improvement statistics also requires special attention if we are unable to devise more stable measures of improvement. If such measures are made the basis of a rigid system of rewards and incentives

---

[8]Another way of combining multiple sources of information about the quality of a school is suggested by Dill (Chapter 10, below). If information on the average improvement score of students in each school in a district were published, the public might form estimates of the quality of learning in each school, combining these average scores with other information available to them.

for teachers or schools, it will soon become evident that they do not consistently identify the same groups of teachers or schools as excellent. The resulting fluctuations in ranking may be seen as normal results of competition; but, if they involve frequent and unexplainable changes in rank, they may lead to disillusionment with the measures. To avoid this disillusionment in the longer run, we should anticipate such results and try to prepare for them. But if we are to make efficient use of improvement statistics, we must also recognize that steady performance as an effective teacher or school may often be revealed only after a period of several years. Reward or incentive systems should therefore be planned so as to provide judgments of performance only after a period of time that permits these judgments to be sufficiently stable; averages over this period, or moving averages, could then be used. The necessary time interval can be estimated through statistical analysis or simulation of the year-to-year judgments, for a given incentive system, over a series of past years' data.

Many trials of indicator-incentive systems and much research based on improvement measures can employ data from existing testing programs. However, some of the recommended research and trials will require additional test administrations. Estimates of the per student cost of this testing vary greatly, from around $.90 to $2.00 per test administration, depending on factors such as the number and grade level of students tested, subject areas tested, the treatment of initial fixed costs, and, last but far from least, the test publisher's pricing policies. Using this range of estimates, states of approximately average enrollment (e.g., Washington, Louisiana, or Minnesota) could test all students in the fall and spring for around $1.4 to $3.2 million. However, since enrollment in such states exceeds the enrollment of all school districts except New York City's, since many states and districts already test several grade levels annually, and since most trials and research will not require such extensive testing, the costs of additional testing in most states and districts would be much lower than the figures cited above. For trials of incentive systems, additional expenses for administration, evaluation, and monetary awards are necessary, but estimates of such expenses vary even more widely than estimates of the costs of testing.

Trial incentive systems must also be used to explore ways of making "improvement" intelligible to educators and the public. Despite the numerous technical considerations necessary in the development and use of incentive systems based on measures of improvement, the policies introduced should be designed so as to emphasize the simpler central principle underlying the evaluation and rewarding of schools and teachers based on measurement of student learning.

SUMMARY

Measures of pupils' improvement can be central to a sound, long-run assessment of the performance of schools and teachers. Without such measures, we risk judging the quality of schools or teachers in terms of pupils' skills at the end of the year alone rather than in terms of the schools' or teachers' real contribution to those skills—thereby failing to guide our schools intelligently to more effective and efficient performance. Furthermore, the procedures adopted so far in various states and districts may not fully realize the advantages of improvement measures because their incentive systems are too centralized, too rigidly tied to test statistics (especially when data are inadequate), and insufficiently related to other sources of information about the schools. If we can develop these systems through repeated trials and careful evaluation, we may be able to monitor and revise our policies so that they can be improved steadily over the years. It is important to use statistical measures of improvement as a basis for assessing where we are and for discovering possible sources of improvement. At the same time, however, we must avoid contaminating these measures by rigidly attaching rewards and penalties to them. Instead, we recommend the research outlined above, the generation of additional data, and trials of evaluation systems that use measures of improvement, so as to be sure that these measures are valid, unbiased, stable, and fairly used. By proceeding carefully in this way, we may be able to design systems of measurement and rewards that will encourage schools and teachers to learn and improve their effectiveness over the long run.

REFERENCES

Alexander, K. L., McPartland, J. M., & Cook, M. A. (1980). Using standardized test performance in school effects research. In A. Kerckhoff & R. Corwin (Eds.), *Research in sociology of education and socialization* (Vol. 2; pp. 1–33). Greenwich, CT: JAI Press.

Alexander, K. L., Pallas, A. M., & Cook, M. A. (1981). Measure for measure: On the use of endogenous ability data in school-process research. *American Sociological Review, 46,* 619–631.

Bacharach, S., Lipsky, D. B., & Shedd, J. B. (1984). *Paying for better teaching: Merit pay and its alternatives.* Ithaca, NY: Organizational Analysis and Practice.

Bellin, S. S., & Bellin, S. S. (1973). Teacher incentives tied to pupil performance. In B. Stein & S. M. Miller (Eds.), *Incentives and planning in social policy* (pp. 117–148). Chicago: Aldine.

Calhoun, F. S., & Protheroe, N. J. (1983). *Merit pay plans for teachers: Status and descriptions.* Arlington, VA: Educational Research Service.

Campbell, D. T. (1984). Can we be scientific in applied social science? In R. Conner, D. G. Altman, & C. Jackson (Eds.), *Evaluation studies review annual* (Vol. 9, pp, 26–48). Beverly Hills, CA: Sage.

Cohen, D. K., & Murnane, R. J. (1985). The merits of merit pay. *Public Interest, 80* (Summer), 3–30.

Coltham, J. B. (1972). Educational accountability: An English experiment and its outcome. *University of Chicago School Review, 81*(11), 15–34.

Cook, T. D., & Campbell, D. T. (1979). *Quasi-experimentation.* Boston: Houghton Mifflin.

Cooley, W. W. (1983). Improving the performance of an educational system. *Educational Researcher, 12*(6), 4–12.

Cooley, W. W., & Bickel, W. (1986). *Decision-oriented educational research.* Boston: Kluwer–Nijhoff.

Cronbach, L. J. (1982). *Designing evaluations of educational and social programs.* San Francisco: Jossey–Bass.

Cronbach, L. J., & Furby, L. (1970). How should we measure "change"—Or should we? *Psychological Bulletin, 74*(1), 66–80.

Dyer, H. S., Linn, R. L., & Patton, M. J. (1969). A comparison of four methods of obtaining discrepancy measures based on observed and predicted school system means on achievement tests. *American Educational Research Journal, 6,* 591–605.

Education Commission of the States. (1984). *Action in the states.* Denver: Author.

Education Research Service. (1979). *Merit pay for teachers.* Arlington, VA: Author.

Epstein, J. L. (1985). *Effects of teacher practices of parent involvement on change in student achievement in reading and math.* Unpublished manuscript, Johns Hopkins University, Center for Social Organization of Schools, Baltimore.

Fennessey, J., & Salganik, L. H. (1983). Credible comparison of instructional program impact: The RAGS procedure. *Educational Measurement: Issues and Practice, 2*(3), 13–17.

Fetler, M. (1986). Accountability in California public schools. *Educational Evaluation & Policy Analysis, 8*(1), 31–44.

Forsyth, R. A. (1973). Some empirical results related to the stability of performance indicators in Dyer's student change model of an educational system. *Journal of Educational Measurement, 10,* 7–12.

Frederiksen, N. (1984). The real test bias: Influences of testing on teaching and learning. *American Psychologist, 39*(3), 193–202.

Freeman, D. J., Kuhs, T. M., Porter, A. C., Floden, R. E., Schmidt, W. H., & Schwille, J. R. (1983). Do textbooks and tests define a national curriculum in elementary school mathematics? *Elementary School Journal, 83*(5), 501–513.

Glass, G. V. (1974). Teacher effectiveness. In H. J. Walberg (Ed.), *Evaluating educational performance: A sourcebook of methods, instruments, and examples.* Berkeley, CA: McCutchan.

Good, T. L. (1983). Classroom research: A decade of progress. *Educational Psychologist, 18*(3), 127–144.

Gronlund, N. E. (1985). *Measurement and evaluation in teaching* (5th ed.). New York: Macmillan.

Guth, J. H. (1984). *The relationship between selected schooling inputs and processes and gains in elementary school pupil achievement in reading, language arts, and mathematics.* Unpublished doctoral dissertation, North Carolina State University, Raleigh.

Haertel, E. (1986). The valid use of student performance measures for teacher evaluation. *Educational Evaluation & Policy Analysis, 8*(1), 45–60.

Hatry, H. P., & Greiner, J. M. (1985). *Issues and case studies in teacher incentive plans.* Washington, DC: Urban Institute Press.

Henderson, C. R. (1975). Best linear unbiased estimation and prediction under a selection model. *Biometrics, 31,* 423–447.

Heyns, B. (1978). *Summer learning and the effects of schooling.* New York: Academic Press.

Heyns, B. (1980). Models and measurement in the study of cognitive growth. In R. Dreeben & J. A. Thomas (Eds.), *The analysis of educational productivity* (Vol. 1, pp. 13–52). Cambridge: Ballinger.

Hoffer, T., Greeley, A. M., & Coleman, J. S. (1985). Achievement growth in public and Catholic schools. *Sociology of Education, 58,* 74–97.

Honig, B. (1984, April 18). Setting the course for school reform. *Education Week,* pp. 59–60.

Johnson, S. M. (1986). *Teacher unions, school staffing and reform.* Cambridge, MA: Graduate School of Education, Harvard University.

Jordan, K. F., & Borkow, N. B. (1983). *Merit pay for elementary and secondary school teachers: Background discussion and analysis of issues.* Washington, DC: Congressional Research Service, Library of Congress.

LeMahieu, P. G. (1984). The effects on achievement and instructional content of a program of student monitoring through frequent testing. *Educational Evaluation & Policy Analysis, 6,* 175–187.

Lieberman, M. (Ed.) (1970). Eight articles on accountability. *Phi Delta Kappan, 52*(4).

MacRae, D., Jr. (1985). *Policy indicators: Links between social science and public debate.* Chapel Hill: University of North Carolina Press.

Madaus, G. F. (1985). Test scores as administrative mechanisms in educational policy. *Phi Delta Kappan, 67,* 611–617.

Marco, G. L. (1974). A comparison of selected school effectiveness measures based on longitudinal data. *Journal of Educational Measurement, 11,* 225–234.

McDonald, F. J., & Forehand, G. A. (1973). A design for accountability in education. *New York University Educational Quarterly, 4*(2), 7–16.

McDonnell, L. M. (1984). *Efforts to improve educational quality: How South Carolina compares with other states.* Denver: Education Commission of the States.

McLean, R. A., & Sanders, W. L. (1983). *Objective component of teacher evaluation: A feasibility study.* Unpublished manuscript, Department of Statistics, College of Business Administration, University of Tennessee, Knoxville.

Millman, J. (1981). Student achievement as a measure of teacher competence. In J. Millman (Ed.), *Handbook of Teacher Evaluation* (pp. 146–166). Beverly Hills, CA: Sage.

Murnane, R. J. (1975). *The impact of school resources on the learning of inner city children.* Cambridge, MA: Ballinger.

Myerberg, N. J., & Splaine, P. (1983). *Annual test report, 1982–83.* Rockville, MD: Montgomery County Public Schools.

Raudenbush, S., & Bryk, A. S. (1986). A hierarchical model for studying school effects. *Sociology of Education, 59*(1), 1–17.

Rogosa, D. R., Brandt, D., & Zimowski, M. (1982). A growth curve approach to the measurement of change. *Psychological Bulletin, 92*(3), 726–748.

Rogosa, D. R., & Willett, J. B. (1983). Demonstrating the reliability of the difference score in the measurement of change. *Journal of Educational Measurement, 20*(4), 335–343.

Rosenshine, B. (1970). The stability of teacher effects upon student achievement. *Review of Educational Research, 40*(5), 647–662.

Rowan, B., Bossert, S. T., & Dwyer, D. C. (1983). Research on effective schools: A cautionary note. *Educational Researcher, 12*(4), 24–31.

Rutter, M., Maugham, B., Mortimer, P., Ouston, J., & Smith, A. (1979). *Fifteen thousand hours: Secondary schools and their effects on children.* Cambridge, MA: Harvard.

Scriven, M. (1967). The methodology of evaluation. In R. W. Tyler, M. Gagné, & M. Scriven (Eds.), *Perspectives of curriculum evaluation.* Chicago: Rand McNally.

Southern Regional Education Board. (1985, July). *Career ladder clearinghouse.* Atlanta: Southern Regional Education Board.

Sproull, L. S., & Zubrow, D. (1981). Performance information in school systems: Perspectives from organization theory. *Educational Administration Quarterly, 17,* 61–79.

Summers, A. A., & Wolfe, B. L. (1977). Do schools make a difference? *American Economic Review, 67,* 639–652.

Summers, A. A., & Wolfe, B. L. (1984). Improving the use of empirical research as a policy tool: Replication of educational production functions. In *Advances in applied micro-economics* (Vol. 3, pp. 199–277). Greenwich, CT: JAI Press.

U. S. Department of Education. (1984). *The nation responds: Recent efforts to improve education.* Washington, DC: U.S. Government Printing Office.

Walton, S. (1984). Mississippi plan links schools' achievement, accreditation. *Education Week,* May 9.

Webster, W., & Olson, G. (1984). *An empirical approach to identifying effective schools.* Paper presented at the annual meeting of the American Educational Research Association, New Orleans, April 23–27.

Wellisch, J. B., MacQueen, A. H., Carriere, R. A., & Duck, G. A. (1978). School management and organization in successful schools. *Sociology of Education, 51* (July), 211–226.

White, B. F. (1975). The Atlanta Project: How one large school system responded to performance information. *Policy Analysis, 1*(4), 659–691.

White, K. P., Wyne, M. D., Stuck, G. B., & Coop, R. H. (1983). *Teaching Effectiveness Evaluation Project: Final Report.* Unpublished manuscript, School of Education, University of North Carolina at Chapel Hill.

Williams, R. H., & Zimmerman, D. W. (1977). The reliability of difference scores when errors are correlated. *Educational & Psychological Measurement, 37,* 679–689.

Wyne, M. D., White, K. P., Stuck, G. B., & Coop, R. H. (1984). *Carolina Teaching Performance Assessment System: Observer's Manual.* Unpublished manuscript, School of Education, University of North Carolina at Chapel Hill.

Wynne, E. A. (1984). School award programs: Evaluation as a component in incentive systems. *Educational Evaluation & Policy Analysis, 6*(1), 85–93.

Zimmerman, D. W., & Williams, R. H. (1982). Gain scores in research can be highly reliable. *Journal of Educational Measurement, 19,* 149–154.

TEN

TOWARD A SYSTEM OF EDUCATIONAL QUALITY CONTROL: NATIONAL ACHIEVEMENT TESTS AND THE "THEORY OF SCREENING"[1]

DAVID D. DILL

INTRODUCTION

Recent major studies of American education and the economy have emphasized the poor performance of American schoolchildren on tests of educational achievement (Boyer, 1983; College Entrance Examination Board, 1983; Goodlad, 1983; National Commission, 1983; Sizer, 1984; Task Force, 1983; Twentieth Century Fund, 1983). The collective evidence suggests that of children the academic knowledge of young people in America is inferior to that in other developed countries, appears to be declining from the levels of previous generations of Americans, and varies substantially by geographical region.[2] One outcome of these reports has been a renewed interest in national achievement tests for monitoring and assessing the quality of American education. Understandably, this interest raises significant social, political, and technical issues. In this chapter I will explore the issue of national achievement

---

[1]I am indebted to Ron Haskins, Lyle Jones, Duncan MacRae, Jr., and Boone Turchi for their constructive comments, but I remain solely responsible for the arguments advanced.

[2]Federally sponsored studies of the achievement levels of American students in the 1960s first revealed substantial variations in levels of achievement by region, between metropolitan and rural areas and by ethnic groups (Coleman et al., 1966; Education Commission, 1971). More recent studies by the National Assessment of Educational Progress, for example in writing proficiency, have reconfirmed regional variations in achievement.

tests and their relationship to the design of a national system of educational quality control.

ACHIEVEMENT INDICATORS VERSUS QUALITY CONTROL

A number of the recent education reports explicitly called for implementation of a national system of achievement tests or exams. For example, *A Nation at Risk* (National Commission, 1983), recommended a nationwide (but not federal) system of state and local standardized tests of achievement, to be administered to students at crucial transition points in their career, particularly from high school to college or job market. Similarly, Sizer (1984), in his national study of American high schools, called for the development of a privately coordinated national system of "exhibitions," in which students could demonstrate what they had mastered during their high school education. As Sizer astutely observed, national exams in other countries provide a powerful incentive for students to excel at the highest level, whereas the lack of such national exams in this country can lead even the ablest students to be satisfied with levels of achievement defined solely at the local level. Finally, in his recent analysis of means to rebuild the American economy, Thurow (1985) argued that all the foreign countries that outperform America economically have national systems of educational quality control featuring national achievement exams. Thurow explicitly recommends such a system for the United States as a crucial link for developing a high quality workforce.

One rationale for a national system of tests would be to institute national indicators to assess changes in educational achievement. Numerous tests or indicators of educational achievement are available (Plisko, Ginsburg, & Chaikind, 1986), including: (a) the National Assessment of Educational Progress (NAEP) managed by the Educational Testing Service; (b) college entrance tests, such as the Scholastic Aptitude Test (SAT) and the American College Testing Program (ACT); and (c) state level (38 as of 1983) minimum competency, assessment or achievement tests (the California Achievement Tests being one well-known example of the last type). Each of these indicators has substantial flaws. While data from NAEP provided invaluable information on overall levels of educational achievement for many of the recent national studies, the current format of NAEP is too limited in that it collects information on aggregate samples rather than individuals, is conducted intermittently, does not evaluate all curriculum areas, and is not currently oriented to the key transition points emphasized in recent studies (Messick, 1985). College entrance exams test only a minority of the relevant population, and explicitly test for verbal and mathematical aptitude rather than academic achievement. By definition, individual state-level exams cannot provide a systematic means of monitoring or assessing national achievement. Thus, if the myriad of current local and state reforms were to increase educational achievement, or even if some of them were to decrease it, we would lack comparative information to show these changes and their causes.

From the perspective of a system of quality control like the one advocated by Thurow, the current collection of indicators is even more seriously flawed. A quality control system usually has three characteristics. First, it specifies standards or objectives against which current or future quality can be compared. Second, it collects information by which conformity or deviation from the standard can be assessed. Third, it provides for corrective actions or initiatives that will be taken if a deviation from the standard is detected. The classic example of this process is a thermostat, in which the temperature set represents the standard, the thermometer represents the means for assessing conformance to the standard, and the mechanism for varying the heat source to correct deviations represents the predesigned set of corrective actions.

While the simplicity of this example appears to belie its application to education, the mechanisms of quality control used in business, not-for-profit, and government organizations, whether for products, services, or people, do not substantially depart from this framework. From this perspective, the current call for national achievement tests has three serious flaws: (a) there is almost no discussion of national educational objectives or standards from which these indicators would be derived; (b) there is insufficient discussion of alternative information collection techniques and their direct and indirect effects on the educational system; and (c) there has been little discussion of a priori corrective actions that might be contemplated when a deviation from standard is observed.

It is noteworthy that the United States is the only developed country lacking a formal national system of educational quality control. I shall argue here that such a system should be implemented, making the following major points. First, there has been an abdication of responsibility at every level of government to implement clear objectives as to what is to be learned in the schools. The existing variations within and between states in educational objectives may contribute to the nation's comparatively low levels of student achievement. A primary task of any attempt to improve educational achievement in the United States must therefore be a national effort to articulate these objectives. Second, the design of national achievement tests together with an educational quality control system would generate both private and public benefits with ramifications for the functioning of the larger society. The national interest in developing such measures would best be achieved if: (a) national achievement tests were federally supported and maintained; and (b) the tests were used, not to classify students, but—with appropriate controls—to assess school performance. Third, the development of standards and measures must be linked with predesigned incentives or corrective actions that will bring deviations in *quality* of school performance into conformance with stated national achievement standards. Finally, given the history and traditions of American society, any effort to develop a system of national quality control of education must be sensitive to state and community rights, and to the expertise of educational professionals. Consequently, successful implementation of a national quality control system would depend upon a strategy emphasizing incremental development, voluntary compliance, and market forces. In the sections that follow, these arguments will be developed in greater detail.

GOALS FOR EDUCATION

One consistent argument in the social sciences is that the most significant cause of improved performance at the individual, group, or organizational level is the explicit setting of goals. Drucker (1973), for example, has argued that for *all* organizations, public or private, commercial or educational, the most significant cause of improved performance at the organizational level is the explicit setting of goals. Similarly, Locke, Shaw, Saari, and Latham (1981), reviewing empirical research on the performance of individuals and groups in business, military, and educational settings, conclude that the single most influential variable in performance is goal setting. This point is worth stressing in any discussion of educational performance because, as a national system, American education is goalless. Any discussion of the development and use of a national system of quality control therefore must be informed by a clear understanding of the nature of the American system of education.

Most citizens are aware that there is no federal policy regarding the nature and quality of educational goals and programs. Indeed, the U.S. Constitution does not include the word "education." Education and schooling were perceived to be a responsibility of the states because of the close ties between religious socialization and local schooling in the early days of the republic. But as Goodlad (1983) discovered in his survey of state and district guidelines for education in the 50 states, the disordered array of topics—goals, activities, instructional resources, and suggestions for evaluation—provide no clear sense of what is essential and what is required. Neither schools nor teachers receive a clear mandate from the state. While it is clear that legislatures and state departments of education intervene constantly with the schools to specify *inputs* to education such as textbooks, courses, financial specifications, and techniques of instruction, they are extremely reluctant to specify the *outputs.* For example, in one single year, the California Legislature introduced 500 bills related to public education, and passed more than a fifth of these (Goodlad, 1983). As a consequence, the 1980 California Education Code contained 42 pages of mandates related to bilingual education, but discussed the subject matter to be taught in elementary and secondary schools in a total of two pages. Goodlad concluded:

> We have assumed since ratifying the Constitution that the states share with local communities responsibility for providing, regulating and guiding public schools. Nevertheless, there remains enormous ambiguity regarding the states' responsibility for leadership and execution . . . the net result is . . . that the schools suffer from lack of a clearly articulated mandate and so are peculiarly susceptible to fads and fashions. (p. 48)

The lack of explicit, consistent goals for American education at the national, state, and local level becomes even more obvious when we examine the means by which education is actually coordinated and controlled. Numerous studies over the past two decades have confirmed the fact that the structure of educational organizations in the United States is "loosely coupled" (Meyer & Rowan, 1978). That is, within the schools there is no systematic coordination of the process, content, or outcomes of teaching. The instructional activities of a school are uncontrolled (in part because there are no explicitly stated goals or standards by which to judge them), and the process of teaching is uninspected. As will be discussed below, this lack of quality standards and inspection is one of the major differences between schools in the United States and in other industrialized countries.

To the casual observer, schools in the United States seem overly controlled, coordinated, and restricted; but we must examine what is closely controlled and what is not. Infinite care is taken to control inputs into education by the use of standardized classifications of curricula, students, teachers, and schools, and by the careful regulation of space, funds, and material allocated to schools. First, a great deal of time and documentation is given to certifying *who* a teacher is (e.g., elementary, secondary, special education), but scarcely any is given to telling whether these teachers actually *do* in the classroom what they are certified to teach. Second, extraordinary care is given to classifying students by grade level, subject area, or special qualities (e.g., gifted and talented, handicapped), but there is little attempt to record what a fifth-grade gifted and talented student actually studies and learns.

Third, extensive rules and careful assignment are employed to control student transitions through the educational system. These categories include place of residence, age, previous education, and ethnic background. But few formal mechanisms exist to ensure that assignments are consistent with the outcomes of instruction, for example, that 12th graders actually do 12th-grade work, or that promoted third graders meet some academic standard. Fourth, each school has a formalized list of curriculum topics. But little effort is given to specifying what a topic actually *means* or to ensuring that each specific topic is taught in a consistent manner. What actually constitutes sixth-grade mathematics can vary remarkably from class to class, school to school, district to district. Fifth, elaborate rules exist to determine what sets of students, teachers and curricular topics may be assembled into, for example, an accredited comprehensive high school. Each such unit is then allocated appropriate funds, space, and materials and detailed records are kept on the nature of all these classifications. But little attention is paid to what actually occurs in the school—whether, for example, the high school is conducting college-level or elementary-level instruction. In short, the American system of education is like an automobile company that carefully specifies who is eligible to work in a plant, what raw materials should be used, what resources each plant receives, and what materials and workers should be in each location of the plant, but never specifies the design of the car, discusses the technology used to construct it, evaluates the process of assembly, or inspects the final product.

How fair is this accusation that the process of instruction and outputs of the schools is uninspected and uncontrolled? A study of a major state school system (Meyer & Rowan, 1978) discovered: (a) less than 3% of the superintendents reported that the district office directly evaluated teaching in the schools; (b) school principals and teaching colleagues have little opportunity to inspect and discuss the work of teachers—85% of surveyed principals reported they do not see their teachers on a daily basis, the majority of principals report no day-to-day working relationships between teachers working on the same grade level, and 83% of the principals report no daily work among teachers in different grades; (c) two-thirds of the surveyed teachers report that they were observed teaching by peers less than once a month, 50% reported similar infrequency of observation by principals; (d) less than 3% of the surveyed superintendents reported using standardized achievement data to evaluate district schools; and (e) 93% of the school principals reported having only general or informal curriculum guidelines for their schools.

In short, the available evidence suggests that in American education, neither teaching nor student learning is subject to serious evaluation or inspection. Belief in the quality and consistency of American education is maintained by a sense of confidence in the elaborate formal classification schemes outlined above.

> For instance, a state creates a rule that something called "history"must be taught in high schools. This demand is not inspected or examined by organizational procedures but is controlled through confidence in teachers. Each teacher of history has been credentialed. There is an incredible sequence of confidences here. . . . The state has confidence in the district, the district in the school, and the school in the teacher. The teacher is deserving of confidence because an accrediting agency accredited the teacher's college. The accrediting agency did not, of course, inspect the instruction at the college but relied on the certification of its teachers, having confidence in the universities which the teacher attended. The accrediting agency also has confidence in the organization of the college— its administrators and departments. These people in turn, had confidence in their teachers, which enabled them to label certain courses as *history* without inspecting them. The claim goes on and on. Nowhere (except in the concealed relation between teacher and pupil) is there any inspection. Each link is a matter of multiple exchanges of confidence. (Meyer & Rowan, pp. 102–103)

But what of the actual knowledge taught? Clearly this is the critical question. It is also the hardest to answer because of the lack of national standards for evaluation and inspection of teachers. However, there is some available evidence with respect to the teaching and learning of mathematics. The most recent comprehensive international study of teaching and achievement is the Second Study of Mathematics (Crosswhite, Dossey, Swafford, McKnight, & Cooney, 1985). This study explored the effects of the mathematics curriculum on the achievement of students in 24 countries by examining a sample of 8th-grade and 12th-grade students in each country. The study examined: (a) the "intended curriculum," that is, what was intended to be taught; (b) the "implemented curriculum," that is, what mathematics was taught by the teacher; and (c) the "attained curriculum", that is, what was learned by the students as demonstrated on a common achievement test.

The international achievement tests confirmed other studies which indicate that while the most able college-bound students enrolled in American 12th-grade calculus courses scored at the international average, the majority of U.S. college-bound students achieved at levels which were exceeded on average by about 75% of the other countries. At the eighth-grade level, the U.S. cohort scored average or below in all five measured areas (i.e., arithmetic, algebra, statistics, geometry, and measurement). Further, U.S. levels of achievement, particularly at the higher cognitive levels, had declined from the original study in 1964.

The following points from the Second Study of Mathematics (Crosswhite, et al., 1985) are relevant to the issue of what is taught in the schools:

- In most other countries the "intended curriculum" is reflected in curriculum guides, course outlines, syllabi, and textbooks adopted by a ministry of education or some similar national body. As the report stated:

  in the U. S., such statements of intended goals or specifications of curricula content are developed in State Departments of Education or at the local school district level. Thus, it is considerably more difficult to describe the curriculum for the U.S. than for almost any other of the participating countries. (p. 3)

- There were sharp differences between what the study's national committee judged a priori to be likely to be covered in an eighth-grade mathematics curriculum and what the surveyed teachers actually covered. As the authors concluded: "This suggests the extent to which the U.S. curriculum lacks a uniform definition in algebra" (p. 29).
- Twelfth-grade calculus students performed at a level comparable to the international average. These calculus classes followed the Advanced Placement Calculus syllabus (p. 83).
- American mathematics is, by most international standards, taught in a highly compartmentalized fashion. The study's authors conclude:

  In most countries of the world a more integrated approach to mathematics is taken in which the subject is presented in a more cohesive and unified fashion. It is plausible that the fragmentation and low intensity found in many of our mathematics programs could be allayed by a more integrated approach to the high school mathematics curriculum. (p. 83)

These brief points from this complex study suggest that: (a) there is greater variability in the "intended curriculum" of mathematics in the U. S. than in any other developed country; (b) the mathematics curriculum within American schools is more highly fragmented and uncoordinated than that of other countries; and (c) the most effective achievement among American mathematics students occurs in calculus courses that follow a standardized Advanced Placement Calculus syllabus. Summarizing this research at the 1986 meeting of the American Educational Research Association, Kenneth Travers, the director of the national coordinating center for the study, argued that American concern with educational reform has neglected the specifics of what is taught in the schools. Travers compared the U. S. with Japan, which educates a larger proportion of its age group at every level than does the U. S., where time devoted to mathematics in the curriculum is less than in the U. S., where mathematics class sizes are much larger, but where achievement levels in every domain are markedly superior. Travers noted that there is much greater homogeneity in what is taught in the algebra curriculum in Japan than in the United States. In short, this international study of mathematics supports the view that part of America's lower educational achievement can be attributed to the lack of consistent national standards for educational objectives, curricula, and teaching materials. If variability and inconsistency exist in the teaching of mathematics, which is the least politically sensitive and most structured of fields, what is likely to be the case in fields such as biology, English composition and literature, and American history, which are subject to local and community tastes, pressures, and conflicts?

To summarize, the American system of education is without clear educational objectives and, perhaps unsurprisingly, lacks means of control and coordination. While each of the national systems to which American education has been compared has stated academic objectives, prescribed curricula, direct inspection of teaching, and consistent tests of student achievement, the United States lacks these collective mechanisms at the national, state, district, or local level. Instead, we have placed our faith in an elaborate system of formal regulations governing inputs to education, but rarely assessing the content and process of instruction or the outcomes of the process.

My major point here is that current proposals for reform of American education avoid facing a major difference between the structure of our educational system and that of other developed countries; namely, the lack of explicitly stated national goals and standards for education and of systematic means for evaluating the achievement of those goals. The proposed national system of educational quality control is a response to that need, but raises substantial questions regarding the appropriate relationship between educational goals, testing, and student learning. These will be addressed below in a section on the components of the system.

THE "THEORY OF SCREENING"

The development of a national system of educational quality control will have both social costs and benefits. One means of understanding these costs and benefits is through an application of the "theory of screening" (Stiglitz, 1975). An extremely important kind of information for the effective functioning of a market is information concerning the qualities of an individual or institution. For example, what is the level of knowledge or achievement of an individual in mathematics, and how effective is a school in educating its students in mathematics? The identification of these qualities of an individual or institution is termed "screening," and mechanisms that sort individuals or institutions according to their qualities are termed "screening devices" (for example, the College Board Achievement Test in Mathematics).

From this perspective, the educational system of the United States performs a screening function for the larger society by identifying the educational qualities of our population. The attainment of a high school degree acts as a screening device because high school graduates supposedly also possess certain qualities that make them eligible for college education, the military, and special types of jobs. As already discussed, however, the lack of stated national objectives makes a high school diploma an unreliable source of information about the qualities of an individual. While corporate recruiters, military recruiters, college admissions officers, and other individuals experienced with high school graduates know that the possession of a high school diploma is an ineffective screening device, the public at large is ignorant of the existing qualitative discrepancies among institutions or areas of the country. A reliable *national* screening device that would provide information on the educational qualities of institutions or regions would help ameliorate this problem.

As Stiglitz (1975) suggests, the development of any screening device has both private and social costs and benefits. A major effect of federally sponsored national achievement tests might be to redistribute income to those who already possess educational advantages.[3] That is, private benefits in the form of further education, "better" jobs, and higher incomes would accrue to those individuals or groups that may be classified by means of a national achievement test as possessing greater skills or knowledge. For this reason there has been understandable hostility to the use of standardized tests as screening mechanisms among groups that consistently score low on such tests. As Stiglitz observes:

> There is thus the possibility that in imparting more skills to the abler students we will simultaneously increase the inequalities of income. This

---

[3]Such a test might conceivably measure achievements that would have been obtained in the absence of education; if so, it might increase the efficiency of the economy, but reward talents and advantages not dependent upon schooling.

has made the organization of the education system and the method by which the levels of screening and skill acquisition are determined, an intensely political question. (p. 294)

If the only benefits of a screening mechanism were private, that is, if the only effect of instituting a national testing system would be to redistribute existing income among individuals and further contribute to social inequities, then the net social return on such a policy would be negative. First, creating a national test system would require substantial federal support. Second, any such mechanism that promised to increase antagonism between racial and social groups would undeniably also have a measurable cost in social unity and goodwill.

However, if the screening mechanism focuses not on the qualities of individuals but on the qualities of *schools*, and if the screening mechanism is part of a larger quality control process designed to improve the quality of education for all students, then conceivably the public policies based on this information could be chosen so as to further equity as well as efficiency. Then it might be argued that the benefits of the system were primarily public. From this perspective, there appear to be five public benefits from a national quality control system.

First, there is the economic benefit derived from the clear articulation of specific measurable goals through the development of a national quality control system. The lack of operational goals at the local and state level, and the variations between states in the focus of their educational systems, have a genuine economic cost in misplaced educational investment, redundant programs (e.g., remedial training in higher education, the military and private industry), and unemployed workers. One concrete example of this problem is the local investment in high school vocational education programs. Several recent studies have criticized vocational education, as currently organized, because it focuses on locally defined, immediately relevant job skills that become quickly obsolete in our rapidly changing, highly mobile labor market (Goodlad, 1983; Sizer, 1984). Instead, these analysts recommend a focus on more substantive skills of language, mathematics and reasoning that will aid the individual over a lifetime. If this critique is valid, and the needed skills are the same throughout the country, a nationally coordinated quality control system could help to deal with it. Such a system could provide all schools, not just the most wealthy or most knowledgeable, with information and incentives to guide the design of a curriculum that better corresponds with the economic realities of the labor market.

Second, state and community-based curriculum development limits the market for educational research and development activities which could benefit the public at large. Currently, for example, school textbook manufacturers orient their publications to states that provide the largest bulk orders, particularly California and Texas, even if other states have different needs. The development of national educational objectives could encourage a national market for teaching materials relevant to numerous states, thereby increasing competition, corporate investment, and eventually the quality of materials available, while simultaneously lowering the costs of their production. Similarly, the availability of consistent national data on educational performance would encourage large-scale research efforts into the effectiveness of various teaching techniques, curricula, and institutional policies. The evaluation, identification, and national diffusion of effective programs and policies would thereby become more feasible.

Third, the development of a national quality control system is a necessary prerequisite to the effective functioning of current market-oriented educational policies. For example, arguments for educational voucher systems, tax deductions for private school tuition, and other policies designed to enhance private choice, presume that sufficient information exists for consumers to select among competing educational alternatives. There is reason to doubt the adequacy of information in the field of education. Families are purchasing a service that is extremely difficult to evaluate in the short term (i.e., until the extended screening devices of college entrance or job offer come into play), and for which there are no national standards. In a situation in which there is so little easily available, standardized, public information on the quality of the services performed, and therefore little ability for individuals to make discriminating market choices, there is much potential for abuse and misrepresentation. The federal government has long provided a public service of labeling on critical commodities such as automobiles (e.g., EPA mileage ratings), foodstuffs (e.g., requirements on the listings of ingredients, cost per measure, etc.) and critical industries such as nuclear energy facilities (e.g., federal safety standards). The development of a national quality control system with appropriate standards, would provide a necessary safeguard for citizen choice on educational alternatives. The public benefit of such a policy stems from what Stiglitz (1975) terms "matching." There is a public economic cost accruing to inefficiencies from a poorly operating market in which individuals and programs are mismatched due to inadequate consumer information. Furthermore, better educated and more wealthy individuals are able to exploit informal sources of information about private schools not available to the public at large. Thus, the development of public policies providing individuals choice in selecting private schools without a commensurate public policy to increase information on the qualities of competing educational services is likely again to lead to the redistribution of income with no gain in social equality.

Fourth, the substantial allocations of federal and state funds for education through various grants, contracts, and cost reimbursement mechanisms are currently made with limited knowledge of the relative performance of educational institutions. Indeed, at the state level, the obvious inequities in financial support between school districts have led to suits and court orders for state intervention to make the funding of public education more equitable. However, the proponents of equitable state funding recognize the inadequacy of such schemes. Equitable distribution of state and Federal funds cannot insure equal educational opportunity. School districts will always vary in: their access to financial resources through local appropriations and voluntary gifts; their access to skilled teachers who inevitably choose to live and work in the most stimulating and rewarding settings; their access to voluntary sources, such as teacher aids, gifts of educational and scientific equipment and community cultural resources; and in their access to motivated and able students. Indeed, logic would suggest that differential funding through special supplements by the federal and state governments would be the only means of achieving relatively equal educational opportunity at the local level (e.g.. special scholarships for professionals willing to work in rural areas).

However, it is unlikely that we could reach any political consensus for the allocation of such supplements. The crudity of discussions about federal supplements is made manifest by the lack of any national standard for assessing the relative educational performance of a school or school district. Therefore, the allocation of federal or state funds for education must be made without knowledge as to the effect of the investment on educational efficiency now or later. The potential for open-ended, wasteful, and ineffective investment in education or educational programs in such circumstances is great. Even if, as is now occurring, a state chooses to use standardized tests as a basis for evaluating its educational investments, there is no way to assure that comparisons of the effectiveness of schools within states are more appropriate than comparisons of similar schools between states. For example, the performance of schools with special environments or clientele, such as schools in an urban ghetto or a university town, may be more effectively compared with the performance of similar schools in other states than to suburban or rural schools in the same state. Furthermore, there is clearly a social benefit to assessing the relative equity of educational opportunity and achievement across states so that federal investments in education can be used most judicially to benefit the national interest. In sum, the utility of national education exams for the development of more effective federal and state policies on allocation of resources to education would be an important social benefit of a national quality control system.

Fifth, there are a series of possible direct educational benefits from a national quality control system that would help standardize course content across the United States. Under the current, decentralized system, what constitutes a course in English for high school sophomores may vary not only from state to state, but from school to school and classroom to classroom within the same school. While this flexibility benefits teachers' academic freedom and creativity, as well as the local control of schools, there are corresponding social costs. A child forced to move from Florida, to North Carolina, to Michigan over a 2-year period, for example, may be inappropriately placed in English classes because of different course content and standards in the respective schools. Even if each school adjusts to this problem of turnover by testing the student for optimal placement, from the child's standpoint (and from society's standpoint), there is no guarantee of an equivalent and appropriately sequenced educational experience among the schools on the basis of what is learned. Furthermore, there is little reason to assume that the child's educational development will be continuous and positive. Similarly, the lack of concurrence on expected performance and content means that teachers have a limited and limiting professional community. Professional development now revolves around discussions of means of disciplining students, and the techniques of pedagogy. Serious discussion of what is to be learned, and how it should be taught, has been limited by the content variations inherent in a decentralized educational system. While only these brief generalizations can be asserted here, the development of a national quality control system also offers the potential for increasing the effective match between the needs of our extraordinarily mobile students and the educational offerings of schools. As well, it may help foster a basis for educational discussion, training, and professional development among teachers on the substance of what will be taught, as will be developed below.

In conclusion, there is substantial evidence that a national quality control system could produce impressive benefits for our society. Therefore, sensitivity to public benefits from the design of such a national system is critical to the successful implementation of the system.

COMPONENTS OF A NATIONAL QUALITY CONTROL SYSTEM

A national quality control system for education must consist of three components: (1) national educational achievement objectives; (2) means of collecting information on achievement which permits the appraisal of performance against standards; and (3) predetermined corrective actions to apply when achievement deviates from the standard.

Objectives

The public schools of the United States are supported primarily by tax revenues from local, state, and national levels, and education is provided free of charge to residents. The maintenance of this publicly supported system rests upon the unspoken assumption that the socialization of all children to a common culture (including the humanities, social sciences, and sciences), and to the essentials of citizenship, is of social benefit to the country. Indeed, if we were not to maintain a common culture, common language, knowledge essential to employment, and knowledge essential to successful citizen participation, the continuation of our society would be at risk. This point was emphasized by several of the recent national critiques of education.

A strong case can therefore be made for assessing achievement in those fields where it can be demonstrated that the knowledge learned provides a social benefit for the country by helping maintain a common culture and the exercise of the responsibility of citizenship. For example, it could certainly be asserted that literacy in written and spoken English, as well as basic knowledge of mathematics and science, knowledge of the history, laws and essential documents of the United States, and at some future point, fluency in Spanish, is knowledge essential for all citizens, the acquisition of which would provide primarily a social benefit. As such, stated national educational objectives for these content areas might fairly be defined for the country as a whole to assess the qualities of students and schools on these factors. As developed below, these objectives would be articulated in the form of syllabi of concepts and topics in each subject-matter field as they are expected to be achieved by students of a particular grade level.

A recurrent fear in the use of achievement tests at the state level is the concern that teachers will teach to the test. In contrast, in other countries, such as England, there is the assumption that both the subject matter covered in classrooms and nationally developed achievement tests will reflect underlying objectives for content developed at the state level and widely disseminated. As one British educator observed: "It is a cardinal principle that the examination should follow the curriculum and not determine it" (Maden, 1985, p. 91). What is lacking in the United States is not the existence of achievement tests, but the absence of publicly stated educational objectives, syllabi of subject topics, and learning materials upon which *both* the student's learning experiences and the achievement tests can be based. An excellent example of the potential for this process is the University of Chicago School Mathematics Project, which is developing pretested course outlines, teaching materials and texts for an integrated mathematics curriculum from kindergarten through the 12th grade.

Information

The identification of national educational objectives in subject-matter fields is a necessary precursor for the development of a national quality control system for education, but also needed are standards against which levels of achievement can be compared, and information to identify deviations of achievement from the standards.

As suggested earlier, the source of information on student achievement would be a nationally designed set of achievement tests in each relevant subject area. These exams would be administered to each student annually at critical transition points, for example, the 4th, 8th, and 12th grades.[4] These tests would be achievement tests, not aptitude tests. In addition, serious consideration should be given to designing achievement exams that involve a mixture of objective and essay questions, the latter being more commonly utilized to assess student achievement in other countries. Feasible mechanisms to implement this idea will be addressed below. A major weakness of existing, objective item achievement exams that employ automatic grading techniques is that the testing process itself does nothing to increase the consensus among educational professionals as to the objectives and topics most worthy of teaching and study. The test process is a private transaction between the test taker and the test maker in which professional teachers play limited role. In contrast, nationally developed achievement tests, designed on the basis of publicly available national educational objectives and standard syllabi, would provide opportunity for professional discussion and debate on course topics, and teaching materials among teachers. Finally, student scores on these achievement tests would then represent reports on performance related to known national objectives that could be compared across schools, states, and regions of the country.

How would this information be utilized? Here the previously drawn distinction between national testing and the orientation of a quality control system can provide guidance. A quality control system should be designed not simply to correct the flaws in a specific unit of output, but rather to use information regarding traits and characteristics of output to determine whether the process by which outputs are produced is effective. Therefore, the information of interest is not individual achievement scores, but average achievement scores for a school.

---

[4]Bias in test results can often be created by those who have a stake in the outcome such as test administrators (e.g., teachers), or those responsible for collecting or disseminating the results (e.g., school officials or state officials) (MacRae, 1985). The implementation and administration of a national system of tests is therefore a critical design component which deserves thoughtful analysis.

Similarly, from a screening perspective, the public interest is in identifying the qualities of schools—whether they are performing effectively—and not in identifying the qualities of individuals. Identifying the qualities of individuals, from which they will receive private benefit in the form of college placements or jobs, should be left to independent testing agencies, the services of which can be purchased at cost by the student. The average achievement level of each school, public or private, however, would be required to be published annually, thus providing public information on the quality of each school.[5]

While we have thus far discussed goals and information, we have not yet defined the standards by which the achievement performance of each school would be judged. One technique would be to set national goals or standards for school achievement scores, and judge schools against this standard. A more pragmatic approach is to recognize that variation is likely to exist among schools, and identify those schools that average especially low or especially high after controlling for factors not within the influence of professional personnel within the school. For example, schools could be grouped nationally into peer groups based upon variables such as type of school (e.g., public or private), socioeconomic level of the community, proportion of English-speaking students and other relevant indicators. Within each peer group an average score could be calculated and schools identified which are significantly above or below the mean in achievement. Alternatively, as suggested by Lester Thurow, an "expected achievement score" could be calculated for each school based upon the income, family educational level, and ethnic background of students. Again, those schools that significantly exceeded or fell short of their predicted score would be identified.[6] Whatever technique is used, these standards, as well as the

---

[5]A number of observers have argued that average achievement scores have serious weaknesses as a proxy for school performance; that achievement gain scores better reflect the "value added" by the school (see Chapter 9, by MacRae & Lanier). I agree with this position, but the complexities and costs of generating gain scores would not be trivial. An alternative might be to link the design of tests administered at various grade levels so that gains between, e.g., 9th and 12th grade, might be assessed. As an example of a potentially relevant methodology, see the new design of the NAEP (Messick, 1985).

[6]Several examples of this procedure exist. See the early study by Klitgaard and Hall (1977). Also, the California Assessment Program uses each school's average reading and math achievement scores to place it on an "expectancy band," which compares its scores with those obtained from other California schools composed of students from similar backgrounds (Hallinger & Murphy, 1986). MacRae has argued (personal communication) that while this approach has obvious appeal, the results are often unstable, and the process has not been effectively implemented for any period of time. While these are important limita-

average achievement scores for each school, would be part of the quality control information for each school published each year.

In summary, a major focus of the quality control system outlined here is to increase the quality and equity in learning opportunities offered by American schools by specifying educational achievement objectives serving the public interest, measuring the performance of students on these objectives, and assessing the relative ability of each school to educate its students to these public interest educational objectives. Individual student achievement scores could still be used within schools for purposes of matching and student placement, but would not be available to third parties, such as colleges or employees, since the purpose of the system is not to enhance the private gain or benefit of the individual student, but rather to enhance the social benefit by increasing the educational equity and quality of the schools.

Actions

What corrective actions would be designed for those schools which might be identified as achievement outliers through the quality assessments? The intent of any quality control effort must be to reward high performance and to take constructive steps to improve quality in low performing units. As Thurow suggests, one means to reward high performing schools would be to set aside a certain amount of federal funds which could be awarded as bonuses to all members of the teaching staffs in those schools. In the case of low-scoring public schools, special federal programs designed to improve the process of education could be applied for, if the school so wished. These could include funds to hire approved consultants to work with the school and community to seek means for improvement, paid summer workshops for the school's faculty members to review materials and curriculum content relevant to the national achievement tests, and other predesigned interventions which could be appropriately provided to assist performance. The major point of this effort is to make available to local schools proven and consistent expertise as a means of improving the educational opportunities for all students.

There are obvious advantages to a system of federal interventions based upon national educational achievement exams. First, rewards or interventions can be concentrated on those schools that deviate from national standards rather than distributing funds or services as a politi-

---

tions, the results from district and state analyses do not necessarily predict results from a national analysis where much greater variance among schools is likely to exist.

cal pork barrel. Second, federal bonuses and national identification as a high-achieving school would provide a significant incentive and a high degree of prestige to public and private schools so identified. Furthermore, this prestige would be identified with the academic achievement of students on material deemed of national importance. Given the low status and pay of the teaching profession, these incentives would not be trivial. Also, low-achieving schools would be publicly identified, thus providing an incentive for concerned local communities, states, and parents, to seek improvement. Finally, school improvement efforts at every school could be explicitly guided by nationally identified achievement objectives and syllabi which are now lacking or unstated at the local or state level. Thus the possibility for improvement in quality for *all* schools would be increased.

In this section, I have sketched the components and design of a national quality control system for education in the United States. As suggested, the system should be oriented to maximizing public rather than private benefits. Thus the quality standards should be established in the form of national educational objectives and syllabi for subject matter fields for which the public benefit can be argued. National achievement exams based upon these objectives should be administered to all students at the 4th-, 6th-, and 12th-grade levels.[7] Consistent with a public interest in excellence and equity in publicly supported education, the achievement test scores for individuals would not be published, nor would they be available for third parties. But the achievement averages for each school would be published and compared with appropriate norms. Finally, predesigned rewards would be given to those schools achieving above a designated achievement standard, and predesigned remedial interventions would be made available to those schools scoring below a designated standard. The implementation problems of this type of quality control system would be substantial. In the following section, some of these issues are explored.

---

[7]L. Jones has suggested (personal communication) the potential of sampling versus exhaustive testing. However, to provide the benefits of a quality control system as advocated here, samples would have to be large enough to provide reliable measures of achievement for each school, which would make the samples much larger than the current NAEP, or any currently proposed revision to this program. Also, while sampling would clearly reduce testing costs and time, it would not provide individual-level information which could be used by the schools for student placement and tracking. Thus, the higher costs of an exhaustive national achievement testing program should be weighed against the benefits of producing individual achievement information which could be used at the school level to improve the effectiveness of learning and teaching. Nonetheless, a sampling design which provided information on the quality of each school would still be superior to the present system in which school quality is unknown.

ISSUES OF IMPLEMENTATION

The difficulties of articulating a quality control system pale in comparison with the difficulties of implementing such a system in the United States—a pluralistic democracy with no tradition of a national educational policy. Consistent with the rest of this article, some suggested means of thinking about these issues are offered. The primary mechanisms for implementing any control system, to paraphrase the argument of William Ouchi (1979), are: (a) a common culture; (b) bureaucracy; and (c) markets.

If control through a common culture alone were possible, no national educational achievement objectives would be necessary because the schools would already be imparting a common body of knowledge reflecting a widely shared common culture. It is noteworthy that the only industrialized country which seems to take this logic of educational control seriously is the United States, whose pluralism seems to belie the existence of a widely shared common culture. For example, Secretary of Education William Bennett has argued that school curricula should be designed around a core of common studies reflecting the masterworks of Judeo-Christian culture (Fiske, 1985). He asserts that if we were to "reason together for a period of time," we "could all agree" on a list of books which would serve as required reading for all our students: "My sense is that among the American people there is agreement on a kind of national curriculum. They are emphatic and consistent about what it is that our children should be taught. . . " (p. 48). This appeal to a preexisting common culture flies in the face of the evidence of a rapidly changing school population, with many students who in no way represent a Judeo-Christian heritage. Furthermore, the increasing number of suits over the content of public school curricula, many of which involve books that "we used to all agree on," raises serious questions regarding the reality of this approach. Finally, even if we were to assume that the rapidly waning vestiges of a shared culture in literature and the arts were sufficient to provide the cultural glue necessary for Americans to function effectively as citizens of the republic, how does this common culture assist us in improving our curricula in mathematics and science? What is our response to the evidence that mathematics in this country is taught in a fragmented fashion, and that our professional teachers have an unusually low level of consensus on what constitutes mathematics appropriate to educate eighth-grade students?

The second approach to implementation is that of bureaucracy. This approach would involve the establishment of federal rules and regulations on what is to be taught, and the required imposition of this national curriculum on all schools. This potential for the nationalization and standardization of education, associated in the popular imagination with a centralized educational bureaucracy such as that in France, has long been a fear of many Americans who desire local and community control of the schools. For example, many of the individuals who opposed the Department of Education in the Carter administration, did so out of a fear of central control over the schools.

A purely bureaucratic control system in the United States is politically unfeasible, but equally unfeasible it appears would be a nonfederally managed control system (cf. proposals in National Commission, 1983; Sizer, 1984). The choice in creating educational control systems in developed countries is between governmental and nongovernmental forms (Clark, 1985). The governmental form is most clearly exemplified in countries such as Germany and Japan, where educational ministries develop educational objectives and exams designed to promote universal, objective educational standards. The nongovernmental form is characteristic of control in the United States where private associations test students for entry to higher education (e.g., the College Entrance Examination Board). The compelling interests of the latter system are the private interests of the universities and colleges to bring order to the business of sorting among applicants, and to legitimate the choices made. As such, this system has a limited interest in standardization, equity, and excellence at the public school level. The choice in terms of developing a quality control system, then, is between a governmental body with a bias toward system-wide fairness and national protection of standards, and a nongovernmental form biased toward institutional control, choice, and autonomy. On this basis the evidence clearly favors a governmental form.

Similarly, a nonfederal governmental entity, such as a state compact (e.g., Education Commission of the States) would face substantial practical impediments. Assigning a national educational quality control system to an agency that would require the individual political support of each state would likely destroy the project before it began. First, the system would require substantial venture capital, which the states are unlikely to provide for an unproven system. Second, the system entails some political risk for the states. The much more limited National Assessment of Educational Progress was strongly resisted in the early 1960s in the South by state school officials who feared (rightly, as it turned out) that these assessments would reveal to the public the lower achievement levels of their students. It is likely that if a nonfederal approach had been utilized in attempts to develop a quality control system for foods and drugs or environmental protection, little progress would have been achieved.

While the social benefits and costs of a national educational quality control system necessitate direct federal involvement and support, they do not mandate federal control. A potentially effective model at the state level is the New York Board of Regents. Though a public agency, the regents have generally maintained a professional and independent stance while conducting quality control evaluation functions including state-wide subject-matter exams. The concept of a national board of regents designed to plan, implement, and manage a national quality control system deserves serious consideration.

The third mechanism for implementing a control system is a market approach. That is, the improvement of education must be tied to the existing public demand for high-quality education. But as suggested by Stiglitz, if limited information exists as to the "qualities" of an entity, then the existing demand for quality education will lead to mistaken investments, public policies, and individual choices. Developing a national system of quality control is an attempt to improve the equity and excellence of education by permitting market forces to work. This logic can also guide the process of implementing a quality control system in the following ways.

First, the selection of subject-matter fields for quality control should be incremental, with the intent of first developing the system, and then extending it as demand warrants. This would suggest that the system should initially concentrate on a few subject areas for which there would be high political consensus as to need and social benefit; mathematics and English grammar and composition are prime candidates. The identification and dissemination of the subject-matter topics, development and administration of achievement tests, and implementation of the system's program of information and corrective action could proceed on this limited agenda. If and when the quality control system achieved a level of integrity and effectiveness in its operation, and as public demand warranted, the system could be slowly expanded to address other areas of achievement for which a public benefit could be articulated.

Second, a strong case can be made that participation in a national quality control system should be required of all educational institutions that receive federal funds, or who are recipients of tax-exempt status as educational organizations. Similar arguments (and parallel procedures) have been utilized to review the performance of educational organizations on equity (i.e., federal monitoring of progress on affirmative action and integration). However, it is also likely that initiating such a program on the basis of voluntary participation would, over time, have substantial impact. This would clearly ease the political divisiveness over developing the system; but if it achieved its potential, public demand for schools to participate in the program would likely be significant.

Third, a market approach to implementation would recognize the potential for creating other markets for the activities of the quality control system. For example, as mentioned earlier, the current method for testing student achievement employs a limiting methodology of machine-scored objective tests, and the limited participation of the test maker and test taker. If the achievement exams designed for the quality control system were to be a combination of objective and essay questions, a market would be created for experienced essay evaluators in the subject-matter fields. This market could be filled by identifying nationally outstanding public and private teachers from subject-matter fields, bringing them together in advance of the achievement tests for training in the syllabi of topics for the field and in the evaluation of essay exams, and finally paying them during the summer months for grading and evaluating the national exams. The effect of this system would be threefold: (1) it would provide national recognition for outstanding teachers; (2) it would provide a basis for professional communication and development of teachers on the subject matter of the national educational objectives; (3) it would provide summer salary supplements for many of the nation's teachers. Finally, the development of this system could be planned with existing subject-matter professional associations, such as the National Council of Teachers of English. By thus opening up the assessment process to educational professionals, additional improvements can be made in the reliability and validity of subject-matter instruction, and additional social benefits can be attained that are not now possible in testing systems organized solely for private benefit.

Fourth, although the system as outlined would articulate national educational objectives, develop and widely disseminate syllabi of subject-matter concepts and topics, and create and administer matching achievement tests, no school would be mandated to adopt the objectives or syllabi so developed. It is assumed that over time the development of an effective quality control system would create a demand for these materials in the schools, as well as for the recommended federally supported consultation for low-achieving schools. Further, it is expected that the quality control system would create a market to encourage research and development, textbook development, and a new market for private consultation and support for the schools. Finally, the incremental development of a quality control system and the emphasis on achievement tests, rather than mandated curricula, would ensure that the local community retained control over what changes (if any) should be made in the schools. Only those subject fields for which there was national consensus as to a national interest and social benefit would be included in the quality control system, and only those schools where the community was supportive would adopt the national syllabi as a standard for their own curricula.

In summary, the pluralistic nature of American society, and the tradition of local autonomy and control of the schools militates against a bureaucratic mandate as to school quality. Similarly, an appeal to a nonexistent "common culture" represents an abdication of any responsibility for ensuring the public interest in equity *and* excellence. A quality control system put into place by a federally supported board of regents, which relies on the logic of a market system to improve the excellence of the schools, is most likely to be an effective strategy of implementation.

MAJOR OBJECTIONS TO A NATIONAL SYSTEM

I have argued that the American system of education lacks coherent goals. A necessary improvement of education in the United States therefore is the development of a national system of quality control featuring stated achievement objectives, publicly available information on school performance related to these objectives, and a policy on incentives and related actions designed to recognize and enhance quality. Public benefit should be a key design criterion for the system, and implementation should emphasize a market rather than bureaucratic logic. Recommendations of this type are provocative if not naïve within the history and context of the United States. Many practical objections to the proposal remain to be explored, but opposition is likely to focus first on questions of ultimate success, and second, on the desirability of local rather than national control of education. In this concluding section, therefore, I will briefly explore these two issues.

Given the political and financial complexities of instituting a national system of educational quality control, is there any reason to expect that such a system would improve the quality of our schools and increase academic achievement among our students? This is a reasonable question. A similar problem is confronted by the Carnegie Forum on Education and the Economy and its attempt to set up national standards for teaching (Shulman & Sykes, 1986). Introducing a new standard in the market for public services is akin to introducing a new product in the consumer market. Demand for the new product is uncertain, yet the new product involves risk and requires venture capital. Most importantly, the worth of the new standard cannot be proven prior to its implementation. In the case of national quality control standards, however, there is some interesting supportive evidence from the experience of the New York State Board of Regents, which performs the closest American analogy to the educational quality control function performed within other countries.

In a study comparing the course taking patterns and achievement

of California high school students with students in New York state and
the country as a whole, Harnischfeger and Wiley (1984, pp. 3–4) made
the following observations:

- California high school seniors' achievement is close to the national
  average in most areas.
- Comparative data for California versus New York reveal that New
  York high school seniors:
  1. Have substantially higher average achievement scores in basic
     reading and mathematics.
  2. Score approximately the same on the verbal section and some-
     what higher on the mathematics section of the *Scholastic Aptitude
     Test*, even though California's test-taking population is more
     selective than New York's (approximately half as many Califor-
     nia students as New York students take the test).
  3. Take college-preparatory mathematics and science courses at a
     higher rate and the more advanced courses (trigonometry, cal-
     culus, physics, and chemistry) at twice the California rate.
  4. Take the College Entrance Examination Board's advanced sci-
     ence and achievement tests at up to four times the California
     rate.
  5. Perform better on the science tests than California students with
     equal aptitude scores.
  6. If they take advanced science tests, are better prepared mathe-
     matically than Californians on the basis of their average mathe-
     matics aptitude scores.

In a presentation of their findings at the American Educational
Research Association, Wiley suggested that the unusual course-taking
patterns and high achievement levels of New York state students may
be attributable to the influence of the New York regents' curriculum,
degree, and testing practices; and that the apparent positive effect of the
regents on student achievement deserves much more serious analysis
than it has thus far received. While the results of this study must be
interpreted with caution, the high achievement levels of New York state
students when compared with the nation as a whole offer some evidence as to the possible benefits of a quality control system similar to
that outlined here.

A second basis for objection to a national quality control system is
the value many Americans place on local control of education. Historically, Americans have assumed that individual, and particuarly religious, freedom could not be preserved in an educational system controlled at the national level, but rather that education should be deter-

mined by the values of the local (presumably more homogeneous) community. This argument led to the tradition of local school boards and community funding for schools. This decentralized structure has successfully dissipated national conflict over educational values, but as suggested herein, behind the veil of local control of schools lurks the anarchy of educational objectives, or the lack thereof, at the state and local level. A number of recent observers have noted that the historical trend toward individual rights and liberties in our political and social life (Bellah, Madsen, Sullivan, Swidler, & Tipton, 1985) and toward purely entrepreneurial approaches to economic development (Thurow, 1985) place at risk the quality and continuity of the larger society. In education as well, the issue is not private versus public benefit, but a recognition of greater balance between the two.

Traditionally, the federal role in education has been to ensure equity and access (Stocking, 1985). Thus federal education initiatives have addressed only special issues of national significance, such as school desegregation and categorical aid to specified sets of students with special needs (e.g., the disadvantaged, the handicapped, those with limited ability in English). With the evolution of the Department of Education, the federal role has been expanded to include an active research, development and assessment program designed to improve education, but equity has continued as the major focus. What is lacking is an appreciation that federal goals for equity in education cannot be attained without federal goals for educational quality. As Rohlen observed in his study of Japanese high schools, "Progress toward social equality that cannot be integrated with the pursuit of general excellence has no long-term viability" (quoted in Clark, 1985, p. 318). This is a new situation in the United States, because the viability of our educational system will be determined cross-nationally, with national systems competing for achievement in schooling as well as in work.

Even if it were possible to ignore international competition and its effect on the viability of our educational system, the issues of equity and quality cannot be separated. As Stiglitz (1975) argues, the principal activity of a school system is providing knowledge and skills. Therefore, the more we rely on education in our society to provide knowledge and skills for the workplace, and the more effective we are in transmitting knowledge and skills, the more "screening" is produced as a natural by-product. In 1950, 50% of white students and 25% of Black students graduated from secondary school, while in 1979 the comparable figures were 85% and 75% (Goodlad, 1983). Access to all the major professions, and increasingly to top business positions, now requires advanced degrees. As a result of these longer periods in school, differences in quality between schools, districts, or states lead to greater inequality between individuals. Given projections that more, not less, education will be required for future generations, a necessary means for encouraging educational equity is a federal effort on quality control in education.

Throughout this chapter, I have examined the issue of national testing and attempted to place it in the context of a national quality control system. There are real and serious questions regarding the validity and reliability of our tests and measures of educational achievement, and regarding the most effective means to implement such systems. But the dominant concern with testing in educational debates within the United States is both misleading and mischievous. It deflects concern from the fundamental underlying issue, which is the goals and content of education. Mathematics, science, English, and knowledge necessary to citizenship, are fundamental expressions of our culture. Knowledge of these can wither and die if the institutions responsible for their definition and defense fail to exercise their responsibilities. The long-term viability of the United States as a collective community is dependent upon the federal government's recognizing its responsibility to support the development of universal, objective educational standards for the nation's schools.

REFERENCES

Bellah, R. N., Madsen, R., Sullivan, W. M., Swidler, A., & Tipton, S. M. (1985). *Habits of the heart: Individualism and commitment in American life.* Berkeley: University of California Press.

Boyer, E. L. (1983). *High school: A report on secondary education in America.* New York: Harper & Row.

Clark, B. R. (1985). *The school and the university.* Berkeley: University of California Press.

Coleman, J. S., et al. (1966). *Equality of educational opportunity.* Washington, DC: U.S. Office of Education.

College Entrance Examination Board. (1983). *Academic preparation for college: What students need to know and be able to do.* New York: Author.

Crosswhite, F. J., Dossey, J. A., Swafford, J. O., McKnight, C. C., & Cooney, T. J. (1985). *Second international mathematics study: Summary report for the United States.* Champaign, IL: Stipes.

Drucker, P. F. (1973). *Management: Tasks, responsibilities, practices.* New York: Harper & Row.

Education Commission of the States. (1971). *National assessment of educational progress* (Reports 1–5). Denver: Author.

Fiske, E. B. (1985). Reagan's man for education. *New York Times Magazine.* December, 22, pp. 30ff.

Goodlad, J. I. (1983). *A place called school.* New York: McGraw–Hill.

Hallinger, P., & Murphy, J. F. (1986). The social context of effective schools. *American Journal of Education, 94*(3), 328–355.

Harnischfeger, A., & Wiley, D. E. (1984, April). *Time and learning: A statewide policy analysis.* Paper presented at the American Educational Research Association, New Orleans.

Klitgaard, R. E., & Hall, G. R. (1977). A statistical search for unusually effective schools. In W. B. Fairley & F. Mosteller (Eds.), *Statistics and public policy* (pp. 51–86). Reading, MA: Addison–Wesley.

Locke, E. A., Shaw, K. N., Saari, L. M., & Latham, G. P. (1981). Goal setting and task performance: 1969–1980. *Psychological Bulletin, 90,* 125–152.

MacRae, D., Jr. (1985). *Policy indicators.* Chapel Hill: University of North Carolina Press.

Maden, M. (1985). England and Wales. In Clark, B. R. (Ed.), *The school and the university* (pp. 77–102). Berkeley: University of California Press.

Messick, S. (1985). Response to changing assessment needs: Redesign of the national assessment of educational progress. *American Journal of Education, 94*(1), 90–105.

Meyer, J. W., & Rowan, B. (1978). The structure of educational organizations. In M. Meyer (Ed.), *Environments and organizations* (pp. 79–109). San Francisco: Jossey-Bass.

National Commission on Excellence in Education. (1983). *A nation at risk: The imperative for educational reform.* Washington, DC: U.S. Government Printing Office.

Ouchi, W. G. (1979). A conceptual framwork for the design of organizational control mechanisms. *Management Science, 25*(9), 833–848.

Plisko, V. W., Ginsburg, A., & Chaikind, S. (1986). Assessing national data on education. *Educational Evaluation & Policy Analysis, 8*(1), 1–16.

Shulman, L. S. & Sykes, G. (1986). *A national board for teaching: In search of a bold standard.* Washington, DC: Carnegie Forum on Education and the Economy.

Sizer, T. R. (1984). *Horace's compromise: The dilemma of the American high school.* Boston: Houghton Mifflin.

Stocking, C. (1985). The United States. In B. R. Clark (Ed.), *The school and the university* (pp. 239–263). Berkeley: University of California Press.

Stiglitz, J. E. (1975). The theory of "screening," education, and the distribution of income. *American Economic Review, 65*(3), 283–300.

Task Force on Education for Economic Growth. (1983). *Action for excellence: A comprehensive plan to improve our nation's schools.* Denver: Education Commission of the States.

Thurow, L. C. (1985). *The zero-sum solution.* New York: Simon & Schuster.

Twentieth Century Fund. (1983). *Making the grade: Report of the Twentieth Century Fund task force on federal elementary and secondary education policy.* New York: Author.

Eleven

REFORMING THE PUBLIC SCHOOLS: TEACHING, EQUITY, AND EDUCATIONAL INDICATORS[1]

DUNCAN MacRAE, JR., and RON HASKINS

A number of common themes appear in the preceding chapters. We shall now summarize them and draw from them a set of common recommendations. In doing so we shall note occasional differences of opinion among the contributors, and supplement their accounts from other sources. Our summary will be organized about the three major issue areas treated in the three parts of this book: policies affecting teachers and teaching; diversity and equity; and information and indicators.

STARTING POINTS

Types of Analysis for Educational Policy

The chapters in this volume lead us not only to suggest policies, but also to examine the role of research and other sources of knowledge as aids in educational policy choice. In guiding public policy, no single study should be used alone (Campbell, 1984, p. 34), and multiple methods of research can also complement one another (Epstein, Chapter 5). In addition to research, we must use the judgments of experienced participants, including teachers and administrators, both for their insights and for the potential support of these groups.

The knowledge we need can originate from sensitive observation

---

[1]For helpful suggestions we are indebted to James J. Gallagher, Joyce L. Epstein, Amy Gutmann, and Edith K. MacRae; they are not, however, responsible for our errors.

as well as statistics, as Ogbu (Chapter 6) has shown. It can arise from a combination of reading of the literature and actual practice. Thus, contributors to this volume use and combine diverse sorts of knowledge. Cooley provides an excellent example of this combination, having worked as a statistician, collaborated with a historian, cooperated closely with school administrators, and studied the work of teachers and social workers who were to use his information.

The knowledge most relevant to policy choice is that which relates explicitly to choices among alternatives. It will be most useful for policy choice if it includes "variables that are school policies," i.e., sets of instructions that tell responsible personnel exactly what they should do (Murnane, 1984, p. 268). Thus, Epstein asks that goal variables in the effective schools literature be translated into "manageable practices based on the alterable structures that teachers can change in their classrooms."

Policy formation or reform, however, often passes through a series of stages at which different sorts of information are available and relevant. For defining a problem and calling our attention to a need for action, descriptive statistics and other knowledge about the existing situation are important; for aid in the design of new policies, knowledge of their expected effects can be of use; and for specific recommendations, information on successful trials of policies is especially needed (Epstein, Chapter 5; Cooley, Chapter 8).

At the initial stage, problem definition, descriptive information about the condition of schools is relevant. Two of our chapters illustrate how such information can be marshaled and presented. Peterson (Chapter 2) presents numerous data on needs, costs, budgets, resources, and test scores, alerting us to the need for funds for school reform. Ogbu also describes school processes to present a twofold problem, including not only cultural domination and bias, but also a need for nonimmigrant minority communities to support their children's academic efforts.

Epstein, Stedman (Chapter 3), and Gallagher (Chapter 7) make specific recommendations as to how schools should be changed. Among them, Epstein makes the most use of research data on trials and evaluations of new programs. Stedman and Gallagher rely more on professional experience than on specific cited studies of policy effects. When Stedman recommends graduate training for future teachers, he draws on his work with schools of education and as an administrator in a university system. Gallagher makes use of his own professional experience with gifted children, and of the opinions of teachers, administrators, and parents as to what provisions should be made for their education.

The third part of the book deals with the use of information and indicator statistics. In this part, Cooley's chapter is based most directly on practical experience. His account of continuing cooperation with the Pittsburgh schools shows that general policies for the use of information can be made to work and to aid the self-improvement of a school district. More speculative are the chapters by MacRae and Lanier (Chapter 9)—assessing the advantages and problems facing indicator-incentive systems—and by Dill (Chapter 10), on national indicator systems. They represent a stage of analysis that precedes practical trials such as Cooley's.

In our recommendations we shall also reach beyond the findings of extant research. Drawing together and supplementing the findings of the other contributors, we propose particular policies and approaches (summarized after each main section below). When such proposals go beyond what has been shown to work, they should be tried and evaluated if possible, in comparison with other policies (including the status quo), before they are proposed for large-scale implementation.

Types of Policy Proposals

The policies suggested by our contributors vary somewhat from abstract, general proposals to concrete examples designed in cooperation with those affected. On the more abstract side are both experimental studies of standard forms of learning programs, and incentive systems. These have been proposed in general terms, since the contexts in which they were tested are likely to differ from the contexts in which they will be applied. Closer to particular situations are Cooley's report of monitoring and tailoring in Pittsburgh, and House and Lapan's (Chapter 4) suggestion of action research controlled by teachers.

The general policy recommendations made here, like many of those in the earlier reports, must be reinterpreted in the context of particular schools. We must do this not only because of differences between central cities and suburbs, between rich and poor districts, or between different grade levels, but also because of differences in local school culture and in political feasibility. The same sort of reinterpretation is often needed for adapting particular locally successful programs and experiments to new contexts. Thus, when our recommendations are couched in general terms, the hard work of designing and implementing specific policies at the state and local level often remains to be done.

Goals

The education reports stressed that what we choose to do depends on our goals and priorities, and how well we do it often depends on the clarity of those goals. Most of our contributors have avoided recommending an overall set of goals for schools, because the choice of goals requires discussion in which the affected parties play a major part. Epstein and Dill, however, have called attention to the need to define our goals as an initial step in making and implementing policies. An example of this process is the Pittsburgh needs assessment described by Cooley. Professionals and the public must refer to common goals if they are to achieve clarity in evaluating past policies and charting future courses of action.

POLICIES AFFECTING TEACHERS AND TEACHING

Teacher Pay: A "Social Contract"

One widespread proposal for improving the schools has been to raise teachers' salaries so as to give them the prestige and standard of living that a profession requires. With reduced public budgets, however, taxpayers have come to ask additional justification for new expenditures; they do so even though teachers' salaries have fallen behind those of competing occupations (Peterson, Chapter 2). Taxpayers and critics have thus argued that pay increases should be matched by evidence of teachers' contributions to students' learning. As a result, political leaders who favor higher pay and better working conditions for teachers "will not, or feel they cannot do so unless the public is persuaded that the teachers they spend more money on are fully capable of doing the job that now needs to be done" (Carnegie Forum, 1986, p. 63). This connection between teachers' contributions and rewards is also shown by Stedman when he notes that a successful career-ladder plan could help "restore the confidence of the legislatures and school boards." Such a plan can constitute a "social contract" between taxpayers and teachers.[2]

The types of quid pro quo that teachers have been required to give are diverse. New teachers can give one sort of assurance to the public by improved preparation, either academically or through guided teaching experience. Those already teaching can take on additional responsibility, garner further academic credits or credentials, or simply acquire years of experience. It is not clear, however, that these sorts of signs of

---

[2]A career-ladder plan involves the potential advancement of a teacher through a series of ranks, in relation to some combination of performance, increased responsibilities, and time spent in a given rank. A "social contract" approach has also been proposed for national poverty policy (Sawhill, 1986).

deservingness really predict students' learning (Hanushek, 1986). But since the recent wave of reform, this quid pro quo has often become more closely related to demonstrations of outputs of teaching. Examples are the measurement of teachers' own knowledge, reflected by tests they must take (as in Tennessee); or their following a recommended style of classroom behavior and management (as in North Carolina).

The Holmes Group (1986) and Carnegie Forum (1986) reports, considering the longer run, have proposed creating diverse ranks within the teaching profession, and awarding high rank and salary only to those who demonstrate special capacities. Teachers may show these capacities by their academic training, by taking newly devised tests early in their careers, by further in-service training, by administrators' and colleagues' judgment, or in other ways. But among these ways, the potentially most important are indications of performance and productivity,[3] against which other means to this end should be checked if possible (Carnegie Forum, 1986, pp. 87–93).

The best indicator of a teacher's accomplishment, if it could be measured and used to guide policy, would be the amount that his or her pupils learned. To make such a guidance system work in practice, however, is not an easy task (MacRae & Lanier, Chapter 9). Present measures of this "value added" by teaching are unstable; standardized tests may be invalid measures; multiple measures are needed; consultation with teachers is required; and repeated trials are needed to design such a system. Among the measures that might be used are not only standardized tests, but also specially designed local tests, and the success of a teacher's pupils in later classes, in admission to college, or on jobs (always with statistical control of ability or prior achievement).

The claim by teachers that such measures are imperfect, and that it is better to use no measures in policy guidance than to use these, may not convince the taxpayer-critics unless teachers gain the power of doctors, lawyers, or professors. Even these latter professions, however, may not be good models—either because teachers cannot attain their power, or because even these other professions are not clearly fulfilling all their responsibilities to the public and also need monitoring of their outputs.[4] Rather, teachers may be able to gain greater authority and pay and better working conditions if they can help give the public an opportunity to judge that they are educating students well.

---

[3]Productivity is output per unit of resources used, and is thus a more valid criterion.

[4]University teachers are motivated to publish by an incentive system, but no comparable system exists for their teaching. Like public-school teachers, they usually feel that devising such systems is not part of their job.

It is not clear, however, that such a "social contract" can be made at present. Though it is urgently needed, no proven means for public judgment of educational effectiveness are yet clearly at hand. It is likely that with careful research and repeated trials, aided by teachers, they can be found and improved. The contract must therefore be negotiated repeatedly over time as better measures of performance become available. As Stedman points out, even when teacher performance measures are not yet ready, pilot career-ladder programs may still be implemented. The contract may then be not simply one between taxpayers and teachers now, but may include a commitment of both to give students in the future the best education then available to them.

We therefore endorse programs of the career-ladder type[5] for teachers, but recommend that major efforts be made to devise procedures for rewarding output and productivity. Furthermore, the administration of these programs must remain flexible so that better and more valid bases for evaluation can be used when they become available.

Procedures for Rewarding Output

Several contributors to this volume have stressed the need to aim educational policies at measures of output, i.e., at teacher or school effects or effects of particular practices (see chapters by Peterson, Epstein, Cooley, MacRae-Lanier, and Dill). To measure outputs, Epstein stipulates that studies of policies that produce effective students require "controls on earlier student ability or achievement," and Cooley notes that "initial student abilities were . . . taken into account in comparing growth" among classrooms.

Measurements of output, i.e., of the value added through instruction, are difficult to use as an incentive, however, as we have noted. How, then, can policymakers encourage a continual search for ways of guiding schools toward improved outputs? We need organizational arrangements and processes that will motivate people to use output measures and to improve them. Ideally, teachers (and members of any profession) should seek to improve their practice, and to a considerable extent they do (House & Lapan, Chapter 4). They do so especially by seeking to fulfill the social roles they have learned through prior education and that are encouraged in the schools where they work.

Yet both actual improvement and the demonstration of this im-

---

[5]As of December 1986, 16 states had begun career ladder programs, and an additional 19 had begun incentive plans of other types (Southern Regional Education Board, 1986, p. 9).

provement to parents and taxpayers seem increasingly to require some external judgment, other than the teacher's own opinion, of what teachers have accomplished. In principle, teachers face such judgments already—from pupils, parents, principals, superintendents, school boards, and those who later teach or employ their students. The more successfully teachers themselves, as a group, can make these judgments and act on them, the less close should be the scrutiny they need from others.

One way to combine the judgments of these other groups with those of teachers would be to create teacher (or school) evaluation committees representing teachers, administrators, taxpayers, and parents. The proportions in which these groups were represented might depend on how successfully teachers and schools could carry out their own internal reviews of performance. School boards might be expected to provide this scrutiny but do not often do so in output terms. These committees' use of output measures could be facilitated by providing the committees with multiple measures of output. Further, the committees should be given professional assistance to help them understand and use the measures. Such output measures might include ratings of teachers; information on pupils' later accomplishment, controlling on prior achievement; and students' judgments as to what they had learned. Over time, a set of output measures could be modified as better ones became available. Initially, only limited rewards might be attached to them, until some agreement had been developed as to which measures were most valid and how best to use them.

The Market for Teachers

Our concern with the outputs from schooling also leads us to seek ways of attracting, training, hiring, and retaining teachers so as to improve outputs—and productivity. The direct approach to this goal requires that the qualities of teachers rewarded by the market be related as closely as possible to the output (learning) they produce; and that the duties of teachers be concentrated as fully as possible on producing that output. Services unrelated to learning (such as lunchroom monitoring or handling of major discipline problems) should be performed by others; and support services and materials that enhance the effects of teaching (e.g., computer data records, audiovisual displays) should also be made available to teachers if needed. These changes will involve expenditures for nonteacher personnel but can increase the productivity (as well as the status) of teachers. Hawley (1986, p. 714) suggests that if we wish to hire able teachers when budgets are limited, as well as to improve teacher effectiveness, some of the best policies open to us are those that "restructure the workplace by granting teachers more collective responsibility, maximizing the time teachers teach, fostering collegiality, and providing increased information about student performance . . .".

The problem remains, however, of how to increase the chance that teachers will be hired and retained on the basis of the learning they induce in students. We might try to give postgraduate education to a select group of prospective teachers (see Chapter 3); if particular university programs of this sort come to be recognized as preparing outstanding teachers, credentials from them will be given greater weight in informal assessments of candidates. It is important, however, that early credentials of this sort not take the place of the measurements of output that need to be developed.

College degrees in subject matter or pedagogy, credits for summer courses, and even current tests of teachers' ability or knowledge, are at best surrogates for assurance that prospective teachers can and will teach effectively to a given set of students. These credentials, if valid, can serve as rough screening devices to remove clearly unqualified candidates from a pool of applicants. We must be careful, however, especially in times of teacher shortage, not to screen out candidates who lack some particular credential but could nevertheless become good teachers. The possibility of further evaluation, as well as training and development, after a teacher is on the job can add to the efficiency of the market as a reflector of teaching productivity.

Thus, Peterson argues, we should try to free up the labor market from hiring conditions that are not closely related to output. A degree from a school of education, for example, should not be a prerequisite for initially hiring a teacher qualified in a technical field, such as science or mathematics. Specific conditions now required for teacher hiring or certification must be re-examined to see whether they hinder productivity by impeding, rather than helping, the efficiency of the market. Able college graduates with needed specialized training may be available for lateral entry into teaching. If they can be induced to enter teaching—partly by removing irrelevant duties from the job—they may become effective teachers. They may need only some transitional learning of their new roles, together with monitoring of their performance and its results.

Several states, led by New Jersey, are now moving toward reform of this type. The New Jersey program, passed by the state Legislature in 1984 to begin with the 1985–86 school year, is a more or less complete implementation of Peterson's recommendation. More specifically, anyone with the B.A. degree who passes the National Teacher exam in a specific subject matter (e.g., history, math, science) can be hired to teach by a local school system. Such employees have the full responsibilities of teachers, although they must be assisted by a team of local teachers and have 100 hours of instruction in education courses during their first year. If they satisfactorily complete the first year, they can receive full certification and be paid at the rate of teachers certified by the traditional methods.

Evaluation data on the New Jersey reform are not yet available. As one might expect, professors of education at state universities and officials of teachers' unions have claimed that the reform exposes children to unqualified and potentially harmful teachers (Goldberg, 1985; Watts, 1986; Winkler, 1985). Even so, if evaluations of the New Jersey program, and similar programs in Texas and elsewhere, show that teachers attracted to the public schools through certification programs of this sort can produce student achievement as effectively as regular teachers, the schools will benefit from a much broader and deeper pool of potential teachers.

Recommendations

We favor the following policies:

1. Career-ladder programs with major efforts to devise procedures for rewarding output and productivty.
2. Formation of local committees for teacher evaluation, giving them professional advice and encouraging them to use multiple measures of output.
3. Elimination of nonacademic teacher duties.
4. Provision of better support services and materials, including computer and audiovisual support.
5. Removing barriers for entrance to teaching when they are not related to output.

It is important that these recommendations, including both benefits and responsibilities for teachers, be considered as a package. Both taxpayers and teachers may be willing to make concessions if they gain something in return. Agreement between them may be aided by consultation and involvement of teachers in the planning of new programs, and by linking evaluation procedures in a "social contract" with appropriations for teachers and schools.

POLICIES CONCERNING DIVERSITY AND EQUITY

The recent wave of educational reform has stressed "effectiveness" and "excellence," but has sometimes been criticized as neglecting the diversity among pupils and schools. Contributors to this volume have dealt with numerous types of diversity. Some such types refer to individual students; their bases can include school performance, attendance, social class, ethnicity, religion, gender, developmental stages, giftedness, and handicaps. Some types of diversity carry negative judgments of deviance (e.g., disruptiveness). Others, contrasting regions, districts, or public and private schools with one another, have been of less concern to the contributors.

When individual students are seen as diverse, the school may either accept or challenge the relevance of this diversity to its tasks. If the school accepts a type of diversity as relevant, it may either treat students differently, or group them together because of their mutual educational influences. If the school denies that relevance, it can group them together because of their common rights (cf. Epstein, Chapter 5).

Movements and emphases concerned with particular types of diversity have often gone their own ways, however, without trying to see various sorts of diversity, and various meanings of equity, in a common perspective. Each of the special groups of children we have listed above is often treated as sui generis, without systematic comparison of their situations in broader terms.

The School's Tasks Concerning Diversity

Most types of diversity treated in earlier chapters are commonly regarded as objective "characteristics of the pupil." More generally, however, diversity refers to social statuses defined by others, including administrators, teachers, and fellow pupils. Pupils placed in such a status may also contribute to this definition by their own self-definitions and actions.

These types of diversity are often transformed into *categories* in which pupils are placed for different treatment: tracks, groupings within classrooms (Dreeben & Gamoran, 1986; Haskins, Walden, & Ramey, 1983), or labels in the minds of administrators, teachers, or fellow students. Even though we come to know close associates as individuals, the larger-scale and more impersonal relations of school administration (and often of teaching) can become those of "street-level bureaucracy" (Lipsky, 1980), whose personnel are led to categorize clients in order to use their time efficiently. Any general treatment of these classifications must recognize that they depend on *sensing* and *interpreting* cues; and that diversity can be created, shaped, or reduced by the school's treatment of a pupil.

In these processes of classification and treatment we seek to further several sometimes conflicting values present in American society. First, we try to sense diversity and its sources *appropriately;* i.e., neither to ignore chances to help by special treatment, nor to stigmatize diversity irrelevantly or unnecessarily.

Second, we want to promote efficiency in every quest for excellence or equity, but especially in the sense of "each child's reaching his or her own potential." This phrase could be translated into efficiency terms if society could define a sum of social well-being (a social welfare function) that it wished to maximize. Its investment in each child's development would then depend on the net benefit of doing so, at the margin (Strike, 1985, pp. 412–413). The best use of our always limited resources would require that there be an equal marginal gain in social welfare, as judged by the community, per dollar spent on any child. Each child's own potential would then be defined in terms of the extent of educational development allowed, for a given budget, under this rule. In practice, the judgment would be made for groups of children as defined by the various types of diversity discussed above. It would require a community to judge, through its representatives and school administrators, whether the gain from spending a given additional sum of money to educate gifted or retarded, majority or minority, would be the same. This is a difficult judgment and can be made only approximately. It may be posed so as to include the distribution of net benefits as well (Dasgupta, Sen, & Marglin, 1972: Chapter 7), but this formulation would still involve maximization rather than compensatory justice (MacRae, 1985, p. 220).

Third, we attempt to promote equity by using a variety of approaches such as:

- Facilitating universal inclusion in school life (Epstein, Chapter 5; Ogbu, Chapter 6); i.e., perceived equal membership or citizenship in the school, including instructional groups. This is not merely a matter of equity in fostering achievement or production, but may also contribute to the functioning of democracy (Strike, 1985; Gutmann, 1986, pp. 5–6);
- Postponing and discouraging unnecessary differentiation in status and opportunities. Epstein warns that "large numbers of students . . . are being ignored, pushed back, or pushed out of school." Both she and Cooley (Chapter 8) propose monitoring systems that can attend to such problems of individual students;
- Examining the expected later social contributions, as well as benefits received, by those given special educational advantages in public schools. We shall thus ask whether gifted students whose special school instruction leads to a higher salary in later life should receive that part of their educational benefits at the community's expense; and whether special attention might be given to

those pupils whose "gifts" enable them to help others, in school or in later life, as well as to earn high salaries.

These approaches will be considered in more specific terms in the following sections.

Policies for Disadvantaged Children

The goal of equal inclusion in school life has been difficult to realize fully for poor children from nonimmigrant minority groups. Among our contributors, Epstein and Ogbu deal most directly with this problem. They treat questions of equity mainly as problems arising within schools. Additional policies have been proposed, however, in the reports and elsewhere, to aid the education of disadvantaged children at the preschool level and of disadvantaged youth who are at risk of dropping out of high school. For greater completeness, therefore, we shall discuss these additional policies as well as Epstein's and Ogbu's recommendations.

Preschool Programs. It is widely believed that preschool education will help solve the problems of unequal educational outcome among diverse groups of children. More specifically, many researchers, educators, policymakers, and public commentators believe that quality preschool programs for poor children would boost their intellectual development and better prepare them for entry to the public schools. Some even argue that preschool programs will reduce rates of delinquency, teen-age pregnancy, school dropouts, and welfare participation (Children's Defense Fund, 1986; Task Force, 1986). These proposals seem to assume that the first 3 or 4 years of human life are critical to subsequent development. A strong form of this view even holds that deprivation of social and learning experience during this period will lead to lifelong deficits, which could be remedied by beneficial experiences during the preschool years, producing long-term benefits.

These assumptions are not, however, strongly supported by research evidence. The arguments against any strong form of the hypothesis that this age interval is critical are now well known among researchers. A growing number of developmental researchers (Brim & Kagan, 1980; Clarke & Clarke, 1976) now believe that continuing change throughout childhood and much of adulthood is the rule rather than the exception, and that preschool experiences by no means determine the course of later development. This more questioning attitude toward the effects of preschool experiences has not, however, become widespread among professionals who make public statements in the media, or among policymakers.

Three generalizations seem to summarize current research findings on the effects of preschool programs. First, quality programs beginning either in infancy or at age 3 or 4 can increase the IQs of children from low-income families by about 8 to 10 points. Second, such increases in IQ or achievement scores, as measured by differences between children who attended preschool and those who did not, disappear after a few years of public schooling. Third, long-term follow-up at ages of 15 and above confirms that the initial differences in IQ and school achievement do not last, but shows that fewer children who attended preschool are placed in special education classes or retained in grade than children who did not attend preschool (Darlington et al., 1980; Lazar, Darlington, Murray, Royce, and Snipper, 1982). There is no widely accepted explanation for this finding, but it does suggest that preschool programs could be cost-effective; they may pay for themselves if the public schools could save money by reducing the need for grade retention and special education classes (Barnett, 1985; Weber, Foster, & Weikart, 1978).

These are encouraging findings. More encouraging still are findings of a study by David Weikart and his colleagues at the High Scope Foundation in Ypsilanti, Mich. In a series of publications extending over nearly two decades, the High Scope team has traced the development of 58 children who attended preschool for either 1 or 2 years and 65 control children who did not. The two most recent follow-ups were conducted when the children had reached ages 15 and 19. The results have no parallel in the literature: Compared with control children, experimental children had higher IQ scores and school achievement scores; lower rates of grade retention, special education placement, school dropout, arrests or detentions by the police, and welfare receipt; and higher rates of high school graduation, postsecondary education, and employment (Berrueta–Clement, Schweinhart, Barrett, Epstein, & Weikart, 1984).

If these results could be achieved among children from low-income families throughout the nation, universal preschool programs for such children would promote equity among diverse class and ethnic groups more than any educational reform ever implemented. But there are at least two reasons for caution. First, a similar preschool intervention study that followed subjects into their late teens found effects that are in many ways quite different from those of the High Scope study. Susan Gray and her colleagues (1982) in Nashville, like the High Scope researchers, did find that children who attended preschool had lower rates of placement in special education classes and higher graduation rates, although these results were confined to females. They did not, however, find any achievement test or IQ test differences in high school;

they found no difference between experimental and control females in pregnancy rates; and they found no differences between the groups in rates of employment or welfare participation.

A second reason for caution in generalizing the High Scope results is that preschool programs implemented on a broader scale have not had similar results. A recent meta-analysis of all published Head Start studies, for example, found that effects on IQ and school achievement were gone after 2 years of schooling, and that there were few substantial differences on any variables between children who attended Head Start and those who did not (McKey et al., 1985). Comparing these results with those of the High Scope and similar studies (Darlington et al., 1980) leads one to judge that outcomes from small-scale, carefully planned projects do not necessarily generalize to similar programs implemented on a national scale. Since the currently popular recommendations on public preschool programs would be implemented on a national scale, caution requires us to conclude that reductions in school failure, teen-age pregnancies, and unemployment would be unlikely.

The proper course of action, as investigators in the High Scope project themselves have recommended (Barnett, 1985, pp. 100–102), is to implement public preschool programs slowly while carefully studying their effects. If early results are promising, the programs should be expanded. In short, the proper recommendation on preschool programs is not to implement them on a national scale but to pursue repeated trials.

Policies for Disadvantaged Youth. The problem of equity in American education is particularly acute for the 900,000 or so 18-year-olds from poor families (in each national cohort of about 3.5 million) who should graduate from high school in any given year. Within this group, those who are minority members, reside in inner cities, or live in single-parent families are especially at risk for a nexus of problems that include school failure, out-of-wedlock birth, crime, unemployment, and welfare participation.

Both the education commission reports discussed in Chapter 1 and the more recent reports on welfare reform (Meyer, 1986; Task Force, 1986) suggest that the public schools could play a major role in the nation's attempt to help these disadvantaged youngsters. In the past 20 years, numerous policies have been aimed at breaking the "cycle of poverty" that victimizes this group of adolescents. These expected remedies have included delinquency prevention efforts, preschool education, guaranteed annual income for poor families, job entitlement programs, antidiscrimination efforts, and reform of the public schools. In each case, initial optimism was followed by despair as program evaluations showed that the effects of intervention were small at best (Aaron, 1978; Murray, 1984).

Even in the midst of a wave of education reform, we should have the perspective to recognize that victories in the war to help these adolescents will be incremental. The best course of action, under the circumstances, is to accept the limited effects that known interventions can produce, and then to move forward to perfecting the interventions we currently use while simultaneously exploring new ones.

Several of the recommendations discussed in this volume are appropriate for implementation on a wider scale. The effective schools literature shows that strong principals, increased authority and flexibility at the school system and building level, and careful monitoring of student progress can be expected to produce moderate gains. Similarly, rapid remediation (Epstein, Chapter 5) can achieve incremental gains, especially as the schools develop their capacity to diagnose and treat problems in reading and math achievement. If we were to implement Ogbu's recommendations concerning family and community involvement in teaching minority children how to go to school, further achievement gains and reduction in dropout rates might be expected. Indeed, moderate progress in the achievement of Black students has already been achieved (Burton & Jones, 1982; Congressional Budget Office, 1986). We see no reason why implementation of the reforms outlined above would not lead to continued improvement in the achievement levels and high school graduation rates of minority students.

Continuing gains in the educational achievement of the poor are important because we expect those gains to improve employment chances and income (Featherman, 1980; but see Jencks, 1979). If only a higher percentage of minority students would stay in school longer, the economic returns to schooling would reduce the amount of income inequality in our society—and without direct government intervention in the economy. In the past, this argument was somewhat flawed because the returns to schooling for Blacks were much less than those for whites; over the past two decades, however, the Black–white gap in returns to education has been substantially reduced (Featherman, 1980; Smith & Welch, 1986).

But how can we keep adolescents from poor and minority families in school longer? Insofar as dropping out is due to students' motivation, perhaps their motives can be redirected by providing greater incentives for graduating from high school. Over and above Epstein's and Ogbu's proposals, we might provide some reward to youth from low-income families who graduated. Few of these youth are likely to continue to college and to have that possibility as an incentive to graduate from high school. But for those who do not plan further education, the job market is the main source of rewards for graduation. Possibly a monetary incentive for further development of job-related skills could be used to increase the rewards from high school graduation for them. This public aid to them would then be analogous to the support that taxpayers already give to students who enter public higher education.

Thus, we propose that, contingent on graduation from high school, students from low-income families be given a grant that might be called a skill development account (SDA). This grant might be given in the form of a voucher to pay for investments in personal skill development. Investments in activities such as skill training, courses at community colleges, and training for professional licenses, would be appropriate. Some portion of the SDA might be used to relocate if economic conditions or local opportunities justified the investment; part might also be used as a small living allowance during training. Unused portions of the SDA could be kept in interest-bearing accounts and would follow workers throughout their employment careers, providing a source of aid for employment should the worker be displaced by international competition or technological change.

Advantages from such a program might include not only those of equity, but also social benefits from increases in economic productivity and from crime reduction, as have been found for the Job Corps (Long, Mallar, & Thornton, 1981). In addition, this program might provide a major and conspicuous incentive for adolescents to finish high school.

Consistent with several of our previous recommendations, we would implement this policy on a small scale with ongoing evaluation. The design and monitoring of such a program must be worked out in detail. If eligible students stayed in school longer to qualify for the SDA, enrolled in appropriate training courses, and had sufficiently higher rates of employment in better jobs than comparison students, the program could be gradually expanded.

Reducing the Social Costs of Misclassifying Pupils

While pupils are in school, they can also be stigmatized by inappropriate classification, with resulting social costs. Schools engage in classification of pupils in numerous ways; in the judgment of some observers, they do this far too much (Dill, Chapter 10). A major policy problem is to propose ways in which this classification should or should not be done. What matters, of course, is not the classification by itself but what is done about it, formally or informally (MacRae & Haskins, 1981, pp. 12–15).

Schools classify pupils at entry into a school, grade, or classroom; continuously during a period of the school year (such as a semester);

and at exit. The formal categories used—those amenable most easily to policy choice—include school grades, courses taken, tracks, and groupings within classrooms. The significance given to any such category is revealed by the treatment of its members by the school and by their fellow students, as well as by members' behavior and self-concepts. At entry to a school, grade, or classroom, classification can be made through first perceptions, through use of diagnostic tests, or through past records. Afterward it can be based on school performance, attendance, and conformity to informal social norms. At exit, students are categorized by possession of a diploma and by their academic, attendance, and behavioral records.

The chance of formation of irrelevant classifications at these stages, and the social costs of acting on them, can be reduced by several types of school policies. We have noted that Epstein proposes rapid remediation to avoid a vicious cycle in which some pupils fall behind. Ogbu also suggests that sensitivity on the part of teachers and administrators, together with learning of "how to go to school" by nonimmigrant minority pupils, can reduce both the number of misclassifications of pupils from these minority groups, and the behavior on their part that leads to placement in lower statuses.

Some unnecessary classifications can also be removed without formal remediation. When multiple statuses are assigned to the same pupil (e.g., quality of performance in various courses as well as in extracurricular activities), the possible "cross-cutting" (rather than cumulation) of these different statuses may de-emphasize irrelevant classifications that label whole students rather than their particular attributes. Thus, as Epstein notes, rather than assigning various groups of pupils to completely distinct tracks, a school can allow different groups of pupils to take some courses together and other courses separately. Similarly, individually paced instruction aided by computers might reduce unnecessary classification that is based on rates of progress. Such policies could increase the extent of equal membership in the school.

Third, careful studies of the diagnostic procedures used in some classifications, and of the actions based on them, may reduce errors of classification. Some classifications involve the diagnosis of causes. When pupils perform differently on similar tasks, especially when they fall below the range of "normal" variation, teachers and administrators may try to find out why. Such a diagnosis may lead to an effort at remediation. It may also lead to a judgment that the cost of improving performance will be prohibitively high; but this judgment can reflect prejudice as well as expertise, as is claimed in the controversies about assignment of disproportionate numbers of Black students to the category of "educable mentally retarded" (Mercer, 1977). Error of this sort might be reduced by closer scrutiny of testing used for classifying students. This would include not only the reliability and validity of the tests but also the differential treatment of students so classified and its results.

Policies for Gifted Children

The meaning and implications of equity can be clarified by examining our policies for educating gifted children and trying to relate them to more general ethical principles. One way to do this is to compare policies for the gifted with those for the handicapped: two different groups with apparently lasting characteristics that cannot be fully equalized by the schools. We might, for example, think of benefits and costs to society (Gallagher, Chapter 7); if so, we might argue that education of the gifted produces a greater benefit to society than the small costs involved. The same sort of argument could be made for special concern for handicapped or retarded children, if society can save the cost of expensive institutional care by mainstreaming or remedial instruction done earlier. We assume, in this type of analysis, that the costs to the teacher and to other students of managing a heterogeneous classroom are taken into account. Gallagher (Figure 3) gives the relative costs of educating various groups, but without specifying the value of the benefits. If the amounts of education used in such a comparison were judged to provide roughly equivalent benefits, then we might give priority to the lower-cost programs.

Equity and the Private Benefits to the Gifted Child. A closer look at the cost-benefit approach to policies for the gifted, however, raises questions of equity. Gallagher points out that we can expect gifted children to make major contributions to society in many ways. He notes the value to society of those who drive "the modern technological engine" and who are given special attention when society focuses on international competition. The education of a child with relevant[6] talents may increase the value of the nation's capacity to compete considerably more than the cost of the additional resources devoted to that education. Of this net social benefit from education, the gain to society at large might exceed the private gain to the child.

---

[6]Talents for music and art, or even for democratic leadership (Giroux, 1984), might not get the highest priority if our only goal were to cope with foreign economic competition.

A question of equity can nevertheless be raised if we ask what the returns to the gifted child are in later life. Who reaps the social benefits? A skilled physician saves lives and improves well-being, but also earns one of the highest salaries provided by our economy. The corporate manager also contributes to production, while receiving a salary even higher than the physician's. Part of this reward is presumably due to their education, perhaps in classes for the gifted; such special classes presumably add an increment to what the gifted person would have learned without them. To what extent, then, should the citizenry at large pay for their extra education? From the perspective of compensatory equity, we might ask that the beneficiaries of publicly financed education for the gifted be required to pay a special tax on that increment to their earnings. To implement such a policy, however, we would first have to ascertain how great those extra private gains were, in relation to the extra social benefits from the additional education received.

Several general ethical principles might bear on policies for the gifted. First, we might be concerned with compensatory equity—the notion that when one person aids or harms another, some compensation is due in return. The economic concern for prices or user charges embodies not only the value of efficiency but a secondary value of compensation or exchange. For most students in school, however, the claim that they should pay for that part of their education that is a private economic good is superseded by a second principle, that of common citizenship. That citizenship is deemed to carry with it equal rights to education, especially at the elementary and high school levels. Insofar as the same amounts are spent on gifted children as on others, these children might then not incur special obligations.[7]

Third—and this is the standard we use here—we could insist that any educational policy that raises students above the level of common citizenship in the school requires special justification. For special programs for gifted students, proponents can argue that policies for gifted students do benefit other members of society. We simply ask that policies for the gifted be more explicitly directed to generating these social benefits, as distinguished from private benefits for the gifted. Such di-

---

[7]We might also invoke Rawls's (1971, p. 83) difference principle, and ask that policies for the gifted be chosen so as to be "to the greatest benefit of the least advantaged." If the taxes supporting education for the gifted do not come from the least advantaged, the extra productive skills gained by the gifted may well bring a net benefit to the least advantaged. This might not make such a policy a Pareto improvement, however, since some taxpayers might have net losses from it. A further principle might suggest that the obligation to repay is greater when the student's family income is higher.

rection would be aided by research on the relative size of public and private benefits and of costs.

Performance: Individual vs. Social. A second reason for seeking some contribution from those who receive special benefits is that such a contribution might be part of a larger effort to encourage mutual helpfulness in schools. We may, for example, be concerned for handicapped children who are capable eventually of living productive lives like other citizens, as having the right to learn to do so—a right that they share with all other children. We would then consider it part of the education of the other children to learn to respect that right. Similarly, we might consider it part of the special responsibility of the gifted to share their gifts with others. From this perspective, we might ask that society devote greater resources to educating those who were gifted in skills that helped other people, in school or in later life.

This approach differs from our usual view of a pupil's success in school, which centers on individual learning or skills. However, children's social skills and social relations are important not only for their own later achievement, but also for benefits they may provide to society in later life and to fellow students in school. Thus, helpful as well as antisocial behavior has a special importance to the school. Schools usually take notice first of disruptiveness, aggression, or vandalism; but we must ask whether helpfulness could also be encouraged more. A major finding of early research on equality of educational opportunity was that the presence of classmates with advantaged background and high aspirations seemed to benefit many minority students (Coleman et al., 1966, p. 305), but the data did not permit exploration of the detailed processes leading to that benefit.

Experiments with groups in which some pupils help others to learn have yielded promising results (Epstein, Chapter 5); but a well-defined and appreciated role for the student who helps classmates—the converse of the disruptive child—needs more emphasis (Hedin, 1986). At a minimum, the educational effect of having able and motivated students who can encourage others in the classroom should be recognized as a positive value; these students' removal, if produced by voucher or tax credit policies, should be counted as a cost (Peterson, Chapter 2). But beyond this minimum, we need to find ways to reward those students who are willing to help others and who have the talents to do so. Some schools have encouraged students to engage in community service or to tutor other students. Schools can reward these activities in various ways (Epstein), not necessarily monetary but including public recognition and educational reading materials or trips. The result may be to emphasize and encourage talents for aiding others.

Recommendations

We recommend the following policies:

1. Incremental implementation of preschool programs for poor children, with careful study of their effects.
2. For disadvantaged youth: incremental implementation of programs for effective schools, and for family and community involvement in teaching minority students how to go to school (Ogbu).
3. Design and trial of a program of skill development accounts for youth from low-income families, contingent on graduation from high school, to be used as vouchers for development of job-related skills.
4. Provision for rapid remediation, as Epstein proposes, to reduce harmful misclassification of students.
5. Avoidance of completely separate instructional tracks, to reduce unnecessary labeling of students.
6. Study of the relation between private benefits, social benefits and costs of programs for the gifted; and especially if private benefits are large, encouragement of these students to help other students in school and to contribute to society in later life. More generally, expansion of existing programs that reward students who help others.

INFORMATION FOR DIAGNOSIS AND ACTION

Indicator Statistics

Not only the final part of this book, but some earlier chapters, deal with statistics that can guide our decisions for educational policy and administration. Peterson presents information on trends affecting education, and Epstein and Cooley write of schools' information systems and of monitoring teachers' practices.

Information and feedback about public education are relevant for guiding choices, both for the nation and at the levels of the state, district, school, classroom, and individual student. Dill proposes defining national goals for education and collecting national statistics to determine whether these goals are achieved and whether student achievement changes over time. At the state and district level, statistics may be used to compare schools, for either accountability, incentives, or internal management. At the level of the school and the classroom, as Cooley shows, statistics can be used to compare performance on various dimensions with what is expected, and to permit needed "tailoring" of the system. Comparison among schools in their degrees of association between socioeconomic status and achievement gains, as Epstein suggests, may throw light on their capacity to be effective for all students.

We recommend that policymakers at every level give more attention to developing and using these information systems. This development requires two coordinated lines of work: (a) the devising of statistical measures to be used, incorporated in convenient forms for access and use; and (b) the cooperative participation of school administrators, teachers, researchers, and public officials in choosing and using the information needed.

The Use of Research Results

The design of educational policies requires the use of the best possible information as to what these policies are likely to accomplish, and at what cost. This information will be useless, however, unless it is put into practice—a step that does not occur automatically.

Motivation for Schools to Change. Changes may be brought about in schools by two sorts of motivation, which may supplement one another. Teachers and administrators may want to change ways of teaching simply in order to do a good job, following the dictates of their professional consciences. But in some instances, external incentives may induce teachers to try new alternatives, administrators to change organizational structures and personnel if necessary, and state legislatures to support changes, including increased funding, that will produce improvement. Indeed, incentive systems based on competition may not be mere matters of "accountability," as they are often perceived, but means of internal stimulation in a state or district school system, analogous to internal competition among units in a corporation. These incentives can increase the receptiveness of participants to relevant research.

Cooperation and Consultation. The effective introduction of research results into educational practice requires an extensive process of consultation, often including teachers, parents, and taxpayers, that may be more necessary in education than in some other types of public policy. This consultation includes, but is not limited to, a dialogue between researcher and client (Cooley & Bickel, 1986, Chapter 3). It can go beyond the direct client, such as a school administrator, to those affected; or to those with whom contracts are made, especially teachers.

The implementation of policies that affect teaching requires consultation with teachers because their behavior and their subjective view of their activities must often change in order for a policy to take effect. Several of our contributors have pointed to the need for experts to participate and consult with teachers and to develop information together with them. House and Lapan (Chapter 4) suggest, as one way to gain teachers' cooperation, the use of action research (Argyris, Putnam, & Smith, 1985). Cooley (1983) and Cooley and Bickel (1986, pp. 183–196) recount a process of consultation with the Pittsburgh school system in developing a new information system; they emphasize the differences between this type of consultation and conventional academic research. This same difference in research style is also reported by Whyte (1986), based on his career experiences in analyzing and introducing reforms in settings as diverse as automobile factories and peasant agriculture.

The need to consult and engage in dialogue is not limited to researchers' work with teachers, however; an analogous dialogue with citizens is needed if any of the recent wave of educational reforms are to be successfully implemented. Timar (1986; Timar & Kirp, 1987), reporting on a multistate study of education reform implementation, finds that South Carolina officials have achieved more than several comparison states because they not only carried out the "authorizing" process (policy enactment) and responded to local initiatives, but also engaged more fully in a "conversation" phase with citizens. It may be in this way that "social contracts" are made. Our final recommendation is therefore that researchers who wish to be effective in improving the public schools link their work closely with these types of consultation.

Recommendations

We recommend the following policies:

1. Policymakers at every level should give more attention to developing information systems to help guide their choices.
2. External incentives should be provided to schools to change in accord with indicator statistics and research.
3. Researchers who wish to give effective policy advice should link their work with consultation with those affected.

A WORD OF CAUTION

Our nation has concentrated its most visible efforts at school reform on major change to be brought about in a short time. But the history of efforts at reform suggests that they need persistence as well as initial resources and momentum. Not only do we need a continued supply of adequate resources, better means of monitoring and modifying our policies, and improved human organization in the schools; we must recognize that the schools follow as well as lead the outside society.

Without jobs, students can learn well yet fail to produce and succeed. Without family support, pupils can be held back by problems or apathy at home. Without equal treatment in the community, minority children can enter school at a disadvantage. Without continuing taxpayer commitment (and intelligent long-term review), needed resources may not be supplied or they may be misused. Let us therefore strive to improve our public schools; but at the same time let us recognize that improvement will require a long and steady effort and will need the aid of our entire society and economy.

REFERENCES

Aaron, H. J. (1978). *Politics and the professors: The Great Society in perspective.* Washington, DC: Brookings.

Argyris, C., Putnam, R., & Smith, D. M. (1985). *Action science.* San Francisco: Jossey–Bass.

Barnett, W. S. (1985). *The Perry Preschool Program and its long-term effects: A benefit-cost analysis.* Ypsilanti, MI: High/Scope.

Berrueta–Clement, J. R., Schweinhart, L. J., Barnett, W. S., Epstein, A. S., & Weikart, D. P. (1984). *Changed lives: The effects of the Perry Preschool Program through age 19.* Ypsilanti, MI: High/Scope.

Brim, O. G., & Kagan, J. (1980). *Constancy and change in human development.* Cambridge, MA: Harvard.

Burton, N. W., & Jones, L. V. (1982). Recent trends in achievement levels of black and white youth. *Educational Research, 11,* 10–14.

Campbell, D. T. (1984). Can we be scientific in applied social science? In R. Conner, D. G. Altman, & C. Jackson (Eds.), *Evaluation studies review annual* (pp. 26–48). Beverly Hills, CA: Sage.

Carnegie Forum on Education and the Economy, Task Force on Teaching as a Profession. (1986). *A nation prepared: Teachers for the 21st century.* Washington, DC: Author.

Children's Defense Fund. (1986). *A children's defense budget: An analysis of the FY 1987 federal budget and children.* Washington, DC: Author.

Clarke, A. M., & Clarke, A. D. B. (Eds.). (1976). *Early experience: Myth and evidence.* New York: Free Press.

Coleman, J. S., Campbell, E. Q., Hobson, C. J., McPartland, J., Mood, A. M., Weinfeld, F. D., & York, R. L. (1966). *Equality of educational opportunity.* Washington, DC: U. S. Government Printing Office.

Congressional Budget Office. (1986). *Trends in educational achievement.* Washington, DC: Author.

Cooley, W. W. (1983). Improving the performance of an educational system. *Educational Research, 12*(6), 4–12.

Cooley, W. W., & Bickel, W. E. (1986). *Decision-oriented educational research.* Boston: Kluwer–Nijhoff.

Darlington, R. B., Royce, J. M., Snipper, A. S., Murray, H. W., & Lazar, I. (1980). Preschool programs and later school competence of children from low-income families. *Science, 208,* 202–204.

Dasgupta, P., Sen, A., & Marglin, S. (1972). *Guidelines for project evaluation.* New York: United Nations.

Dreeben, R., & Gamoran, A. (1986). Race, interaction, and learning. *American Sociological Review, 51*(5), 660–669.

Featherman, D. L. (1980). Schooling and occupational careers: Constancy and change in worldly success. In O. G. Brim & J. Kagan (Eds.), *Constancy and change in human development.* Cambridge, MA: Harvard.

Giroux, H. A. (1984). Public philosophy and the crisis in education. *Harvard Educational Review, 54*(2), 186–194.

Goldberg, D. (1985, April 26). New teacher certification program bypasses traditional education degree. *Washington Post,* pp. E1–E2.

Gray, S. W., Ramsey, B. K., & Klaus, R. A. (1982). *From 3 to 20: The early training project.* Baltimore: University Park Press.

Gutmann, A. (1986). Distributing democratic education. *Working Paper 10, Democratic Values.* Project on the Federal Social Role. Washington, DC: National Conference on Social Welfare.

Hanushek, E. A. (1986). The economics of schooling. *Journal of Economic Literature, 24*(3), 1141–1177.

Haskins, R., Walden, T., & Ramey, C. T. (1983). Teacher and student behavior in high- and low-ability groups. *Journal of Educational Psychology, 75,* 865–876.

Hawley, W. D. (1986). Toward a comprehensive strategy for addressing the teacher shortage. *Phi Delta Kappan, 67*(10), 712–718.

Hedin, D. (1986). *Students as teachers.* Washington, DC: Carnegie Forum on Education and the Economy.

Holmes Group. (1986). *Tomorrow's teachers.* East Lansing, MI: Author.

Jencks, C. (1979). *Who gets ahead? The determinants of economic success in America.* New York: Basic Books.

Lazar, I., Darlington, R., Murray, H., Royce, J., & Snipper, A. (1982). Lasting effects of early education: A report from the consortium for longitudinal studies. *Monographs of the Society for Research in Child Development, 47*(2–3, Serial No. 195).

Lipsky, M. (1980). *Street-level bureaucracy.* New York: Russell Sage Foundation.

Long, D. A., Mallar, C. D., & Thornton, C. V. D. (1981). Evaluating the benefits and costs of the Job Corps. *Journal of Public Policy & Management, 1*(1), 55–76.

MacRae, D., Jr. (1985). *Policy indicators: Links between social science and public debate.* Chapel Hill: University of North Carolina Press.

MacRae, D., Jr., & Haskins, R. (1981). Models for policy analysis. In R. Haskins & J. J. Gallagher (Eds.), *Models for analysis of social policy* (pp. 1–36). Norwood, NJ: Ablex.

McKey, R. H., Condelli, L., Ganson, H., Barrett, B. J., McConkey, C., & Plantz, M. C. (1985). *The impact of Head Start on children, families, and communities* (DHHS Publication No. OHDS 85–31193). Washington, DC: U.S. Government Printing Office.

Mercer, J. R. (1977). Cultural diversity, mental retardation, and assessment: The case for nonlabeling. In P. Mittler (Ed.), *Research to practice in mental retardation* (Vol. 1, pp. 353–362). Baltimore: University Park Press.

Meyer, J. A. (Ed.). (1986). *Ladders out of poverty* (Report of the Project on the Welfare of Families). Washington, DC: American Horizons.

Murnane, R. J. (1984). A review essay—comparisons of public and private schools: Lessons from the uproar. *Journal of Human Resources, 19*(2), 263–277.

Murray, C. (1984). *Losing ground: American social policy, 1950–1980.* New York: Basic Books.

Rawls, J. (1971). *A theory of justice.* Cambridge, MA: Harvard.

Sawhill, I. V. (1986). *Anti-poverty strategies for the 1980s.* Unpublished manuscript, The Urban Institute, Washington, DC.

Smith, J. P., & Welch, F. R. (1986). *Closing the gap: Forty years of economic progress for blacks.* Santa Monica, CA: Rand.

Southern Regional Education Board. (1986, December). 1986—Incentive programs for teachers and administrators: How are they doing? *Career Ladder Clearinghouse.* Atlanta: Author.

Strike, K. A. (1985). Is there a conflict between equity and excellence? *Educational Evaluation & Policy Analysis, Z*(4), 409–416.

Task Force on Poverty and Welfare. (1986). *A new social contract: Rethinking the nature and purpose of public assistance* (Report to Governor Mario M. Cuomo). New York: Author.

Timar, T. B. (1986, October). *Managing educational excellence: State strategies to reform schools.* Paper presented at the annual meeting of the Association for Public Policy Analysis and Management, Austin, TX.

Timar, T. B., & Kirp, D. L. (1987). *Managing educational excellence.* New York: Falmer.

Watts, D. (1986, December 17). Alternate certification 'places children at risk.' *Education Week,* p. 18.

Weber, C. U., Foster, P. W., & Weikart, D. P. (1978). *An economic analysis of the Ypsilanti Perry Preschool Project.* Ypsilanti, MI: High/Scope.

Whyte, W. F. (1986). On the uses of social science research. *American Sociological Review, 51*(4), 555–563.

Winkler, K. J. (1985, March 13). New Jersey's schoolteacher plan alarms schools of education. *Chronicle of Higher Education,* pp. 1, 18.

Author Index

Subject Index